TRADITIONAL HOODOO & CONJURE

A HANDBOOK OF SPIRITS, SPELLS, & ROOTWORK

ABOUT THE AUTHOR

Witch, author, and teacher of the metaphysical, **Miss Aida** is a priestess of Santeria and Palo. Magical practice has always been a part of her life. She was raised in a practicing Cuban family and specializes in spiritual eradications, as well as spiritual cleansings and protection. Beyond her books, her work has been featured on numerous radio shows, television networks, and independent films.

TRADITIONAL HOODOO & CONJURE

A HANDBOOK OF SPIRITS, SPELLS, & ROOTWORK

MISS AIDA

FOREWORD BY LELIA MARINO

Chicago, Illinois

Paperback ISBN: 978-1-964537-60-3
Hardcover ISBN: 978-1-964537-98-6

Library of Congress Control Number on file.

Published by:
Crossed Crow Books, LLC
518 Davis St, Suite 205
Evanston, IL 60201
www.crossedcrowbooks.com

Printed in the United States of America.
IBI

OTHER BOOKS BY THE AUTHOR

Hoodoo Cleansing and Protection Magic
Banish Negative Energy and Ward Off Unpleasant People

Hoodoo Justice Magic
Spells for Power, Protection, and Righteous Vindication

Cursing and Crossing
Hoodoo Spells to Torment, Jinx, and Take Revenge on Your Enemies

Destroying Relationships
Hoodoo Spells to Break Up, Separate, Hot Foot, and Drive Off Your Foes and Rivals

Figural Candle Spells
Conjuring Magic with the Power of Fire

This book is dedicated in loving memory
to the best friend of my life and the brother
that I never had. He was also one of the very best
physicians that God has ever put on this planet.

Dr. Thomas Edward Zima

CONTENTS

FOREWORD

As a descendant of Hoodoo and Obeah practitioners from Alabama, South Carolina, and Panama, I am thrilled to be tapped to write this foreword. My grandmother and great-grandmother were incredible teachers who imparted so much knowledge and spiritual wisdom to me. They taught me a great deal about various practices such as spiritual healing, divination, dream interpretation, herbal remedies, and conjure work. Through this powerful lineage, I have been able to honor the legacies that have come before me through my work as a practitioner of conjure, diviner, birth worker, and Master Herbalist. My hope is that this foreword can provide readers with insight into the diverse, fascinating, and powerful practices of my ancestors, so that they too can gain an understanding and appreciation for the unique gifts these traditions have to offer.

It was years ago that I met Miss Aida and began learning about her life and work. I am grateful for the experience of having met her and continue to be inspired by her knowledge. Miss Aida is a priestess in the African diaspora of Santeria and Palo, as well as being a renowned expert in the African American folk practice of Hoodoo. With a unique insight and years of experience in Hoodoo, Miss Aida is able to provide meaningful advice and valuable resources to those seeking to learn more about the subject.

After reading Miss Aida's breakdown of the diasporic traditions brought to the Americas and their islands by enslaved Africans, I was immediately captivated. I am certain many people who claim these traditions have never been exposed to this rich cultural history and the resilience of these people. I was particularly moved by the beauty of the dance, music, and storytelling, as well as how it was all passed down generation to generation, even amidst the oppressive circumstances. It was an eye-opening experience that left me with an even deeper appreciation of the African diaspora which I hail from.

Traditional Hoodoo is a love-letter to the practitioners of Hoodoo—those that have come before us and set the course for this spiritual practice. Through research, interviews, and exploration, Miss Aida explores the historical context, evolution, and use of Hoodoo in its many forms. Her ultimate goal is to honor and pay tribute to the traditions of Hoodoo, the history and prominent people, as well as its modern-day evolution, while providing readers with a deep understanding of this powerful craft. She is dedicated to preserving and honoring Hoodoo. And, to that end, this book is a celebration of its practitioners, past and present.

Lelia Marino, CD, CPD,
Yaya Nkisi Malongo
Owner of The Sacral Healing Garden & Ma Lucerita's Magica Shop

ACKNOWLEDGEMENTS

My sincere gratitude is extended to all of my loyal clients and to my followers on social media, who are just like my own family. I love each and every one of you so much. All of you are so very special to me. You are my good friends. Thank you for being in my life.

Speaking of good friends, Lelia Marino, who has deep familial roots in the practices of Hoodoo and Conjure, tolerated my constant questions about slavery. Her beautiful and heartwarming forward has deeply touched my soul. Thank you, Lelia!

My gratitude is also extended to Andrea Whipple, who encouraged and motivated me to write this book. Thank you!

Lobo "Junior" von Hexenmeister (who has assisted me in writing five other books) and Jakob der Hexenmeister are my loyal German shepherd dogs. They have patiently awaited play time while this project was in the works. However, in my defense, they did enjoy extra treats for being good boys!

Last but not least, a remembrance to my Asha. She was my twelve-year-old German shepherd dog who was born on my lap and, sadly, in December 2021, passed away peacefully on my lap. She was the sunshine of my life. Her son, Junior, and I miss her so very much. Rest in peace, baby girl. We love and miss you, my little angel from Heaven.

Athena's Asha vom Atlas
(Oct. 2, 2009–Dec. 15, 2021)

INTRODUCTION

My mother was born and raised outside of Havana, Cuba. She was a practitioner of Santeria, Palo, and Cuban Brujeria. Both Santeria and Palo were birthed in Cuba by the African slaves. *Brujeria,* meaning "Witchcraft" in Spanish, is a mixture of metaphysical practices arising from the indigenous people, including the Ciboney Native Americans, as well as Catholicism, European, and African magic. Brujeria, in my opinion, is an Earth-based magical practice, because the practitioners work with whatever is available to them.

Although many Cubans (mostly those with strong European roots) possess a misguided view that magical practitioners are either paupers, low-class, or prostitutes, my mother's family was wealthy. The truth is that many wealthy people in Cuba engaged in at least one form of the aforementioned practices. For example, Desi Arnaz, the co-star of the show *I Love Lucy,* frequently paid tribute to the Orisha/African deity "Babalu Aye" through song. In fact, that extremely popular song talks about an *ebbo,* or "offering," to the Orisha in order to get what Arnaz desires. Surprisingly, the words to the song reveal the actual spell's ingredients.

Metaphysical practices were more accepted in Cuba because the vast majority of the population either believed in the crafts, respected them, or practiced them. Unlike in the United States, it wasn't a crime to be a practitioner.

My mother arrived in the United States prior to the rise of the communist regime in Cuba, and my Aunt Isabel shortly followed her. Their arrivals into the United States were quite a culture-shock for both of them. The Afro-Americans couldn't understand their Spanish language, so they felt alienated by what they considered to be their own people. Even worse, they learned that practicing magic in the United States was illegal. In fact, up until the late 1970s, people in my home state of Michigan could go to jail or even prison just for being fortune tellers!

With the perpetual fear of either being deported or going to jail, they temporarily ceased their practices of Santeria and Palo. Additionally, they lacked access to the resources needed for proper offerings to the entities. In Santeria, the Orishas were syncretized with Catholic saints. Therefore, the Yoruba or Catholic names of these entities were (and still are) oftentimes referred to interchangeably. They had Catholic religious statues displayed while their white visitors just assumed that they were devout Catholics. To this day, many Cuban households (especially those of the elders) do the same, leaving many to curiously ask themselves "Hmm, I wonder if this person is a priest/priestess of the religion, or do they simply love the saints?"

My mother and aunt later met other Cuban Santeros and Paleros who showed them how to practice their beloved crafts without being "caught" and where to locate the resources needed for offerings. Thereafter, their magical practices continued in secret for the rest of their lives.

I was born and raised into this household of magico-religious practices and later became a priestess myself. However, my preference was for Brujeria, because Santeria and Palo required animal sacrifices, which was taking its toll on my conscience. After discovering Hoodoo, another African-based metaphysical practice, it elated me to witness the similarities of Hoodoo to Santeria, Palo, and Cuban Brujeria. Why? Because the core philosophies of all the aforementioned practices are derived from Africa, a familiarity that was ingrained into me since childhood. This made me immediately fall in love with Hoodoo and its splendor.

The beauty is in collaborating with the spirits of our ancestors and spiritual court. Communicating with the spirits of plants, minerals, insects, and animals give us a special insight into God's creations.

The spells can be simple or complex, depending on our desires. In its simplest forms, we can choose to work with what is around us. One could easily compare the simpler rituals to the enchanting, nature-based magical practices of many Pagans. In its most complex forms, the spells can become as task-oriented as we choose them to be. Nevertheless, whether simple or complex, the spells are effective.

Most importantly, the beauty of Hoodoo lies within understanding its rich history while appreciating the endurance of the people who birthed and nurtured this craft. I often think of how my mother and aunt practiced their magic in both fear and silence. It makes me realize that is what the slaves did too, but with a much greater magnitude of worry and privacy. The difference being that the slaves had much more to lose if discovered: torture, or even death.

So, join me on this journey as we explore the amazing and diverse trails that the forefathers experienced to create the craft of Hoodoo and Conjure. The narratives are as enchanting as they are emotional. We will also explore authentic ritual practices, magical spells of past and present, and how to work with the many spirits who exist in our world.

CHAPTER ONE

HOODOO AND HOW IT BEGAN

The Big Question

Tons of radio show hosts and podcasters have asked me the burning question that seems to be on everyone's minds: "What's the difference between Voodoo and Hoodoo?"

Unfortunately, the answer is not simple because, when we explore the topic of "Voodoo," the question grows in complexity. It exists throughout the world in diverse forms of practice, as well as various spellings. Originating from the African Traditional Religion (ATR) of West African Vodoun, the practice was brought to the Americas and evolved into what is known today as "African Diaspora Religions." They are:

- Brazilian Vodum
- Cuban Vodu
- Dominican Vudu
- Haitian Vodou
- Louisiana Voodoo

These practices strongly adhere to the principles of Vodoun. Hoodoo, in contrast, is a derivative tradition with a strong Christian foundation that has adopted other magical belief systems

What is Hoodoo?

Hoodoo, also known as "Conjure" or "Rootwork," is a form of folk magic comprised of a system of divination and herbalism that is practiced in North America. Predominantly derived from African magic (mainly from Central and West Africa), Hoodoo also incorporates Islamic, Christian, Jewish, European, Native American, Asian, and even Caribbean metaphysical beliefs and practices.

Honor and Respect

If you wish to be a decent and effective Hoodoo practitioner, just performing the spells isn't enough. It is not only important but virtuous to understand, respect, and honor the history, as well as the treacherous journey taken by others to get Hoodoo to where it is today.

Additionally, knowledge helps us to understand and appreciate the craft and its roots. Knowledge gives value to our work. Knowledge helps us to respect others and earns us respect. Knowledge is empowering. Knowledge is power!

Know the Facts

We will briefly explore the truth regarding the birth and rise of slavery. This is because it is just as important to understand and appreciate the roots, culture, and history of Hoodoo's founders as it is to understand their magic. Without this knowledge, the rituals have no meaning. But, because we will be armed with the facts, we will be ready to explore the journey of both the people and the magic of Hoodoo...

Africa and the Africans Before Slavery

First and foremost, it is imperative to know that it is an unadulterated myth that the history of the Africans was solely a one of primitive savagery. It is propaganda—the dissemination of rumors and lies to influence public opinion—in order to encourage people to embrace and/or accept slavery without guilt or remorse. Now, let's explore the truth. Here's what REALLY happened...

Centuries prior to the arrival of Europeans, Africa and the Africans had a rich and diverse history. They had large and powerful political structures in the more populated areas, while smaller areas, such as villages, relied on agreements between its people. According to an article published by Ferris State University entitled "Africa Before Slavery" in conjunction with the university's Jim Crow Museum, "Art, learning, and technology flourished, and Africans were especially skilled with medicine, mathematics, and astronomy. In addition to domestic goods, they made fine luxury items in bronze, ivory, gold..."

Africans also had a vast knowledge of astrology. It is widely believed by historians that the discovery and practice of astrology actually occurred in Ancient Egypt in the African continent and later taught to the Greeks. Sadly, the Greeks, in turn, claimed astrology as their own discovery. Nevertheless, as you can see, the Africans were a highly educated, intelligent, proud, well-cultured, and noble people.

As with almost all cultures, the Africans also had a long history of magico-religious practices. In many villages, magic was practiced overtly on a daily basis. People depended on their magical practitioners for advice, health care, spiritual care, spiritual teaching, and, of course, their magical needs. These practices were known by different names depending on the region of Africa and the varying belief systems. By all accounts, most are classified today as African Traditional Religions (ATRs).

The Trans-Atlantic Slave Trade

How did this monumental slave trade begin? Unlike the depictions made by the uninformed screenwriters of movies in which we view ridiculous stories of village chieftains selling their own tribal members as they primitively flee through the jungle, the truth is instead far more disturbing. Please don't be swayed by what the uneducated and narrow-minded people in the movie industries wish us to believe.

What really happened? For centuries, prior to the "big" Trans-atlantic Slave Trade, hundreds of Africans were already being captured by other cultures. So, capturing slaves from Africa was not a new idea. But this is how the idea of bringing slaves to Northern America was birthed...

The Africans had been trading goods with European merchants for centuries. Around the year 1619, Europeans needed help to work their lands, so they provided a host of bribes to the traders, such as textiles and other goods, in exchange for slaves. Initially, less than one hundred people, mostly impoverished ones, were taken. Unfortunately, as the greed escalated, these same African traders became rich. Other Africans—those who were either leaders, had some power themselves, or craved that power—wanted "a piece of the action." This barbaric greed created rivalry between the African traders and the powermongers who eventually prevailed. Those who triumphed formed an alliance with the Europeans who, in turn, gifted them with vast numbers of weaponry.

With these weapons, powerful troops were created to subdue and capture entire African communities and completely change the political structure in many areas of Africa. The class system no longer existed, and virtually any able body was "fair game." People of all walks of life were snatched from their homes. Any influential person who was deemed a threat to the existing powers was captured. This included priests of the African magico-religious practices, tribal chieftains, Islamic leaders of religious and/or and magical practitioners, Christians, political rivals, and especially those born into royalty, such as the famous Prince Abdul Rahman Ibrahima ibn Sori.

As word spread, the demand for free slave labor ensued, resulting in the birth of African slavery into the Americas. Sadly, between the seventeenth and nineteenth centuries, a vast slave trade was created in which traders kidnapped and enslaved African victims. These Africans were then transported mainly into the Americas, which included countries such as Brazil, Portugal, and Spain. They were also sent to Northern America and the islands throughout the Caribbean, such as Cuba, Haiti, Barbados, etc.

How far was this greed carried out? It is roughly estimated, according to the Trans-Atlantic Slave Trade Database, that 12.5 million enslaved victims were transported. However, only 10.7 million survived the ghastly, unspeakable acts of torture they endured on their journey. It's mind-boggling to realize that the horrifying treatment of these people during the voyages alone resulted in the deaths of nearly two million poor souls.

Slavery in North America

Of the 10.7 million slaves who made it to the Americas alive (mostly departing from Central and West Africa), approximately 388,000 (or 3.6%) were shipped directly to North America, which is a smaller figure compared to the immense number of slaves who were shipped to the aforementioned countries and islands.

In the beginning of this chapter, both the definition and the inclusion of other magical systems of Hoodoo were described. To better understand how these other magical systems were integrated into the practice of Hoodoo, it is first important to know exactly where the importation of Africans occurred in what is now known as the United States of America (USA).

When the slave trade began, the United States was then called "British North America," and what we now call the "States of the Union" were referred to as "colonies." When the slaves were initially brought to British North America, they were sent into the Southern Colonies of:

- Georgia
- North Carolina
- South Carolina
- Virginia

As time passed, the colonies/states to adopt slavery grew to include:

- Alabama
- Arkansas
- Delaware
- Florida
- Kentucky
- Louisiana
- Maryland
- Mississippi
- Missouri
- Tennessee
- Texas
- Virginia
- West Virginia (the state of Virginia was divided into two states)

Sadly, 388,000 slaves were not enough to satisfy the insatiable greed of numerous slave owners, especially those in the Southern Colonies. But they didn't purchase more slaves; instead, they created a more despicable and economical ploy to increase their slave count. In Douglass's book *Narrative of the Life of Frederick Douglass, An American Slave,* he stated that there was a credo amongst slave owners that any children born of "negro" women were to be considered "negroes" and, thus, destined for slavery.

This core mindset encouraged white slave owners to rape African and/or African American women or force them into prostitution for the sole purpose of impregnation. These atrocious acts thus produced more slaves without having to pay the purchase price. According to Douglass, even though this procreation practice resulted in lighter skin-colored children who often resembled their fathers, the slave owners didn't care that they were torturing their own biological children.

As a result of these ongoing procreation acts, by the year 1860, there were over 4.4 million slaves living in the Southern States. It's sickening to learn that the country with the least number of slaves entering the Americas ultimately produced more slaves than any other slave country or island. Additionally, the statistic of 4.4 million living slaves does not account for those who had died, escaped, gained their freedom, or lived in the Northern States. These factors provide a probability that even more slaves had been procreated within North America than what has been published.

What the Africans Brought into the Americas

As previously stated, the African people had immense knowledge of art, technology, medicine, mathematics, astronomy, and more. It appears obvious that many slaves were intellectually superior to their owners. The enslavers knew this, so many barbaric measures were employed to keep the people submissive and isolated, unable to engage in anything other than manual labor. Yet, the slavers could not eradicate their intellect, faith, wisdom, or the knowledge of their magical-religious backgrounds.

To get a better idea of their tenets, let's first explore their religious and/or magical-religious belief systems...

In the past, although there were many religions practiced in Africa, the three predominant ones were:

1. The least popular of the three religions practiced by the first African slaves to enter the Americas was Judeo-Christianity. This religion expanded, especially on the West Coast of Africa, in the eighteenth century. It was basically birthed when christianized slaves from Europe and the Americas returned to Africa and preached the "new" religion to others. They were predominantly Catholics. Later, Christian missionaries entered Africa to preach and convert.

2. Countless of captured Africans were Muslims or had exposure to the religion of Islam. In fact, the very first contact made in Africa between the white Europeans and Africans was on the West Coast of Africa. The Africans who made the first contact with white Europeans were called "black Moors" because they were of the Islamic faith. Most of the black Muslim slaves believed in the powers of Witchcraft and brought the knowledge of crafting magical (written) words, charms, amulets, and talismans with them. In fact, Muslim slaves in the Americas were highly acclaimed for the immense powers of their magical charms.

3. The predominant faith of the first slaves to enter the Americas was a combination of magic integrated with religion. This system is known today as "magico-religious practices." Mirriam-Webster defines this as "belonging to or having the character of magical practices to cause a supernatural being to produce or prevent a specific result." Magic was an integral part of their religious lives. Although there were variations in the viewpoints and practices from town to town or even village to village, the core beliefs were basically the same. Similar to Catholicism, they believed that there is one ultimate higher power and underneath this higher power is a pantheon of entities, or supernatural beings, who are worshipped and petitioned for assistance with the needs of the devotees.

From past to present, many of the African magico-religious worshippers, such as those who practice the Yoruba religion, engage in voluntary spirit possession. The human hosts allow benevolent entities, such as their deities, to temporarily 'borrow" their bodies. The purpose of the actual possession, or "being mounted," is to provide a favorable benefit for the human hosts and/or those around them.

Sometimes, the mounting will occur from a simple mutual agreement between the entity and the host. In other cases, mounting is accomplished by summoning rituals that included rhythmic drumming and dancing, prayers, shouting, singing, and so on.

Practitioners of the magico-religious faiths also had an intimate relationship between the supernatural and natural or mundane, world. They were skilled diviners and herbalists. Many of these Africans were experts on the uses of herbs, barks, leaves, and roots (therefore, sometimes referred to as "root doctors"). They believed that all plants and roots have spirits who are ready, willing, and able to communicate with the herbalist, telling them what they are capable of accomplishing.

Not only did the slaves bring their knowledge of divination and herbalism to the Americas, but also their expertise in crafting talismans, charms, and magical charm bags for almost any need. Most notably, their knowledge of how to appeal to their deceased ancestors for assistance was of the utmost importance (to be discussed in the next chapter).

The Diaspora of the African People and their Magico-Practices

It took me awhile to grasp the interpretation of the term "diaspora" because it has been oftentimes used out of context. According to the Oxford Dictionary, it is a simple definition: "The dispersion or spread of people from their original homeland." Therefore, the diaspora of African religions and traditions simply mean the dispersions of these practices outside of Africa. Now that this has been made perfectly clear (at least to me) let's explore this diaspora!

The slave owners of the Americas and their islands tried to completely wipe out all forms of African culture. They attempted to do so because they believed that if they allowed the African culture to endure, there would be a unity of power amongst the Africans. This unity could eventually create a rebellion against their slave owners.

As stated earlier, North America brought in the least amount of people from Africa. These slave owners didn't own many slaves, making it easier for them to separate African families and friends from one another. The slave owners even separated those who spoke the same languages in order to completely isolate each slave from any type of familiarity. The strategy of these actions, along with the brutality of nearly perpetual torture for even attempting reminiscence, was to eradicate the remembrance of both Africa and its beautiful culture. Slave owners believed that these actions would facilitate submissiveness and cause future generations to become indifferent to their heritage. However, this strategy wasn't completely successful, as you will later see...

In contrast, other countries in the Americas brought in an enormous number of slaves—so many that most slave masters owned large groups of slaves, including complete families and those who spoke the same languages. The acts of brutal torture were not as frequent or profound as it was in North America. As a result of these actions, it was more difficult to completely eradicate African culture and religious beliefs.

Fortunately, African slaves outside of North America were therefore better able to preserve their fundamental beliefs, rituals, and styles of worship, but not in their original forms. Instead, they were modified to fit their new environments. The adaptations were successful, largely in part through syncretism. The merging of the African magico-religious with that of the religious and spiritual beliefs of the hosting countries gave birth to modified, or new, African Diaspora Religion (ADR) or African Derivative Traditions (ADT).

The Nigerian slaves who were brought into Cuba, a predominantly Catholic country, saw numerous similarities between their African deities (or "Orishas") with that of the Catholic saints. For example, the Orisha Oshun had many attributes and qualities similar to that of the Virgen Caridad del Cobre, the patron saint of Cuba. This gave rise to the syncretism of Oshun with the Virgen Caridad, and they are often both referred to and worshipped interchangeably by many, including myself. This ingenious syncretism of the Orishas was applied to almost all the Catholic saints, allowing African worshipping styles to be secretly rooted into Catholic customs. This practice gave birth to the ADR of Santeria. Similarly, the merging of Catholic saints and African deities in Haiti gave birth to the ADR of Haitian Vodou. As you will later see, Haitians and Cubans play a significant role in the growth of Hoodoo in North America.

In the meantime, let's take a look at just some of the ADRs and ADTs, as well as those which were birthed in the Americas and its islands:

- **Bahamas:** Obeah, Haitian Vodou
- **Belize:** Dugo Obeah

- **Brazil:** Batuque, Candomble, Catimbo, Macumba, Quimbanda, Umbanda
- **Columbia:** Columbian Yuyu (Juju)
- **Cuba:** Santeria, Palo, Abakua, Arara
- **Curacao:** Montamntu
- **Dominican Republic:** Dominican Vudu
- **Guyana:** Comfa, Obeah
- **Haiti:** Haitian Vodou
- **Jamaica:** Kumina, Myal, Obeah
- **Puerto Rico:** Sense Espiritismo
- **Saint Lucia:** Kele
- **Suriname:** Winti
- **Trinidad and Tobago:** Trinidad Orisha, Obeah
- **Venezuela:** Venezuelan Yuyu (Juju)
- **USA:** Hoodoo, Louisiana Voodoo

The above list does not account for all of the countries and islands that accepted slaves, nor does it contain all of the innumerable ADRs and ADTs. The intention of this abbreviated list was just to give you an idea of the diverse and wondrous African influences throughout the world.

As you can see, both Hoodoo and Louisiana Voodoo were birthed in the United States. So, let's continue to explore the slaves' journeys to see how this happened.

The Slaves' Experiences in North America

These few succeeding pages do not remotely account for all of the hardships suffered by the slaves at the hands of their owners. This is, instead, my respectful intention to open the eyes of the uninformed, to incite curiosity, and, hopefully, to entice others to further research the topic of slavery and its aftermath. In the meantime, here's a brief overview...

The Hardships

The unrelenting and hideous physical torture, as well as mental abuse imposed upon these people by their slave owners, was only the beginning. Most slave owners employed brainwashing techniques as an attempt to achieve unconditional compliance, cooperation, and even gratitude from their slaves.

Can you believe it? The slavers had the audacity to expect gratitude from their slaves! But the process of handling slaves had been meticulously calculative in its attempt to achieve all desired goals. Slave traders had this down to a science, and operated in three phases: slave raiding/trading, slave breaking/making, and slave labor/slavery. The attempted brainwashing occurred in the slave breaking/making phase.

In this phase, there is attempted deculturation—a process by which an ethnic group is forced to abandon their languages, culture, customs, religions, and belief systems. As previously mentioned, the first slaves were immediately separated from their friends, family, or anyone who shared the same languages or familiarities. Additionally, this tactic also produced isolation, as it is a documented fact that humans are hardwired to interact with others. When we are isolated, we crave any type of social interaction, whether positive or negative, making us vulnerable to adopting radically different beliefs.

Next, the attempted imposition of a different belief system began when the Christian slave owners and/or representatives of their churches continuously upheld the notion that it was an act of providential mercy for the Africans to have been rescued from their lives of "savagery" in Africa.

Thereafter, the first slaves and their descendants were taught by the Christians that this type of servitude is honorable and noble because it is "God's will" and is, thus, pleasing to Him. How was this accomplished? By teaching only select versus of the Christian Bible—those that were out of context to the body of the parables.

For instance, a very popular verse taught to the slaves was as follows:

> *"Bondservants, be obedient to those who are your masters according to theflesh, with fear and trembling, in sincerity of heart, as to Christ; not with eyeservice, as men-pleasers, but as bondservants of Christ, doing the will of Godfrom the heart, with goodwill ldoing service, as to the Lord, and not to men, knowing that whatever good anyone does, he willreceive the same from the Lord, whether he is a slave or free."* (King James Bible, Eph. 6.6–8)

The above example illustrates the blasphemous attempts at achieving gratitude from their slaves. As a matter of fact, in the British West

Indies Islands, the entire Holy Bible was disassembled and reconfigured specifically for slaves (for further reading, see *Unholy: The Slaves Bible* by David Charles Mills).

Their Endurance

While the slave owners believed that they were successfully eradicating all remembrance of African culture, most slaves still retained memories of their magico-religious practices. The first slaves quickly learned how to communicate with one another. Not only did they discuss their spiritual beliefs, but also practicing their magic in secret locations. Due to new environmental factors and constraints, the original practices of Africa were obviously altered. This appears to be the birth of Hoodoo and the start of its preservation through oral tradition.

Occurring concomitantly throughout the antebellum era of slavery, the missionaries and other Church representatives insisted that all people of color turn to Christianity. However, most owners disapproved of these mandates and feared rebellion if slaves were taught that all men were created equal. So, compromises were made between the slavers and Church representatives. As a result of these mutual concessions, Africans and their descendants lived amongst a plethora of ever-changing, conflicting, and confusing "biblical" codes of behavior dictated by their Christian owners, representatives of the churches, and even the government. Depending on the individual slave owner or the location, the religious doctrines taught to the slaves were obscured in ambiguity.

Most slaves were kept illiterate. Some slaves were severely beaten if they did not follow the blasphemous reorganized scriptures that were preached to them. In fact, Frederick Douglass once said that the non-religious slave owners were not as cruel as the religious ones because the latter would take biblical scriptures out of context as an excuse to further torture their victims. Slaves must have wondered, "How can their God be so cruel? This doesn't sound right!"

In other locations, slaves were either allowed or forced to attend church services. While church leaders were reluctant to preach the gospel to them, the slaves, in turn, grew weary of the white preachers' repetitive sermons that included nonsense such as "Obey your Masters," "Servitude to your Master is akin to servitude to God," or other similar ideas.

Nevertheless, despite the best efforts of the slave owners, the African people and their descendants were not fooled. In fact, they were profoundly underestimated. Despite the brutal repercussions if discovered, they were determined to keep their culture alive at any cost—and many did pay the price. Yet, they continued to face the deceptions of pseudo-Christianity by acting submissive, successfully deceiving their owners into believing that they had completely alienated their heritage and beliefs.

A great example of the resilience of slaves' attitude toward Christianity is that of a few documented cases of Muslim slaves. As an attempt to continue observing their religious beliefs and practices, they would "humor" the Christians by saying that God is Allah and Jesus is Mohammed. Same players, different names? Or was this the beginnings of pseudo-syncretism between Islam and Christianity in an attempt to fool the slave owners? No matter how one interprets these responses, it's no doubt an act of perseverance. The intelligence, strength, and fortitude of the slaves prevailed.

Their Perseverance

As continuous religious and political pressures demanded the conversion of slaves into Christianity, many Christian churches allowed them to worship. During services, the slaves tended to express religious emotions and actions similar to that of African religious behaviors. They exhibited acts of singing, praying, shouting, and rhythmic dancing. These behaviors were later famously termed "Ring Shouts" or "Danced Religions."

Additionally, while performing these acts, they were also calling upon and welcoming the Christian Holy Spirit into their bodies. Sound familiar? Well, that sure sounds similar to a magico-religious summoning ritual to me! African traditions were clearly being brought into Christianity. However, equally important is that Christianity was also being bought into the African belief system.

Because religious leaders were reluctant to teach slaves the Holy Scriptures, they instead taught select (mostly illiterate) slaves a negligeable portion of scriptures. Later, minimally prepared, these people were sent to preach the scriptures to fellow slaves. Many of the selected people were also Hoodoo practitioners and integrated their magical knowledge into the translation of Christianity, becoming phenomenal preachers.

As a result of their remarkable preaching techniques, countless of followers could identify with the plight of Moses leading the escaped slaves into the promised land. Thousands believed that the Holy Bible was a mystical book filled with magical recipes and remedies. Optimism for a better future was awakened. The combining of Hoodoo and Christianity resulted in a complimentary marriage.

Perseverance is the act of continuing in spite of difficulties, failures, or opposition. Having faced the gravest of dangers, against all odds, the Africans and their descendants have achieved what millions would not dare to tackle. They preserved their traditions and beliefs as much as they could. These people were amazingly resilient!

The Migration and Growth of Hoodoo

Now we know how Judeo-Christianity and Islamic practices became integrated into the tradition of Hoodoo. However, that wasn't all that was happening. Other magical belief systems were also combined into the craft. Let's explore what else happened before, during, and after the introduction of Christianity into Hoodoo...

How did people share information with others before the age of telephones or computers? Through eavesdropping, intimate verbal, and/or visual interactions. When people migrated from one area to another and interacted with natives of differing cultures, new information and ideas were shared. As we already know, the exchange of communication expands our knowledge base. The growth of Hoodoo also did so in this manner.

Native American Influence

Native Americans of the Chickasaw, Cherokee, Choctaw, Creek, and Seminole nations, historically called "The Five Tribes," owned black slaves. This occurred in the Native territory which is now modern-day Oklahoma. The owners engaged in the same forced reproductive practices (as did many white slavers) and also viewed these offspring as being racially distinct from themselves and more akin to their slaves. As a result of this practice, thousands of mixed-raced slaves were produced.

However, Native Americans were also enslaved, particularly the Wando, Kiawah, Stono, Etawan, Edisto, Tuscaroras, and Yamassess tribes of the Lowcountry (the Carolinas). During the Colonial Era, thousands were captured and sold. By the year 1708, South Carolina had an enslaved population of twenty-nine hundred African descended slaves and fourteen hundred Native American slaves. Intimate relationships ensued, and there were oftentimes intermarriages of Native Americans to Africans. This practice was not limited to the Carolinas and, frequently, both races could be found on auction blocks in areas such as Louisiana.

Both cultures had an immense knowledge of magic and spirituality. These interactions enriched both the craft of Hoodoo and Native American practices.

European Influence

Most people living in North America were of European heritage. Thus, there was a profound interaction between Europeans and slaves, resulting in a melding of magical beliefs and practices. Dr. E. Franklin Frazier had published his dissertation as a book entitled *The Negro Family in the United States.* One excerpt from his extensive research reads, "Magic and folk beliefs of the rural Negroes in the United States, some African elements have probably been retained." He also inserted that, due to the extensive interaction between the two cultures, it was a very difficult task to separate African from European magic and folk beliefs.

Likewise, in his dissertation entitled *Slave Religion,* Albert J. Raboteau elaborated on Dr. Frazier's findings, stating "Many Afro-American Witchcraft beliefs are European in origin. The capacity of folk beliefs from different peoples to parallel and mutually influence one another makes the enterprise of separating one from another difficult..."

Noteworthy were the magical contributions to Hoodoo from the Pennsylvania Dutch. Erroneously called "Dutch," they were a German cultural group with many of their own magical practices. They settled in North America from the seventeenth through nineteenth centuries. As native Pennsylvanians intensely interacted with slaves and helped to fight for their freedoms, the sorcerers were also exchanging magical knowledge. However, did you know that the Pennsylvania Germans had also been influenced, to some degree, by Jewish Kabbalah mysticism?

Jewish Influence

The Sephardic were the first of the Jewish people to immigrate from Europe to North America. As early as the 1600s, while settling in the Northern Colonies, many also settled in the Colonial South, including Georgia, Texas, Virginia, North Carolina, and South Carolina—the colony with the longest history of Sephardic settlement. As time passed, the Ashkenazi Jews followed suit. Though most Jewish immigration took place after the Civil War, several small settlements arose throughout the country.

Due to the lack of synagogues and, therefore, a formal religious community, the practice of Judaism wasn't as structured as it is today. Their belief systems were instead heavily based on mystical and magical practices. The mystical Jewish texts of the Kabbalah, Zohar, and Sefer Yetzirah were gladly shared with the non-Jews in the new world. These texts were not only heavily influenced by the Germans of Pennsylvania, but also helped to shape the growing philosophies and value systems of North America.

However, some Jews also became slave traders, while many were slave owners. According to the website *My Jewish Learning,* while their population was relatively small at the time, over 75% of Jewish families living in Charleston, South Carolina; Richmond, Virginia; and Savannah, Georgia owned slaves. Furthermore, nearly 40% of Jewish households across the country were also slave owners. ("Where the False Claim that Jews Controlled the Slave Trade Comes From"). Yet, the interactions and sharing of magical knowledge between the Jewish people and the Africans (as well as their descendants) contributed to the growth of Hoodoo.

Caribbean Influence

Colonial Louisiana was originally under Spanish rule and later became maintained by the French in 1699. Slavery was then introduced by the French colonists in 1706. Their first targets were the indigenous people of Louisiana. Thousands of defenseless Native Americans were killed, and even more were captured and enslaved, including the Atakapa, Bayogoula, Natchez, Choctaw, Chickasaw, Taensa, and Alabamon peoples. Between 1710–1721, the French introduced African slaves, predominantly arriving from the French West Indies into Louisiana.

These slaves also attempted to preserve their magico-religious practices. Having been integrated into the religious beliefs of both the French and Spanish Catholics, the belief system now adopted Native American magical practices. What is now known as Voodoo—not to be confused with the spiritual practices of Haitian Vodou or African Vodoun—was birthed in French Louisiana. At that time, Voodoo was considered both a cult as well as a magical system of practice.

In 1768, the Spanish re-established their rule of Louisiana and banned the trade of Native Americans. But they did not abolish the African slave trade. What did they do to acquire more slaves? They replaced the prospective Native American slave population by shipping in Romani slaves. Now there is interaction, as well as a possible sharing of magical practices, with yet another cultural group of people.

Between 1792–1803, there was a successful insurrection by self-liberated slaves against the French colonial rule in Saint-Dominique, a Caribbean island of Hispaniola which is known today as Haiti. Thousands fled to New Orleans and produced a profound catalyst to the practice of Voodoo.

When Louisiana became a territory of the United States in 1804, New Orleans shortly thereafter began its reputation as the capital of Voodoo and Hoodoo. This is why many people of today believe that these terms are all synonymous, but they are not. Voodoo has deep African Haitian origins, whereas Hoodoo (although it is alive and thriving well in Louisiana) does not.

The Cuban people also play a role by introducing and integrating their ADRs into the craft of Hoodoo. Some Cubans migrated to Louisiana with the Haitian people during the time of slavery, while others arrived in the United States after emancipation. However, they play a much larger role, along with people from other Caribbean islands, as you will later see in this chapter.

Asian Influence

After slavery was abolished in the United States, the importing of Chinese people (some arriving from Cuba) became the new labor supply in the South. Many worked alongside the freed African American slaves. Because numerous Chinese people had their own magico-religious beliefs and practices, yet another exchange of magical knowledge ensued.

The Flexibility of Hoodoo

In exploring the etiology and journey of Hoodoo, we've barely scratched the surface of its migration. Most of the slave states had their own differing systems of Hoodoo practices due to the integration of various cultures and with whom the slaves associated. Other considerations were the environmental availability of herbs, roots, minerals, etc. Books have been published on the magical practices of the Gullah people, an African American ethnic group predominantly residing in Florida, Georgia, South Carolina, and North Carolina. Other published books include the practice of Hoodoo in Memphis, Tennessee, South Carolina, and other states, yet each book differs in its approaches to spellwork.

Obvious examples of varied approaches to Hoodoo spells are illustrated by one of the most prolific researchers on the topic of Hoodoo: Harry Middleton Hyatt, M.A., D.D. He was an Anglican minister who collected folklore as a hobby and travelled to many states to gather information about the craft. From 1936 to 1940, he interviewed approximately sixteen hundred African American Hoodoo practitioners from the states of Alabama, Arkansas, Florida, Georgia, Illinois, Louisiana, Maryland, Mississippi, North Carolina, South Carolina, Tennessee, and Virginia. Hyatt collected over 13,458 separate Hoodoo spells and folkloric beliefs and published them in a five-volume, 4,766-paged collection entitled *Hoodoo, Conjuration, Witchcraft, Rootwork.*

In numerous instances, the approaches to spellwork and the rituals differed, depending on the location of the informant.

Clearly, Hoodoo is neither a rigid magical practice, nor is there only one single "correct" way of performing a spell. It is, instead, a diverse, evolving craft that adjusts to time, location, and other people. However, the core beliefs are African, and many of their descendants bravely kept the craft alive just as they did with their heritage—through oral tradition.

The Ups and Downs of Hoodoo

Following emancipation was a period in history called "The Reconstruction Era," taking place approximately between the years of 1863–1900. It was a time when the United States attempted to cohesively integrate millions of newly freed African Americans into the existing social, political, and labor systems of the country. However, in the beginning, the attempts made by the "powers that be" to deculturize the African Americans continued.

Immediately following emancipation, clergy and educators from the Northern States were called upon to repudiate the practice of Hoodoo. The cultural reformers, both black and white, attacked the craft by declaring Hoodoo as merely a slave superstition. Knowing that the freed slaves desired racial advancement, the reformers asserted that the belief in the craft was both degrading and reminiscent of the demoralizing experiences of bondage. These affirmations successfully persuaded many—but not all—freed slaves to abandon their magical belief systems.

As a result, from approximately 1863 until the early 1880s, Hoodoo was nearly forgotten. While many African Americans who were striving for racial advancement lost their interest in Hoodoo, a smaller population, including many escaped slaves, kept the craft alive by passing on their knowledge to their descendants and close friends. Then, in the mid-1880s, Hoodoo again regained popularity amongst many of those who had either lost interest in the craft or had no knowledge of it. However, that popularity yet again declined after the turn of the century, regaining popularity from 1920 to 1940, and suffering another downturn from 1940 until 1970.

The eras experiencing a decline in the interest of Hoodoo was mostly a result of intellectual and cultural shifts. Additionally, there was an unwillingness of the middle class African Americans to abandon scientific progress. They detested and feared having their identities attached to the stigma of being influenced by superstition. Thankfully, it was the working class African Americans who continued to keep Hoodoo alive.

In the 1930s, acclaimed anthropologist and author Zora Neal Hurston's most important and extensive research was on the topic of Hoodoo. She ultimately proclaimed that Hoodoo was primarily African in nature and a vital element of the black people's racial identity. Unfortunately, the middle-class African Americans had no regard for her suppositions. However, today, Hurston's research is highly regarded by countless of African American people of all classes, as well as Hoodoo practitioners.

In the 1970s, Hoodoo again regained its popularity when an influx of Afro-Cubans immigrated into the United States and brought their African Diaspora Religion of Santeria with them. As the Cubans associated with others, portions of their practices integrated into Hoodoo and revived an interest in the craft. Later, the same occurred with the immigration into the United States of Bahamians and their practice of Obeah; The Puerto Ricans and Sense Espiritismo; Trinidadian's Shango; Brazilian's Candomble; and another influx of incoming Haitians and their practice of Vodou. Since the 1970s, Hoodoo remains popular.

The Politics of Hoodoo

Is Hoodoo a closed practice? Is Hoodoo only allowed to be practiced by African American people?

The prevalent argument amongst the African American people is that Hoodoo was brought into the United States by the African people. Their descendants created it, suffered to nurture it, and kept it alive. Therefore, the craft belongs solely to them.

The counterargument from other races is that Hoodoo has too many other magical systems integrated into the craft. It is not pure African, but, instead, a potpourri of differing magical systems, along with the religious worship of Christianity. Therefore, it is an "All-American" folkloric practice.

You, the reader, have been given the facts. The decision is now yours. If you do choose to practice Hoodoo, please first allow me to share my personal opinions...

My mother was Afro-Cuban and my father was white. The Cubans called me *La Americana* ("the American"), while most white people called me "The Cuban." Always having been in the middle, it was easier for me to see both sides of a coin. Here again, it is easier for me to see both sides of the argument. However, there are weaknesses to either side that ought to be addressed.

Hoodoo does indeed have too many other magical systems integrated into the craft for it to be professed as being a pure African practice. For groups requiring initiations into the craft, such as the Gullah people and those practicing Louisiana Hoodoo, yes, it's a closed practice because their secrets remain secrets. But overall, there are tens of thousands of magical Hoodoo spells that have been openly disclosed for over a hundred years.

If you had read the introduction, you already know my history with the African Diaspora Religions. Palo is a closed practice, as there are numerous secrets in the religion that should never be shared with an outsider. Why? Because there are too many factors that require years of knowledge. Neophytes attempting to practice Palo can be compared to a medical student attempting to perform open heart surgery. All aspects of Palo ought to be closed to non-initiates.

Santeria, on the other hand, is the worship of the Orishas/saints. Everybody is welcomed to love, honor, and respect the deities. Outsiders are welcomed to give offerings to the deities and ask for favors. However, to acquire more knowledge about the belief system and gain a closer relationship with the Orishas, secretive initiatory practices ensue, and those particular aspects of Santeria become a closed practice.

Sadly, Palo and Santeria are being exploited on social media by popular criminals, con artists, drunks, and drug addicts. With thousands of followers, these people have caused the practices to become grossly misrepresented and misinterpreted for the sake of the almighty dollar. It's infuriating to watch them being blasphemed. Since the same is happening to Hoodoo, can you blame others for demanding it to be a closed practice?

One cannot simply read a book or two about Hoodoo, profess expertise, then refer to oneself as a "Root Doctor," "Trick Doctor," "Conjure Doctor," "Two-Facer Doctor," "Two-Handed Doctor," or "Wangateur." Yet, many do. Is that insulting to the African Americans? Of course, it is! Others practice Hoodoo in ways that show contempt and disrespect toward the African American people. It's unadulterated hypocrisy.

My advice to all is that if you plan to practice Hoodoo, know its history and respect the craft, its journey, and its people. Remember the old adage "The Negro is a man without a history?" Well, my friends, the truth is the exact opposite: The African American is a person with a rich, diverse, challenging, and breathtaking history. RESPECT THE PEOPLE!

CHAPTER TWO

YOUR ANCESTORS AND SPIRITUAL COURT

Most practitioners of the African traditional and diaspora practices honor their ancestors, one higher God, and a pantheon of deities to call upon for assistance, comfort, and spiritual as well as day-to-day guidance. Thanks to the Judeo-Christian influences, Hoodoo also provides a plethora of entities to call upon for the same purposes, as well as assisting us with our magical spells.

These entities are your spiritual court and include:

- Your Ancestors
- God, Our Father
- Jesus Christ
- The Holy Spirit
- Moses
- Holy Angels
- Your Guardian Angels
- Your Spirit Guides
- Your Affinity Spirits
- The Archangels
- The Saints

Of course, there are numerous deities in the African diaspora religions and traditions that many Hoodoo practitioners also honor and petition. This practice is perfectly acceptable. However, always make sure that you know exactly who the deity is. Thoroughly research any unknown entity, as you may inadvertently call upon an entity that is not benevolent. So, be careful. The same advice applies to angels and saints. There are around two hundred fallen angels that are demonic in nature, yet some are referred to as "saints."

One last piece of advice: Never pray in a language that you don't understand, and never take someone else's word for it. There are many instances where people have been tricked into calling upon something malevolent. Except for your ancestors, all the aforementioned entities understand all the languages of our world.

Now that we are properly prepared, we are ready to explore our Spiritual Court...

Honoring Your Ancestors

"We become who we are by standing on the shoulders of those who came before us."
Old Yoruba Proverb

In addition to God and the pantheon of deities, numerous African people also worship their ancestors. It is believed that ancestors, both those who died long ago and those who passed more recently, have the power to intervene and mediate between the living and the pantheon of deities. The ancestors have this power because they are spirits and, therefore, have faster accessibility to the aforementioned entities.

The Glue That Keeps Us Together

In parts of Africa, honoring one's ancestors was and still is a daily discipline, as well as part of annual celebrations. It is believed that each generation has the responsibility for preserving the wisdom of their ancestors. From youth to elder, every member of the family unit has an important designated position in ancestral ritual activities. They all respect and depend on one another for the knowledge and expertise that each individual holds in their roles.

Within the perspective of ancestral veneration in the African religious practices, there is a strong belief in reincarnation. It is believed that people reincarnate within their own family lineage and are, therefore, the ancestors of their own future reincarnations. Because the deceased return to their own family lineage, the living try to make the location that they helped to shape a better place than they had left it. It is important to keep family traditions and shared memories alive through ritual and verbal communication in order to help each other remember their past lives. Otherwise, all would be forgotten because, as humans reincarnate, we tend not to remember. It is also believed that calling on one's ancestors going back seven generations will enable everyone to identify with previous incarnations.

When the African people were captured and forced into slavery, the ritualistic roles each had in ancestral veneration were destroyed for both the slaves and the family members left behind. Many of the first African slaves wished for death, believing that would enable them to return to their native lands.

The African diaspora practices throughout the Americas have spent years reintroducing ancestral veneration, but with many modifications. Of course, depending on the demographics and location of the practitioner(s), there are slight variations in prayers and offerings.

Everyone Has a Right to Honor their Ancestors

As with the African diaspora practices around the world, many Hoodoo practitioners also engage in ancestral veneration. We turn to our ancestors for spiritual enlightenment, healing (physical and emotional), comfort, protection, survival, character improvement, and guidance when we are experiencing any type of difficulties. We can also turn to different ancestors for different issues. Everybody, even those not affiliated with any religion or magical craft, has the right to communicate with their ancestors. It is our birthright, and it is impossible for anyone to take that right away from us.

A Glimpse into the Experienced Practitioner's Practice

Before teaching you how to begin your practice of ancestral veneration, questions may arise that need to be addressed before proceeding. You might say "Well, that isn't the way I saw John Doe do it," or "I saw Jane Doe do many things that you didn't teach me." So, allow me to address the most common observations made by a newcomer.

Someone might have an ancestral pot containing rocks because it is believed that rocks have the ability to amplify prayers. Or, you might see a long, decorative cane without a handle. In some homes, depending on the practice, you might see a pot, cane, and/or altar in either the bathroom or the basement. These are all tools and locations to represent ancestral veneration. Oftentimes, you'll see a lit cigar used as an offering or for cleansing.

Don't be alarmed if you see food offerings on a cracked plate: it's not disrespectful. That crack represents the body of the deceased that had been discarded when the soul was elevated. Many times, you'll see someone offer libations by pouring water or some sort of alcoholic beverage in a bottle cap, then use their fingers to drizzle it on the floor as an offering. Or they may instead put the libation in their mouths and spray it onto one of their ancestor tools.

The aforementioned actions are all easily explainable ritualistic tools and behaviors of either initiates or highly experienced practitioners. However, all these experienced people started their ancestral rituals from the very beginning. They began their journey in simple steps, so that's where we'll start too...

Ancestral Veneration for the Beginner

Step One: Know Who You're Going to Summon

Only call upon ancestors that you know are of good character. Do not call on those with unquestionable oddities, such as histories of criminal behavior, emotional instability, or had exhibited destructive or self-abusive behaviors such as alcoholism, drug addictions, and the like. Any predominant behaviors of the invoked ancestors will directly affect your situation.

For example, my great-great grandmother poisoned her husband, my great-great grandfather, for repeatedly cheating on her! Although she was a lovely woman, she's also a murderess, and I would not wish to receive any homicidal energies from her.

Also, do not call on any ancestors that you know nothing about. Someone may have undesirable traits that could unfavorably affect you. It's a good policy to simply wish them well and move on.

Step Two: Make Four Lists

Write out four lists, one with all the known deceased female ancestors from your maternal side and then another of all the known deceased males. Repeat the process for your paternal side. Try to use the women's birth names if you can. Arrange the lists in chronological order, from the most recently deceased to all the way back to the most distant past, or visa-versa—it's your personal choice.

Do not include relatives that have died within the last year. Highly experienced practitioners called "Elders" perform specific ceremonies so that the recently deceased do not become earthbound ghosts. It is my preference to allow these spirits to rest for a year so that they may return with the ability to freely come and go as they please.

Last, next to each name, write down their accomplishments. As an example, let's pretend that John Doe is one of my ancestors. I would say: "John Doe, who was born and raised in Kansas, moved to Texas in adulthood, attended the University of Texas, then moved to Houston, worked for NASA, and became a rocket scientist."

Simply make notes about each person on your list. It may sound tedious at first, but remember the African people's rationale for doing so: to keep family traditions and remembrances alive through ritual and verbal communication

Step Three: Include Affinity Spirits if you Have them

Awo Falokun Fatunmbi coined the term "affinity spirits" to describe any historical figure who has inspired an area of your life and continues to guide you. It is my preference to only include those that will remain part of my ancestral spiritual court. Many African Americans, for example, include affinity spirits such as Harriet "Mama Moses" Tubman, Frederick Douglass, Dr. Martin Luther King, Rosa Parks, and other notable supporters of civil rights.

Anybody can call on anyone, no matter your gender, race, religion, or political views. Do not allow people to tell you otherwise. If you truly honor and respect the spirit, they will most likely help you. Just don't take advantage of their willingness to help.

Here is an example of how to call on an affinity spirit: "Albert Einstein, who was born in Germany, later moved to Italy, and then to Switzerland to study mathematics and physics. You later immigrated to the United States and became a world-renowned scientist."

Out of respect for your ancestors, your affinity spirits are called on last.

Step Four: Setting Up Your Altar

First, determine a permanent location in your home for your altar. It is preferable to select a quiet location, such as a bedroom or even a bathroom. Once you have determined where the altar will be placed, you will need the following items:

- A small wooden table
- A white cotton cloth
- Clear glass candle holder
- White candles
- A clear drinking glass
- Clear or plain white ceramic cup
- Plain white ceramic dish
- Clear flower vase
- Fresh white flowers (preferably carnations)
- A smooth small waterproof mat
- Your four lists

Place the cloth over the table. The candle holder with the candle ought to be centered, but slightly toward the back of the altar. Place the vase with water and the white flowers on one side of the candle and the glass container with fresh water on the other side. Place the mat on the floor in front of the altar so that it slightly touches the front feet of the table. Have your lists ready. You will need the rest of the items later.

Light the candle and wait five minutes before dedicating your altar. The purpose of waiting is because the flame of the candle serves two purposes. First, it pierces the veil between the spiritual world and our mundane world, and gives the flame time to pierce that veil. Secondly, the flame can feed the entities energy from the fire.

Step Five: Invoking Your Ancestors

Knock on the altar three times to grab their attention, then call on your ancestors and affinity spirit(s). If you are female, call on the females of your maternal side first, followed by the males of your maternal side. Then, call on the females of your paternal side, followed by the males of your paternal side.

If you are male, call on the males first of your paternal side, followed by the females on your paternal side. Then, call on the males of your maternal side, followed by the females of your maternal side, as previously directed.

If a male and female are present together, such as siblings, the male would call on all the ancestors, both male and female, on the paternal side. Then, the female would call on the ancestors of the maternal side, as previously directed. Call on your affinity spirits last.

Once the invocation is completed, try to sing either a religious or spiritual song. You will sing the same song each time they are invoked to create familiarity.

Next, tell them who you are, announce that you are dedicating the altar to them, and tell them it will be their permanent home when they visit. Also, let them know that they are free to come and go as they please, because your home is their home. Then, tell them to enjoy their candle, flowers, and fresh water that you have offered. You do not need to stay with them for the entire time, but remain at least for fifteen minutes. For the first few times, refrain from engaging in conversations or asking for favors. Allow time for your ancestors to get used to you.

The candle ought to be lit for at least two hours. When you are ready to extinguish the candle, knock three times on the altar. Then, dismiss them as a group by simply addressing them as "My ancestors" or "My ancestors and ____ [name of affinity spirt(s)]." Thank them for visiting and, if they wish to leave, to go in peace. Then, snuff out the candle (never blow out a candle, as it is disrespectful to the fire spirits).

Fresh water needs to be given daily. After all, how would you like it if you stopped by someone's house and they provided you with a glass of stale water?

Step Six: Offering Meals to Your Ancestors

After the first invocation, it is a nice idea to offer your ancestors food and libations thereafter. Spirits will consume the essence from the offerings, which gives them nourishment and energy.

Repeat the invocation process described in Step Five, followed by the song, then bestow your offerings. It ought to be a portion of the meal that you had made for yourself and/or your family. Always give the ancestors the first portion. The food is placed on the white ceramic dish, and the libation—such as coffee, tea, or an alcoholic beverage—is poured in a cup. Ensure that hot beverages are not too hot, just as if you're offering it to the living. Place these offerings either on the altar or the mat on the floor. Tell them what you're giving them and say something like "Enjoy your meal."

When you're ready to extinguish the candle, ensure that you ask for their blessings first. Then, repeat the dismissal verbiage in Step Five.

The food and libation ought to stay where it is for twenty-four hours, no more, no less. Then, take everything somewhere outdoors where wild animals can enjoy the "leftovers." Do not discard anything in the garbage, as it implies that the food your ancestors enjoyed was simply garbage. It's insulting.

Food and libations ought to be offered to your ancestors at least once a week. If you start accidentally dropping food on the floor, it means that one of your ancestors wants the same food. Offer it on the altar or the mat. Later, you might begin to smell food or libations. It is another indication that an ancestor desires something to eat or drink. The same applies to the odor of cigars or cigarettes. Light the tobacco, lay it on a clear or white ceramic ashtray, and place it on the altar.

As time goes on, you may sense a desire to place more decorative items on your altar. Just remember to always keep everything clean and uncluttered. You may also increase your communication with them, just as if living relatives are in your home. Feel free to talk openly. Ask for guidance, blessings, and assistance. However, do not ask for many things at one time. It's confusing and insulting.

That's the process, and it's not as difficult as many fear it to be. Eventually, you'll become comfortable performing the ritual and, of course, your communication skills will improve. It will just take a little bit of time.

Communicating With Only One Ancestor

If you need to communicate with only one ancestor, invoke only that spirit in the invocation process followed by your song. Then, offer food and libation. Begin the communication process. You can ask for help or guidance in any type of matter, but restrict your bidding to just one problem or question per sitting. Patiently wait for an answer. If nothing is given to you in the first twenty minutes, you will most likely receive the answer later. Remember to thank your ancestor and ask for a blessing before you extinguish the candle, which ought to be at least two hours after first igniting it.

Answers to your query may come to you immediately, hours later, in the course of a day, or even days later. The answers could be given to you in dreams, in the movement or behaviors of animals, sudden changes in the weather, or many other ways. It is a bad idea to look for signs because anything and everything around you could be misinterpreted as such. Instead, let the signs come to you. If you didn't get a sign or couldn't interpret what a specific sign meant, ask your ancestor for clarification.

God

Addressed by countless of names such as: Allah, Adonai, Elohim, Jehovah, Yahweh, etc.; God is the creator of the universe, everything in it, and of all living creatures. Some Hoodoo practitioners have claimed their success as a result of a special revelation from God. Other practitioners believe that an essence of God is within all human beings, and our ability to perform magic successfully is a result of the powers contained within that very essence.

The belief that all humans possess an essence of God also extends to Catholicism. Decades ago, my deceased husband's cousin attempted to take advantage of me. Hesitant to continue helping an ungrateful person, I sought the advice of a Catholic nun. Expecting her to say "Turn the other cheek and help her," she instead became angry and, almost yelling, declared: "God is within each and every one of us. If you allow her to take advantage of you, then you are allowing her to take advantage of God. That is the TRUE sin. Stay away from that woman!" It was a valuable life-lesson.

Most Christians are familiar with "The Lord's Prayer," which is a perfectly acceptable invocation to God. However, there is an abundance of other prayers in both the Hebrew and Christian Bibles. Amongst them are the Psalms. It is widely believed by most Hoodoo practitioners that the Book of Psalms is a collection of magical incantations. Either recited orally or sung, these prayers are designed to appeal directly to God for specific favors. Later on, we'll be discussing the powers of the Psalms, along with individual ones that can be recited for specific needs or desires.

Jesus

Also referred to as Jesus Christ or Jesus of Nazareth, He is the central figure of Christianity. He was a Jewish rabbi who had performed many miracles during his lifetime.

The most common representation of Jesus is either a crucifix—a man affixed to a cross—or just the cross. This is because He was executed by being nailed to a cross and tortured. It is believed that He was willingly executed for both the past and future sins of all mankind. In other words, He took on the punishment for our crimes against God the Father. The third day after His physical death, He was resurrected, and His presence was witnessed by several people. His followers spread word of His teachings, the miracles He had performed, and His rebirth. Thus, more followers were gathered, and, ultimately, the religion of Christianity was born. The first formal Christian Church was created around the year AD 300. Today, Christianity is the world's largest religion.

It is said that Jesus was conceived by the Holy Spirit, born of The Virgin Mary, and, after His resurrection, ascended into Heaven, from where He will return to judge the living and the dead. Because of these declarations, some Christians believe that Jesus is God incarnate, while others believe that He is the son of God.

The Christian Bible tells people that they should pray to God the Father using the name of Jesus because He is the mediator between man and God. Therefore, millions of people pray to Jesus for their needs and desires.

Jesus and the Conversion Process

For various slave groups, especially those who were to be baptized into Protestant Christianity, religious experiences were required from one another as proof of worthiness to join the Church. One former slave stated that "Nobody can talk about the religion of God unless they've had a religious experience in it." (Raboteau)

These conversion experiences entail entering secluded areas and concentrating on their queries. The similarities of what each person had experienced included having feelings of heaviness or sadness from the weight of sinfulness, followed by receiving visions, and/or falling into trances. They were then transported into Hell while interacting with a threatening demon. Later, an emissary from Heaven becomes the savior and rescuer, revealing Heaven and God while informing the person that they have been saved. Many see Jesus as the emissary, and one slave even reported witnessing Jesus read the Bible. Once saved, the slaves were worthy for baptism.

Today, in some areas where initiations into Hoodoo are obligatory, one prerequisite within the initiation process is to partake in a ritual called "Seeking Jesus." This ritual includes a combination of Christian practices similar to the conversion process practiced by the slaves and West African customs.

The Holy Spirit

As previously mentioned, some Christians believe that Jesus is God incarnate. This is because they view God as triune, expressed as God the Father, God the Son (Jesus), and God the Holy Spirit (or Holy Ghost). This triune is referred to as the "Holy Trinity." However, others see them as separate or independent agents.

It is believed by some Christian religions that the Holy Spirit as an extension of God can mount a human being and take possession of them. Many engage in this practice to provide a favorable benefit to the hosts or to the community. The mounted hosts might speak in languages unknown to the hosts or to others. This is called "speaking in tongues," and is referred to as a heavenly language. Partaking in spirit possession by the Holy Ghost was also a common practice amongst the slaves in the early Black-Christian churches.

The image of the Holy Spirit is often depicted as a white dove...

As many of my readers know, my love for German shepherd dogs (GSD) is vehement. Most of my dogs have been titled in Schutzund, a sport designed specifically for the GSD, entailing expertise in tracking, obedience, and protection.

My boy, Lobo, was very good with obedience and protection, but he continuously faltered in tracking. Every single time he would compete in the sport, his terrible tracking techniques disqualified us from further activities within the first five minutes of the contest.

Having failed with everything that experts advised me to do, it became my mission to take matters into my own hands. The best course of action, in my humble opinion, was to combine spellwork with an appeal to the Holy Spirit.

The Spell

Five nights before an upcoming competition, a yellow nine-inch candle was cleansed with Florida Water, followed with holy water. It was blessed in the name of the Father, the Son, and the Holy Spirit.

With a pencil, the candle was inscribed from bottom-to-top with the word "success" nine times. Lobo's picture was also inscribed once, with the words: "I will have a passing score in tracking." His picture was placed face up in a candle holder. Then, the candle was placed directly over his picture.

Without extinguishing the candle, which burned for about twenty-eight hours, I prayed to the Holy Spirit every few hours and begged for Lobo to pass the tracking phase. When the candle finally extinguished itself, the wax remains showed what appeared to be a dove in flight. The remaining wax and picture were buried in my front yard.

The Astonishing Results

On the day of the competition, Lobo had the highest tracking score of any other dog: 99 out of 100. He then obtained the highest score in obedience.

After all dogs completed the first two phases, it was lunchtime. For the rest of my life, I'll never forget what happened next. Someone exclaimed: "Oh my God, Aida! There's a white dove on top of the barn and it's looking right at you!" I looked up and my eyes locked onto the bird's gaze. This continued for about five minutes, then it flew away.

Lobo went on to get the highest score in protection and came home with five trophies. My only request was to pass tracking, but the Holy Spirit must have looked favorably on my pleas. By the way, Lobo never faltered in tracking again for the rest of his life.

White doves are rarely seen in these areas. Nobody knows where it came from, nor do we know where it went. Here is the prayer:

Prayer to The Holy Spirit

"Breathe into me, Holy Spirit, that my thoughts may all be holy. Move in me, Holy Spirit ,that my work, too, may be holy. Attract my heart, Holy Spirit, that I may love only what is holy. Strengthen me, Holy Spirit, that I may defend all that is holy. Protect me, Holy Spirit, that I may always be holy.
(Ask your petition)
Amen."

Moses

"In all the signs and the wonders, which the Lord sent him to do in the land of Egypt to Pharaoh, and to all his servants, and to all his land, and in all that mighty hand, and in all the great terror which Moses shewed in the sight of all Israel."
(Deut. 3.11–12)

One of the most memorable movies ever produced was *The Ten Commandments,* a 1956 religious classic starring Charlton Heston as

Moses. The movie depicts many miracles performed by Moses through the use of his magical staff. Some of the phenomena included converting the staff into a snake, turning the Nile into blood, creating lice, locusts, frogs, and many other astonishing feats. The most dramatic scene of the movie, however, was the parting of the Red Sea.

It's been a comical habit of mine to jest with my religious Jewish friends when discussing Moses. My response to any topic concerning Moses always begins with "Yeah, yeah, yeah, I saw the movie!" But the truth is, although an incredible classic, it gives the viewers just a modest glimpse into his life, history, and knowledge of mysticism. Many academics and Jewish scholars who study Moses are familiar with his understanding of the magical practices, as were the African American slaves.

The Hebrews were enslaved by the Egyptians for around four hundred years. Moses, a Hebrew, was found, adopted, and protected by the Pharoah's daughter—the childless Queen Twosret. She became his mother, thus making the Pharoah his uncle. This lineage placed Moses as the second in line to the throne—the Pharoah's son being the first.

Moses was raised in nobility as an Egyptian, acquiring his royal training from scholars. It is speculated by many academics that this band of scholars also included the Pharoah's court of male sorcerers—the magicians of Egypt. Therefore, we can highly suspect that Moses was a masterful sorcerer. Sadly, Moses wasn't considered to be a wise man by Egyptian standards. This is because the Pharoah's sorcerers were considered the wise men given their knowledge and skills of eloquence. Moses, unlike his teachers, had a severe speech impediment.

Following the death of Moses's uncle, his cousin became the new Pharoah. While Moses was tremendously bothered by the torture endured by the Hebrews, he later learned that he, too, is a Hebrew. Moses forfeited his life of riches and luxury to free them. Moses met God, who helps him with the task by giving him magical powers. In the Book of Exodus, God said to Moses "See, I place you in the role of God to Pharoah…" (Ex. 7.1).

Moses appealed to the new Pharaoh to free his people, but he was refused. He then demonstrated his magical abilities by turning his staff into a snake—an Egyptian magical symbol. However, Pharoah was not impressed, as his magicians demonstrated the same ability. Did Pharoah believe this to be an old parlor trick? Even when Moses's snake consumed the magician's snake—implying that his magic is more powerful than that of the magician—the Pharoah remained indifferent.

Because the Egyptians viewed the Nile as the bringer of life, Moses next used his staff to turn the Nile into blood. However, the Pharaoh's magicians were able to do the same. Following that event, Moses turned all the dust of the earth into lice, fleas, and pestilence, impressing the magicians. Thereafter, Moses outperformed the magicians with one unique miracle after another, including causing boils on people's skin, thunderstorms of hail and fire, manifesting swarms of locust, and creating three days of darkness. These feats converted the Pharoah's magicians into believers.

Finally, when the Angel of Death took the lives of the first-born males of Egypt, the Pharoah finally allowed the exodus. Moses led his people into freedom and, during their voyage through the desert, continued to perform many magical feats.

The African American people were wise to the symbolism behind the stories and honored Moses as the great Conjure Man, who, despite his speech impediment, was able to conquer all obstacles to free his people from slavery. In fact, other African descendants of slavery also honor Moses. For example, in the Haitian diaspora of Vodou, a deity named "Damballa" is honored as their snake God. He is looked upon as an intelligent, patient, wise, and kind deity. Damballa's syncretism is Moses.

The Catholics, as well as many other religious denominations, believe that it is perfectly acceptable to pray to Moses for assistance. Numerous Hoodoo practitioners pray to him for help to obtain magical powers.

Holy Angels

Angels, as believed by many religions, are celestial beings who stand by, worship, and serve God. There are countless angels, and their specific roles depend on their standing in the hierarchical structure. The traditional hierarchy of angels, ranked from lowest to highest, comprise of nine orders: angels, archangels, principalities, powers, virtues, dominions, thrones, cherubim, and seraphim.

Angels are mentioned throughout the Holy Bible. For example, in the Book of Luke, angels proclaim the birth of John the Baptist as well as the birth of Jesus (Lk. 1.11–2.20). Why do angels have such prominent roles in the Bible? Because the duties of many are to serve as messengers of God, act as intermediaries between God and humans, and/or to intervene and intercede on behalf of mankind.

Some angels are "psychopomps," those with the responsibility of escorting newly deceased souls of humankind from earth to the afterlife. Having been a trauma nurse for many decades, I have witnessed numerous patients conversing with unseen forces before passing over. When asked who they're talking to, they would proclaim that they were talking to angels.

Many Christians believe that angels also serve to save individuals in perilous times. Have you ever heard of someone being involved in a tragic accident whereby, for some "unknown" miraculous reason, the person survived? Most likely, angels were involved in the rescue.

We can certainly pray to angels for help and praise them, especially when they have granted our petitions. They don't seem to get the acknowledgement that they duly deserve. Even St. Pope John Paul II once suggested that modern mentality should come to see the importance of angels.

Avoid the Fallen Angels

If you're unfamiliar with an angel from whom you wish to petition, always research the name and history first. There are around two hundred angels who had fallen out of grace with God and were kicked out of Heaven. After their downfall, they turned demonic in nature. They follow Satan—also known as *Iblis* in the Islamic faith—"the King of the Demons." The predominant names are well known, so it's neither a time-consuming nor difficult task to investigate.

If you cannot find the name of an angel, then assume it's an unknown entity. Never call upon unknown entities by name, as you may take the chance of inviting something malevolent into your life.

Your Guardian Angels

A profound opening statement of *Ancient Aliens,* a television program on the History Channel airing since 2010, reminds me of our guardian angels. The announcer, referring to extraterrestrials on Earth, exclaims: "We are not alone. We have *never* been alone." This statement also applies to every individual person because we all have guardian angels assigned to us from the time our souls entered our bodies.

Our guardian angels, the lowest on the hierarchical structure of angels, are assigned to watch over us and to warn us when we face impending danger or unscrupulous people. Their role is also to protect us, as clearly stated in Psalm 91: "For he shall give his angels charge over thee, to keep thee in all thy ways. They shall bear thee up in their hands, lest thou dash thy foot against a stone." (Ps. 91.11–12)

In addition to protecting us, they serve as our personal psychopomps, escorting us into the afterlife when we die. In a nutshell, they are with us pre-birth to post-death.

Our guardian angels are acknowledged by many religions, including Judaism, Christianity, Islam, Zoroastrianism, and even Thelema. While some believe that we are assigned anywhere from one to ten guardian angels (depending on the religion or faith), it is my personal belief that we are each assigned two.

When we have what is perceived to be a "gut feeling" to abstain from an activity or to avoid certain people, it is in actuality a warning from our guardian angels. Many times, I have ignored a bad "gut feeling," and it turned out that the warning was correct. How many times has it happened to you? How many times was the message ignored, and then later regretted? On 2 October 2014, even Pope Francis told his gathered crowd of thousands that people sometimes have those "gut feelings." He said: "Oftentimes we have the feeling that I should not do this, this is not right, be careful," explaining that these feelings are actually "the voice of your guardian angel." ("Homily for the Feast of Holy Guardian Angels")

It is highly advised by both religious leaders as well as many metaphysical practitioners to not only trust your guardian angels, but to express gratitude for their efforts. Establishing a quick verbal relationship with them by acknowledging their presence on a regular basis is a good start. Have you seen the numbers 111 or 1111? Many practitioners say it is a sign that your guardian angels wish for their presence to be known. When you see these numbers, verbally thank them for protecting you, because it aids in developing a much stronger bond between you, them, and God.

Your Spirit Guides

There are many schools of thought on the definition of spirit guides. In most of the African magico-practices (and as was taught to me), it is believed that spirit guides are humans that have died, crossed over to the other side, and return to Earth to help others. Animals that have passed can also return as spirit guides.

You may have known the spirit guide during that person or animal's lifetime. The entity may have been a teacher, a friend, co-worker, relative, admirer, lover, partner, or pet. Sometimes, a spirit guide who owed you a karmic debt from a previous incarnation may watch over you until an opportunity arises to repay that debt.

As a rule, spirit guides come and go out of our lives, depending on our particular needs. For instance, during my tenure as a trauma nurse, there were times that I had saved lives without ever learning how to perform a particular life-saving technique. Yet, they were performed impeccably. They were probably spirit guides of doctors or nurses with advanced degrees assisting me with the procedures. Or they could have been the patient's spirit guides or guardian angels attempting to save their lives.

Some spirit guides will stay with a person for their entire lifetime. Many mediums and psychics proclaim that their abilities to communicate with the spiritual realm is due, in part, to the assistance of their lifelong guides.

Most spirit guides are teachers and are available to any person upon their request. Simply ask God through prayer to send you a teacher who is an expert in the topic of which you desire to gain knowledge and/or comfort. There are also many instances where they will automatically find and teach us something that they believe is imperative toward our physiological, emotional, spiritual, social, or academic growth.

Your Affinity Spirits

As previously mentioned, the term "affinity spirit" is used to describe any historical figure who has inspired you in any area of your life. My favored affinity spirits include Geronimo, the great and brave warrior, and the masters of science: Albert Einstein and Nikola Tesla. These people have always inspired me because of my love of science and the high value placed on defending both my rights and the rights of others.

Affinity spirits can also include ascended masters—those who were once human, but have achieved great spiritual growth. They are leaders in the spirit world, acting as guides and teachers to mankind. Examples of ascended masters include Mohammed, Buddha, and Vishnu.

The Archangels

Archangels, or "Chief Angels," are those who serve God directly. Because of this prestigious title, there's a common misconception that they are the highest ranking in the order of the hierarchy of angels. But, as previously discussed under the "Holy Angels" section, they are the second-lowest ranking in that hierarchy.

Although St. Raphael the Archangel states: "I am Raphael, one of the seven angels who stand in the glorious presence of the Lord, ready to serve him," disagreements exist as to the number of those in existence (Tob. 12.15). Some religions adhere to the belief that there are indeed seven, others believe that there are ten or more, while the Eastern Orthodox tradition mentions "thousands."

We'll probably never know the exact number of existing Archangels, but we can always petition them for assistance with our needs and desires. Archangels are also regarded as saints, the most popular or well-known being St. Michael, St. Raphael, and St. Gabriel.

The Saints

When most of us think of saints, we think of a deceased person canonized by the Catholic Church. Canonization is a procedure by which the Church declares a Christian to be united with God in Heaven, an intercessory to God on behalf of the living, and worthy of veneration. Quite a few African magico-religious deities have syncretism with Catholic saints.

People belonging to other organized religions can also be held in the same regard, but they are not called saints, as this title originated in Christianity. They are given different titles but share the same attributes with the saints, such as being a wonder worker and possessing a special relation with the Holy Spirit.

The title has also been informally designated to hundreds of deceased people who the regional populaces believe to be worthy of the honor. These spirits, referred to as "folk saints," had characteristics in life similar to those of canonized saints. They are also considered to be intercessors with God on behalf of the living.

However, many unscrupulous people, as well as demons, have been categorized as "folk saints." So, you are once again reminded to extensively research any entity for whom you wish to petition.

A Word About the Man at the Crossroads

Although not a member of everyone's spiritual court, he is highly regarded by most Hoodoo practitioners. People meet him at the crossroads to perform spellwork, make deals with him, and ask him to deploy—or to carry on—their spellwork.

As we already know, Santeria is an ADR which derives from the Nigerian religion of Yoruba. We believe that the man at the crossroads is Eleggua, a loving Orisha who exists in other ADRs with similar names.

Eleggua has twenty-one paths. Although a few of those paths are that of a trickster, he can also reside in our garbage or guard the crossroads. However, many Hoodoo practitioners believe that the Man at the Crossroads is the devil. Although not a fact, it is my personal belief that this reputation was erroneously acquired through Eleggua's antics as a trickster.

When going to the crossroads to petition him, he can simply be addressed as "Man of the Crossroads." Just remember that if one calls upon the devil, one will most likely acquire the devil or one of his demon followers. So, please be mindful when calling upon entities by their names!

Be Respectful

No matter who you petition within your spiritual court, always be respectful. Be humble, honest, and appreciative. Remember the expression, "you can catch more flies with honey than with vinegar."

In the next chapter, we will explore the most successful ways of gaining favor from the saints. The same respectful actions ought to be applied to any benevolent entity who has the power to help.

CHAPTER THREE

THE SAINTS AND THEIR PRAYERS

"And the smoke of the incense, which came with the prayers of the saints, ascended up before God..."
(Rev 8.4)

Saints, like angels, are able to interact directly with God. They do not directly answer our prayers, but instead take our prayers directly to God. We can think of saints as representatives of mankind's needs and desires.

My personal interpretation of this structure is akin to that of a court case. The saint acts as an attorney seeking a favorable ruling from God, the judge. However, there are phases involved to establish the ideal attorney-client relationship:

Phase One: The Attorney's Experience

The correct attorney for the job must have experience in the field for which one needs representation. A real estate attorney would not do well in a medical malpractice case, right? So, their experience is extensively researched before they are chosen.

Phase Two: The Consultation

The attorney and the client get to know each other. The lawyer then decides if the prospective client is worthy of their services. Therefore, the client must be on their best behavior.

Phase Three: The Down Payment

If the attorney decides to take the case, a down payment, or "retainer fee," is required. A mutual agreement is established regarding further payment as the job progresses.

Phase Four: The Attorney Hears Your Case

One doesn't briefly tell the facts to their legal counsel just one time. The client and their attorney spend many cumulative hours or days together until the facts are clearly understood.

Phase Five: The Judge Hears Your Case by Your Attorney, the Intercessor

The attorney stands before the judge, relays the client's case, character, and integrity, then pleads for a favorable ruling.

Phase Six: Payment in Full

If the attorney wins a favorable ruling, the client pays the remaining debt.

Your Attorney, the Saint

When petitioning saints, similar principles apply to the above phases of the attorney-client relationship. We will now employ these same techniques toward achieving a favorable outcome with our requests.

Selecting a Saint

The history of almost all of the saints can be easily found online. Most saints have led lives of specific hardships for which they serve as champions for those who suffer similar hardships. Other saints are commanded by God to help us with specific needs. Their "patronage" is the area for which they give support. One of the best webpages I have found on specific saints and their patronage is *Catholic Online.*[1]

1 www.catholic.org/saints/patron.php

However, please don't *just* research their domains. Read about their lives as well, because being acquainted with a saint's life, experience, or purpose for serving others helps to establish a closer relationship. It fosters a mutual understanding of one another.

Once you familiarize yourself with the saints, never petition two saints at the same time for the same purpose. This behavior casts doubt on your faith in the saints' abilities, it's insulting to them, it could cause confusion, and your petition may not be granted. How would a judge feel if two different attorneys approached them on different days for the same case?

Again, remember that some entities proclaiming to be saints do not have honorable intentions. Avoid any saint for whom you cannot find information, or if the information seems ambiguous. Always be suspicious of obscure entities, and do not petition them. Charles Horton Cooley (17 August 1864–7 May 1929), a famous sociologist, once said "...Unless we can understand something as to how the motives that issue from this obscurity are generated, we can hardly hope to foresee or control them" ("On Self and Social Organization," 22).

Consulting the Saint and Making the Down Payment

Once you have chosen a saint, it is important to first establish a rapport and provide a down payment without asking for anything in return. We do this by first offering either a five-day, seven-day, or nine-day glass-encased vigil candle and a fresh glass of water replenished daily. The flame of the candle provides energy and nourishment, while the water is refreshing.

Since white is a neutral color, a white candle can be offered to any entity. Many spiritual shops, as well as Latin grocery stores, carry saint candles. They are of various colors depending on the saint's preferences. First, be conscientious of fire safety. Place your candle inside a candle holder, then place this on a metal container, such as a pie plate, that sits over two stacked cork coasters. Other practitioners scatter sand on the altar, then set their candle holders atop.

Light the candle. Offer the glass of water and recite the saint's prayer aloud. In many African diaspora practices, prayers are shouted. It is my personal belief that sound is energy more easily transmitted into the spiritual realm.

Before saying "amen," which closes a prayer, introduce yourself and tell the saint to enjoy the candle and water. Do not tell the saint anything else. Then, close the prayer. Repeat daily, around the same time each day, without extinguishing the candle. By the time the wax has been totally consumed, the saint has had time to study your character.

Once your down payment has been delivered and prior to explaining your case, think about what the full payment ought to be. Unless otherwise specified, full payment could consist of one or several of the following ideas:

- Donating money or food to the needy in the name of your chosen saint.
- Donating money to a church bearing the name of your saint.
- Publicly thanking the saint on various social media platforms.
- Offering white roses or carnations on your altar.
- Buying a statue or framed picture of your saint and proudly displaying it in your home.
- Offering prayers to God for nine consecutive days in praise of the saint.

The Novena—Relaying Your Case

A *novena* is an ancient tradition of praying. Derived from the word *novem,* meaning "nine" in Latin, it is a nine-day prayer. They are popular throughout the world, including in Latin America, the Philippines, Melanesia, and Africa. The magico-religious influences still hold firm in areas of Africa because the novenas are also accompanied by singing, clapping, waving, or "shout offerings."

But why nine days? Most Christians explain that the number nine represents several miraculous Biblical events. However, this number is also significant in other religious and metaphysical practices. For example, in Hoodoo, it represents mastery and wisdom, while other practices proclaim that the number nine embodies triple perfection. Nevertheless, this time frame allows you ample opportunity to make your case perfectly clear to your saint.

People often ask me how it's possible to believe in God, yet practice magic. My response is always the same: "If you pray novenas, then you are practicing a magical ritual that just has a different name..."

Timing

With exceptions such as St. Martha who requires nine consecutive Tuesdays, almost all novenas are performed on nine consecutive days. Although not critically required, the start day is usually consistent with the saint's preferred day of the week.

The time of day usually doesn't matter. However, you must ensure that the start time selected for the ritual is the same each day. Because prayers are interpreted as music in the spiritual world, imagine that your favorite song is aired on the radio at exactly 1:00 pm daily. Wouldn't you tune in to hear that song every day? Well, it is believed that saints do the same to hear your prayers.

The Candles

Due to the ever-changing profit-making demands of candle production companies, nine-day glass-encased candles are rarely available, as they are costly to make. Therefore, it will be important to buy two five-day or seven-day candles in order to complete the novena. Do not allow the first candle to extinguish itself. Once the amount of wax is barely visible, the second candle should be lit to ensure continuity. If the second candle hasn't extinguished after completing the nine-day novena, just allow it to continue burning.

The Process

Light the candle and place a fresh glass of water on your altar. Because the flame of the candle pierces the veil between our world and the spiritual world, it may take a few minutes. So, wait five minutes before starting the novena.

Remember that all prayers must be recited aloud. Call the saint's name three times, then begin your prayer. Unless otherwise directed in the prayer, before saying "amen," which closes the prayer, tell the saint who you are and plead your case. Talk to the saint as if a child is talking and pleading with a parent to gain their pity and favor. Be humble, respectful, and display humility. Tell the saint everything that happened and make your request. Then, tell the saint what your payment will be if your petition is granted. Tell them to enjoy the candle and the fresh water. Thank the saint, then close the prayer with "amen." Repeat every day for a total of nine days.

Everything you say and promise ought to be consistent for the entire time. Don't change your mind or add more to the request. Remember, this is a song. How would you feel if your favorite recording artist changed the words to your favorite song on any given day?

To avoid forgetting what your payment will be, write it down. Once the candle wax has been consumed, place that paper in the candle container and keep it until your petition is granted. This way, the paper will remind you of the promissory payment.

Example

Let's pretend that John Doe has a heart condition and prays for healing. So, he appeals to St. Raphael, the healer, for help.

He places a fresh glass of water on the altar, lights the candle, and waits about five minutes. Then, he recites the formal prayer aloud. Before saying "amen," he pleads his case. He says:

"St. Raphael, I am John Doe, born on January 1, 1808.
I have a heart condition and have been to four different doctors who all say that I cannot be healed.
I beg of you, St. Raphael, to please help me.
Please help to heal my heart and make it healthy again.
I have a wife and three small children who need me.
My wife is not healthy and unable to work, so, without me, my family could possibly become homeless.
My children need their father.
Please, St. Raphael, please help me.
If you grant me this favor, I promise to donate $100 to a church named after you.
Thank you for listening to my prayers.
Enjoy your candle and your fresh water.
Amen."

He repeats the exact prayer, pleas, and promise for a total of nine consecutive days. When the novena is completed, he places the paper with the promissory payment in the candle container.

The Case is Heard by God

Once your novena is completed, the saint will present your case to God. This may take time, because the saint may have other cases to present before yours, and we don't know what the wait time is for the saint to be heard before God. Therefore, you must have patience and not pester the saint for immediate results. Think of it this way: how would your attorney feel if you kept calling every day and pleading for immediate answers when he doesn't even have a court date?

If there is no movement within a few months, God may not have ruled in your favor. But if your petition is granted, then payment must be made.

Make Payment in Full

Honor your promissory payment, light a taper candle anointed with olive oil, and recite the formal prayer to the saint. Then, vehemently thank the saint for helping you and tell them how and when payment will be or was made.

In the future, always refer to that saint with respect. Never say "I used this saint," as it is both presumptuous and disrespectful. Instead, it is most appropriate to say "The Saint helped me."

A frequent question amongst my followers is if it's true that a saint will punish a person if they fail to make payment. The answer is a resounding "NO!" These entities are good, righteous, and holy. However, failing to make payment and then appealing to the saint for another favor will be performed in vain. Most people have reported that, not only did the original saint ignore their petitions, but so did all the others. In magico-religious practices, it is believed that only thieves expect to get something for nothing...

Common Difficulties

This book contains only the most prevalent conditions or illnesses endured by many of my clients throughout the years. A brief history of the saint ruling the specific domain will be delivered, along with their novena prayers. For conditions not mentioned, simply conduct an internet search using the words: "Patron saint of ___ (occupation, condition, or specific illness)," or search the website provided earlier.

Abusive Relationships

St. Rita of Cascia was born in Italy around the year 1381. At an early age, she begged her parents to allow her to enter a convent, but was instead arranged to marry a cruel man named Paolo. Young Rita became a wife and mother at only twelve years of age, and her husband was a man with a violent temper. In anger, he often mentally and physically abused her. Paolo had many enemies, but Rita's influence over him eventually led him to be a better man.

Following the deaths of Paolo and both of her sons, Rita joined a monastery. She died in 1457 and is buried at the Basilica of Cascia. Centuries following her death, it was discovered that her body was incorrupt, or almost perfectly preserved. Rita was canonized by the Catholic Church in 1900.

St. Rita had endured much pain in her lifetime and can certainly have empathy for those who are abused. She is also able to tame the abusers.

Day of the week: Sunday

Prayer for Abusive Relationships

"St. Rita, worker of miracles, from thy sanctuary in Cascia,
where in all thy beauty thou sleepest in peace,
where thy relics exhale breaths of paradise,
turn thy merciful eyes on me who suffer and weep!
Thou seest my poor bleeding heart surrounded by thorns.
Thou seest, O dear Saint, that my eyes have no more tears to shed, so much have I wept! Weary and discouraged as I am,
I feel the very prayers dying on my lips. Must I thus despair in this crisis of my life? O come, St. Rita, come to my aid and help me.
Art thou not called the "Saint of the Impossible," an advocate to those in despair? Then honor thy name, procuring
for me from God the favor that I ask.
(Explain your case and plead your petition here)

Everyone praises thy glories, everyone tells of the most amazing miracles performed through thee, must I alone be disappointed because thou hast not heard me?
Ah no! Pray then, pray for me to thy sweet Lord Jesus that He be moved to pity by my troubles and that, through thee, O good St. Rita, I may obtain what my heart so fervently desires.
AMEN."

Animal Conditions and Illnesses

St. Francis of Assisi was born around 1181 in the town of Assisi, Italy. He was the son of a rich man and a charming, spoiled "party-boy" who always got his way.

However, when God called to Francis to follow Him, he did so. Donning the clothing of a poor shepherd and surrendering his worldly goods, Francis began preaching to the people about peace with God, with one's neighbor, and with oneself.

He loved nature, slept in the open, and preached the brotherhood with all of God's creations. Francis believed that nature and all God's creations were a part of His brotherhood. Any animal was as much his brother, and he intermingled with them as such.

There are two famous stories relating to Francis's interaction with animals. He once preached to hundreds of birds about being thankful to God for all that they have. The birds stood still as he walked among them, only flying off when he said they could leave.

The second story involved a wolf that had been eating human beings. When the townspeople wanted to kill the wolf, Francis intervened and talked the wolf into never killing again. The wolf became a pet of the townspeople, who made sure that they always had plenty to eat.

By the time that Francis had died in 1226, he started a new religious order called "The Franciscans" and helped St. Claire of Assisi to start the order known as "The Poor Claires." He bore the stigmata on his own hands, side, and feet, correlating with the five wounds of Jesus on the cross.

Canonized by the Catholic Church in 1228, St. Francis of Assisi was declared the patron saint of animals.

Day of the week: Monday

Prayer for Animals

"Heavenly Father, our human ties with our friends of other species is a wonderful gift from You. We now ask You to grant our special animal companions Your fatherly care and healing power to take away any suffering they have. Give us, their human friends, new understanding of our responsibilities to these creatures of Yours. They have trust in us as we have in You; our souls and theirs are on this Earth together to give one another friendship, affection, and caring. Take our heartfelt prayers and fill your ill or suffering animals with healing light and strength to overcome whatever weakness of the body they have.
(Explain your case and plead your petition here)
Your goodness is turned upon every living thing and Your grace flows to all Your creatures. From our souls to theirs, goodness flows, touching each of us with the reflection of Your love. Grant our special animal companions long and healthy lives. Give them good relationships with us, and, if You see fit to take them from us, help us to understand that they are not gone from us, but only drawing closer to You. Grant our prayer through the intercession of the good St. Francis of Assisi, who honored You through all Your creatures. Give him the power to watch over all our animal friends until they are safely with You in eternity, where we someday hope to join them in giving You honor forever.
AMEN."

Blockages in Your Path

St. Peter was born around AD 1 as "Shimon Bar Yonah," sometimes called "Simon." He became an Apostle of Jesus, who renamed him "Peter"—a nickname meaning "rock." Jesus says to him: "And I say also unto thee, that thou art Peter, and upon this rock I will build my church," going on to say, "and I will give unto thee the keys of the kingdom of heaven..." (Mat. 16.18–19).

After Jesus died, St. Peter began preaching Christianity and did indeed build the first Christian Church in Rome, becoming its first Pope. Sadly, somewhere between AD 64–68, he was crucified upside down on a cross and died.

Because St. Peter holds the keys to the pearly Gates of Heaven, he can unlock all doors and open all roads.

Day of the Week: Monday

Prayer to Open the Roads

"O Holy Apostle, because you are the Rock upon which Almighty God has built His Church, obtain for me, I pray you: lively faith, firm hope, and burning love, complete detachment from myself, contempt of the world, patience in adversity, humility in prosperity, recollection in prayer, purity of heart, a right intention in all my works, diligence in fulfilling the duties of my state of life, constancy in my resolutions, resignation to the will of God, and perseverance in the grace of God even unto death, that so, by means of your intercession and your glorious merits, I may be made worthy to appear before the Chief and Eternal Shepherd of Souls, Jesus Christ, Who with the Father and the Holy Spirit, lives and reigns forever.
(Explain your case and plead your petition here)
AMEN."

Bullies

St. Alexis (*San Alejo*) was born around the year AD 380. The only son of a wealthy Roman senator, he learned to be charitable to the poor and eventually walked away from all of his worldly possessions. He spent the rest of his lifetime amongst the poor, living as a beggar.

During his life, he faced constant persecution and ostracism for being a beggar, but remained steadfast until his death somewhere around AD 430. For what he had endured, he has great sympathy for those who are also ostracized by bullies, and he will drive them away.

St. Alexis was canonized by the Catholic Church in an unknown year, and he was declared the patron saint of beggars.

Day of the week: Sunday

Prayer to Drive Away Bullies

"Oh, glorious St. Alexis, virtuous and blessed Saint,
that, inspired by the Lord, you walked away from family life
and you knew to give up everything to live alone and in begging.
Blessed St. Alexis, you who have the power to move away
everything bad that surrounds the servants of the Lord, I beg you to
protect and defend me and give me energy, strength, and courage.
Kind St. Alexis, you who found favor before Mary,
today I need your help, please don't leave me abandoned. In all
humility, I ask you to take away the enemy and evil from my side.
Get me away from Satan, liars, the ruin of treacherous people,
curses, evil eyes and tongues, of the traitors, the slanderers, and the
harmful ones. Get me away from everyone who wants to see me
rendered and sunk. Keep me from envy, evil, and injustice.
Keep me from jealousy and resentment, of rejection and loneliness.
Hide me where they can't find me from those who want to cause my
downfall. Oh, Glorious St. Alexis, called "The Man of God,"
bring me closer to Jesus and Mary, so that with their Divine
Goodness, they cover me with all their goods to guide me and set me
free of all spiritual and earthly evil, and help me get the grace that I
humbly request of you today.
(Explain your case and plead your petition here)
Blessed St. Alexis, by the grace of the blessed Virgin Mary and the
grace of the Holy Spirit, please have mercy on me.
AMEN."

Cancer

St. Peregrine Laziosi was born in 1260 in Forli, Italy. He was initially anti-papal, once striking a holy man representing the Pope right in the face! The holy man's kind response changed the life of Peregrine forever, and he joined the priesthood.

Later, Peregrine developed metastatic cancer of the foot and was scheduled to have it amputated. However, in a dream, Jesus touched him and his diseased foot. He woke up the following morning completely cured of the cancer. He died many years later in 1345. Four hundred years after his death, Peregrine's body was found to be incorrupt.

Canonized by the Catholic Church in 1726, St. Peregrine was declared the patron saint of cancer and is lovingly referred to as "The Cancer Saint."

Day of the Week: Sunday

Prayer for Cancer Victims

"O great St. Peregrine, you have been called 'The Mighty,' 'The Wonderworker,' because of the numerous miracles which you have obtained from God for those who have had recourse to you.
For so many years, you bore in your own flesh this cancerous disease that destroys the very fibre of our being,
and who had recourse to the source of all grace when the power of man could do no more. You were favoured with the vision of Jesus coming down from His Cross to heal your affliction. Ask of God and Our Lady the cure of the sick, whom we entrust to you.
(Explain your case and plead your petition here)
Aided in this way by your powerful intercession, we shall sing to God, now and for all eternity, a song of gratitude for His great goodness and mercy.
AMEN."

Communication

St. Gabriel, the Archangel, is mentioned in the Hebrew Bible, the Quran, and the Christian Bible as the communicator who appears before mankind. He is honored by the religions of Judaism, Islam, and Christianity for delivering God's messages to humanity throughout history. For these reasons, he is known as the patron saint of communication.

Oftentimes, people will stop communicating with one another due to misunderstandings or arguments. When this happens, St. Gabriel can help to foster communication, if he is asked to intercede.

Day of the Week: Sunday

Prayer to Open the Lines of Communication

"Archangel St. Gabriel, please teach me how to communicate effectively with other people when I have something important to say to them and to listen well when other people have something important to say to me. Show me how to successfully build relationships of mutual understanding and respect with people, in which we can learn from each other's stories and perspectives and work together well, despite the differences between us.
Whenever the communication process has broken down in one of my relationships due to a problem such as misunderstanding or betrayal, please send me the power I need to overcome the issue and start communicating well with that person again.
(Explain your case and plead your petition here)
Thank you, Gabriel, for all of the good news from God that you bring into people's lives, including mine.
AMEN."

Demonic & Evil Spirit Attacks

St. Benedict of Nursia was born into a noble family around AD 480 in Nursia, located in central Italy. Benedict chose to live a quiet life of prayer and devotion to God after disapproving of the immoral lifestyles he encountered as he aged, leaving his family and friends behind to be alone. He lived a sequestered life in a cave for many years. Later, many other monks joined him, eventually building monasteries together.

Even though he lived a life devoted to God, Benedict was constantly tempted by the devil. He was able to defeat the devil numerous times throughout his life, earning him the title of protector against evil spirits, temptation, and evil Witchcraft.

His death date is around the year AD 548. St. Benedict of Nursia was canonized by the Catholic Church in 1220 and declared patron saint of several domains.

Day of the Week: Saturday

Prayer to Ward Off Evil Spirits:

"In the name of God the Father Almighty, through the intercession of St. Benedict, keep away from me and my loved ones, evil spirits; Good spirits, shield us against them! Malign spirits, you inspire wrong thought to men. Malicious spirits, liars, you lead them into deception. Mocking spirits, you play with human's credulity. I reject you with all the power of my soul, and I close my ears to your suggestions. I call upon me the Mercy of God. Good Spirits, I implore you, assist me in this battle. Give us strength to resist evil influences. Shine your light on the snares of evil spirits. Keep us from pride and evil arrogance. Good spirits, do not let jealousy, hatred, malevolence, or any other feeling but love grow in our hearts, for these feelings open the doors to the spirits of evil. (Explain your case and plead your petition here)
AMEN."

Drug Addiction

St. Maximilian Kolbe was born on 8 January 1894 in the Kingdom of Poland, which was part of the Russian Empire at the time. He became a Polish conventual Franciscan friar. During World War II, he was arrested by the German Gestapo multiple times for hiding Jewish people. He was ultimately transported to the Auschwitz concentration camp.

His openness as a Catholic priest brought him severe treatment. Ultimately, in 1941, he was murdered by the Nazis via a lethal intravenous injection of carbolic acid into his left arm. Kolbe is often depicted in a prison uniform with a needle being injected into his arm.

Canonized by the Catholic Church in 1982, two of the domains belonging to Maximilian Kolbe are patron saint of drug addicts and prisoners.

Day of the week: Sunday

Prayer for Drug Addiction

"St. Maximilian Kolbe, turn your gaze on us
who honor you and have recourse to you.
Radiating with the light of Mary Immaculate,
you brought countless souls to holiness and introduced them to
faithful endeavors for the victory of good over evil.
Your life of love and service was cut short by a lethal
injection, given in a prison cell in Auschwitz.
Pray that God will help break the chains
of addiction that hold me bound.
May His grace strengthen me in resisting this dependence
that prevents me from living a life of health and happiness.
Guide me to the resources I need to find healing and wholeness.
(Explain your case and plead your petition here)
AMEN."

Emotional and Mental Disorders

St. Dymphna was born in Ireland in the seventh century. When she lost her mother at the age of fourteen years old, it caused her wealthy father, Damon, to become afflicted with mental illness. Due to this mental illness, Damon decided to marry Dymphna. Frightened by his bizarre behaviors and intentions, she escaped and fled to Belgium with a Catholic priest, who is now St. Gerebernus.

Damon pursued them and when they were found, he decapitated Gerebernus. Then, he tried to persuade his daughter to return to Ireland and marry him. When she refused, he decapitated her too. She was only fifteen years old.

Canonized in the year 620 by the Catholic Church, St. Dymphna was declared the patron saint of mental illness.

Day of the week: Monday

Prayer for Emotional or Mental Disorders

"Good St. Dymphna, great wonderworker in every affliction of mind and body, I humbly implore your powerful intercession with Jesus through Mary, the health of the Sick, in my present need. (Explain your case and plead your petition here). St. Dymphna, martyr of purity, patroness of those who suffer with nervous and mental afflictions, beloved child of Jesus and Mary, pray to Them for me and obtain my request. AMEN."

Enemy Warfare

St. Joan of Arc was born in France around 1411. She was a victorious military leader and warrior. During her lifetime, England, along with Burgundy, controlled most of France. At the age of around thirteen years old, Joan of Arc started receiving visions from St. Michael, the Archangel, and other holy deities. They urged her to help the true King of France reclaim his throne.

With the help of St. Michael and the other deities, she led French troops from one victorious battle to another against England and Burgundy. Finally, her military leadership brought Charles VII to the throne as the true ruler of France.

In the year 1431, at the age of only nineteen years old, Joan of Arc was executed by the English and burned at the stake. Canonized by the Catholic Church in 1920, St. Joan of Arc was declared the patron saint of France. Additionally, she is oftentimes called upon to assist with victories in national wars or individual personal battles.

Day of the Week: Tuesday

Prayer for Victory Against Enemies

"St. Joan of Arc, in the face of your enemies, in the face of harassment, ridicule, and doubt, you held firm in your faith. Even in your abandonment, alone and without friends, you

held firm in your faith. Even as you faced your own mortality, you held firm in your faith. I pray that I may be as bold in my beliefs as you, St. Joan, I ask that you ride alongside me in my own battles. Help me be mindful that what is worthwhile can be won when I persist. Help me hold firm in my faith. Help me believe in my ability to act well and wisely.
(Explain your case and plead your petition here)
AMEN."

Health and Healing

St. Raphaël the Archangel, is a healer. In fact, the name Raphaël means "God has Healed." St. Raphaël serves people who need to heal physically, mentally, emotionally, and spiritually. In the New Testament, his incredible healing powers are mentioned in the Gospel of John. It speaks of the pool at Bethesda, where many ill people rested, awaiting the moving waters. Then, "...An angel of the Lord descended at certain times into the pond; and the water was moved. And he that went down first into the pond after the motion of the water was made whole of whatsoever infirmity he lay under." (Jn. 5.1–4)

Day of the Week: Sunday

Prayer for Healing

"Glorious Archangel, St. Raphaël,
great prince of the heavenly court,
you are illustrious for your gifts of wisdom and grace.
You are a guide of those who journey by land
or sea or air, consoler of the afflicted,
and refuge of sinners. I beg you, assist me in all
my needs and in all the sufferings of this life,
as once you helped the young Tobias on his travels.
Because you are the medicine of God, I humbly pray
you to heal the many infirmities of my soul and the ills that afflict
my body. I especially ask of you the favor:
(Explain your case and plead your petition here)

And the great grace of purity to prepare me to be the temple of the Holy Spirit.
AMEN."

Prisoners

As previously discussed under "Drug Addiction," *St. Maximilian Kolbe* was a prisoner of Nazi Germany and, was ultimately murdered by them. Not only is he the patron saint of drug addiction, but also of prisoners, due to the suffering that he himself endured as a prisoner.

Day of the Week: Sunday

Prayer for Prisoners

"O Prisoner-Saint of Auschwitz, help me in my plight.
Introduce me to Mary, the Immaculata, Mother of God.
She prayed for Jesus in a Jerusalem jail.
She prayed for you in a Nazi prison camp.
Ask her to comfort me in my confinement.
May she teach me always to be good.
If I am lonely, may she say, 'God is here.'
If I feel hate, may she say, 'God is love.'
If I am tempted, may she say, 'God is pure.'
If I sin, may she say, 'God is mercy.'
If I am in darkness, may she say, 'God is light.'
If I am unjustly condemned, may she say, 'God is truth.'
If I have pain in soul or body, may she say, 'God is peace.'
If I lose hope, may she say, 'God is with you all days, and so am I.'
(Explain your case and plead your petition here)
AMEN."

Protection

St. Michael the Archangel, is venerated in Judaism, Christianity, and Islam. St. Michael is a warrior saint who battles for righteousness in the name of God. There are various biblical accounts of his battles and victories over evil and injustices, and he is often depicted conquering Satan in war.

Day of the Week: Sunday.

Prayer for Protection

"St. Michael the Archangel, defend us in battle,
be our protection against the malice and snares of the devil.
May God rebuke him, we humbly pray;
and do thou, O Prince of the Heavenly host, by the power of God,
thrust into hell Satan and all evil spirits who wander through the world for the ruin of souls
(Explain your case and plead your petition here)
AMEN."

Slavery: Physical or Spiritual

St. Josephine Bakhita was born in Africa in 1869. Her uncle was the brother of a village chief. Because the Arab-Muslim slave trade still existed many decades after the Atlantic slave-trade, she was kidnapped at a young age and sold into slavery.

In Africa, Josephine was forced to convert to the Islamic faith and sold several times. Josephine endured horrific and unthinkable acts of torture by many masters. Finally, she was sold to a kindly Italian consul.

Later she was sent to help the consul's friend, Augusto Michieli, whose wife was expecting a baby. After the baby was born, Augusto took Josephine and the baby to Italy as a temporarily measure. They stayed with the Canossian Sisters, where Josephine was baptized as a Catholic. She chose to remain with the nuns and joined the order herself, remaining there for fifty years.

In her last days of life, her mind regressed to her youth in slavery, and she believed that she was still in chains. Right before her death in 1947, the Virgin Mary appeared to Josephine. This visitation created a happy death for St. Josephine.

Canonized by the Catholic Church in 2000, St. Josephine was declared patron saint of Sudan and of human trafficking survivors. Additionally, the Catholics advise that all victims of slavery ought to petition her for help. This includes victims who cannot escape abusive relationships or those enduring spiritual slavery—i.e. acting in a way that others demand of a person in order to be accepted without any positive rewards or fulfilling their soul's purpose.

Day of the Week: Sunday

Prayer to Escape Physical or Spiritual Slavery

"St. Josephine Bakhita, as a child,
you were sold as a slave and had to spend
untolddifficulties and suffering.
Once freed from your physical slavery,
you found the true redemption in your
encounter with Christ and his Church.
Oh, St. Bakhita, help those who are trapped in slavery;
intercede on their behalf before God so that
they are freed from the chains of captivity.
May God free anyone who has been enslaved by man.
Provide relief to those who survive slavery, and
allow them to see Him as a model of faith and hope.
Help all survivors to find healing for their wounds.
We beg you to pray and intercede for those
who are enslaved among us.
(Explain your case and plead your petition here)
AMEN."

Speedy Results

St. Expeditus, also known as St. Expedite, was a Roman centurion (a Roman military officer) in Armenia. Not much is known about his roots or upbringing, but it is suspected that he was also born in Armenia and his name was "Elpidius."

Expeditus had converted to Christianity and was executed for doing so around the year AD 303. Venerated by the Catholic Church for having been martyred in the name of Christianity, he was elevated to sainthood during the pre-congregation era.

According to tradition, it is believed that, the day St. Expeditus was to convert to Christianity, the devil appeared to him as a crow. The devil said to convert the following day by saying *cras,* which means "tomorrow" in Latin. St. Expeditus crushed the crow while responding *hodie,* meaning "today." In other words, he doesn't waste any time!

St. Expeditus is the patron of many domains, including emergencies, expeditious solutions, and opposition to procrastination. Later in this book, we will discuss other matters in which he will intercede. However, he does not assist with emotional problems. Remember, this is a military officer who does not have time for these types of matters.

Day of the Week: Thursday

Note: It is strongly advised that payment to St. Expeditus include a slice of poundcake, preferably the "Sara Lee" brand.

Prayer for Speedy Results (From the Catholic Share Website)

"St. Expedite, Noble Roman youth and Martyr,
you who quickly brings things to pass, you
who never delays, I come to you in need:
(Clearly express what you want and ask
him to find a way to get it to you)
Do this for me, St. Expedite,
and when it is accomplished, I will as
rapidly reply with an offering to you.
(Make a promise to give St. Expedite a specific
offering when your desire is granted)
Be quick, St. Expedite! Grant my wish
and I will glorify your name.
AMEN."

God: The Final Decision Maker

Our spiritual court is powerful, and that power is needed to assist us in attempting to manifest out desires. However, I will usually summon God only if nothing else worked. This is because:

1. God is the highest-ranking entity. We do not seek the help of God and then appeal to a lesser ranking entity for the same purpose. If you were in the military, would you go to a four-star general seeking help, then immediately afterward ask a buck sergeant for the same thing? Of course not! If all else fails, then we pray to God. It's the same as asking the buck sergeant first, then continuing up the hierarchy until asking the general for help.

2. God is the ultimate judge. He may refuse the intercessor but, appealing to him personally, may change his mind. However, if he says "no," then that is the final answer, and there is nothing else that we can do. Afterwards, entities will not intercede for us and—most likely—our spellwork will be performed in vain. So, it's better to try other means of achieving our goals before appealing to God.

Specific prayers to God will be addressed later in this book. We'll save the most important for last. But, in the meantime, let's explore our own roles toward achieving successful spellwork...

CHAPTER FOUR

BECOMING A FORMIDABLE SPELLCASTER

"The most common way people give up their power is by thinking they don't have any."

—Alice Walker, Author of The Color Purple

The Power Source

When asked how their magic worked, numerous expert Hoodoo practitioners from the late 1800s to the early twentieth century replied that their powers came from God. Many others declared that they received "a special revelation from God." These typical responses, found in the book *Slave Religion,* remind me of an incident that happened decades ago...

An in-law who had previously taken advantage of my kindness developed metastatic cancer. Although we had neither seen each other nor spoken to one another in years, she sought free nursing care from me. While my feelings toward her were contemptuous, a mutual friend attempted to convince me to nevertheless help her.

Feeling guilty, I had discussed the matter with a pious Catholic nun, Sister Mary K. Rather than telling me that it was my "God-fearing" duty to help her, she instead said what I had least expected to hear. Sister Mary K. said that God is within each and every one of us. Therefore, when allowing others to take advantage of us, we are committing a sin, because we are also allowing them to take advantage of God.

Based on the aforementioned responses, there's no denying that Hoodoo and Christianity are complementary to one another within numerous core philosophies. Obviously, one of those fundamental tenets is that each and every one of us have special powers derived from the Divine within us. However, having that power is not the same as being able to effectively utilize it.

When You Know Better, You Do Better

If someone bought you a piano, you couldn't become a musical sensation overnight. Instead, it would be imperative to learn the instrument, study the musical notes, and practice. Therefore, to become an impressive pianist, it takes knowledge and perseverance.

Furthermore, mistakes must be made. Mistakes not only teach us to avoid making the same ones in the future, but they gift us with the foundation of experience. During my lifetime, there were voluminous mistakes that ultimately rewarded me with growth and wisdom.

The same principles apply to spellwork. Effective manifestation of your desires takes knowledge and practice. You have the proverbial "magic wand," but knowing how the wand works and how to use it effectively will separate you from the others as a formidable practitioner.

Protect Your Power Source

All of us have an energy field called an "aura" that act as a shield to protect us from outside negative influences. It also prevents us from losing energy. When that shield is radiant, we are loaded with spiritual power. However, when it is dim and suppressed, so is our power source.

Negative influences, such as emotional or psychological illnesses, can suppress the aura or even create holes or tears in the shield. Therefore, it is essential to keep ourselves in optimal physical condition while avoiding others who negatively influence our emotions.

Spiritual slavery is another aura suppressant. It is damaging when our behaviors are compliant with other people's expectations, especially to an excessive degree. This is because we are behaving or performing in a manner that is contrary or hurtful to our true personalities, goals, desires, and/or life purpose. It is also the most common way that spiritual slaves surrender their power because the slave masters make them believe that they have none.

Protect your power by nourishing your aura. This can be accomplished by seeking medical care for physiological needs and seeking methods of relieving emotional tensions.

Spraying oneself with holy water, Florida Water, or salt water will rid many unwanted negative energies. Reciting prayers aloud, such as Psalm 37, is also beneficial to the aura because they rid us of negativity. Drinking nettle tea, which has both antibacterial as well as spiritual uncrossing properties, is also beneficial.

Be Aware of Spiritual Obstacles

As with anything in our mundane world, most of what we attempt to accomplish seems to always meet us with challenges. Well, it's no different when we're attempting to magically manipulate or change an outcome. So, before discussing the mechanics of magic, the behaviors, and the actions necessary toward realizing successful spellwork, we must first ask ourselves an important question: Is the magical spell even worth performing?

If your magic is directed toward another person—or "target," as we say in the metaphysical practices—one must be aware of the strengths that the target may possess. Those strengths can resist any and all attempts to produce the desired results.

Sometimes we can tear down the obstacles, but, sadly, there are times that we cannot. Being aware of the oppositions gives us an opportunity to either approach the spellwork in a more vigorous manner or to simply realize that any attempted spellwork could be futile. The three most common obstacles are the strength of the target's aura, the protection they may have established, and the target's free will.

The Target's Aura

We already know that everyone has an energy shield that protect us from outside negative influences. The healthier and more radiant the shield, the more difficult it is to penetrate it in order to influence the target's behavior, attitude, or decision-making process.

This obstacle can be approached by performing continuous spellwork in order to weigh down the aura and finally penetrate it. Think about the slaves who practiced Hoodoo. They never surrendered, but instead continued performing spell after spell until they achieved their desired outcomes. Their freedom wasn't granted overnight through spellwork. It took a lot of spells, time, energy, and perseverance to finally achieve their goals.

Spiritual Protection Surrounding the Target

The good news is that most people neither practice magic, wear items for protection, nor pray for defense. Those who do so are either metaphysical practitioners, aware of the practices, or religious.

The optimal time to perform spellwork is when the targets are sleeping. It is a time of vulnerability because their guards are down and, many times, they disrobe their protection apparel. Additionally, midnight to 3:00 am is known as the "witching hour," a time when the powers of a Witch or practitioner are the strongest.

Free Will

This is the most difficult obstacle to overcome. It is because God gifted all of us with a free will to make our own decisions. Additionally, many religions stress the fact that it is a product of the intrinsic human soul.

Free will is also influenced by our individual core value system. If the target is vehemently opposed to an idea or behavior, practitioners can either minimally manipulate the target toward a desired goal or the magical spell won't work at all. Here's a true story of what happened to me...

I once knew a practitioner who totally appalled me. He was physically unattractive, an emotional wreck and carried more proverbial baggage than ten people combined. Additionally, it was later discovered that he hosted ritualistic satanic sexual orgies. His views on sexual conduct and religious beliefs totally collided with mine. After being told to keep his distance, he instead placed a love spell on me.

After waking up one morning and holding warm thoughts of this disgusting man for several hours, it occurred to me what he had done. His love spell was immediately removed. Two months later, he tried again, and that too was immediately eradicated. There is no way under the sun that we could ever be together. The free will that God had gifted me prevailed.

Now, had this been a man with a good soul and a great personality, the spell may have worked, because I would have already liked the guy. But if he later displayed values that conflicted with mine, my free will would once again prevail, and he would be GONE!

Your Greatest Obstacle? You!

Oftentimes, inexperienced neophytes will engage in spellwork aimed towards unrealistic expectations and fast results. These types of spells are doomed to fail. Although easier said than done, refraining from the need to fulfill improbable desires or demanding immediate gratification must prevail.

Avoid attempting impossible results. Just the other day, a new client desired a love spell on a happily married man who once smiled at her thirty years ago, yet has never seen him again. She was immediately refunded for the reading, as this was not only an impossible task, but also unethical. Another example of an impossible task is attempting to gain the love of a famous celebrity who doesn't even know the petitioner. Your petitions must be within reasonable boundaries.

A common mistake made by many is integrating differing metaphysical practices into one spell. This behavior is akin to making one spaghetti sauce from differing recipes. The sauce will, most often than not, flop, as will the spell.

Distrusting your spiritual court by becoming impatiently angry or even going to other entities could cause you to lose their support and assistance with future spellwork. In fits of impatience, some people have even turned to demons seeking to fulfill their requests. The results are usually disastrous.

Last but not least are the threats such as: "If God doesn't grant me this petition, I will NEVER believe in him again!" This is a common provocative statement suggesting that these people believe themselves to be superior to the entity. It also clearly suggests a lack of faith, which is essential for a positive outcome.

Now that we have explored what to avoid, let's examine how magic works and the positive behaviors and actions necessary toward realizing successful spellwork.

Magic is Energy Output

Have you ever seen television programs and movies that involve a magic wand? The Witch says a magical incantation aloud while waving a wand that emits lights and sparkles? Well, there's some truth to that scenario. The lights and sparkles released from the magical wand represent energy output, while the Witch's words emit even more energy through sound.

Energy is the force that causes movement as it travels through waves from one location to another. The intention of spellwork is to transmit as much energy as possible to a specific location or person. Thus, the more energy output involved, the better the chances of manifesting your desires.

Power sources are everywhere. A savvy practitioner knows where to find them and how to utilize them effectively. In the next chapter, we will explore tools containing energy, such as fire, smoke, plants, minerals, items possessing vibrational properties, etc. However, even without tools, we can transmit energy from our own power source.

Vibration is another power source. According to many parapsychologists, even thoughts can transfer from one person or entity to another through vibrations. They believe this is because all thoughts have substance, and the substance of thought is vibration, which is emitted through energy transferences in the air. Thus, another reason to think and believe that your spell has already manifested!

"Ring shouts," a ritual practice derived from Africa, is a clear example of utilizing one's own power source. Originally practiced in North America by the enslaved, the ecstatic ritual consists of moving in a circle while stomping and/or shuffling the feet, clapping, singing, and praying. Shouts are still practiced today by many Gullah people and several Black churches. Most Africans and their descendants knew, as they know today, that energy can be emitted through movement, emotions, intentions, visualization, and, most importantly, through sound.

Sound

Drumming rituals in the African Traditional and Diaspora practices is a great example of how highly skilled people produce and manipulate energy through sound. Have you ever seen a glimpse of these rituals on television? Numerous men play rhythmical drumbeats, varying in tone, tempo, and vigor. They do this in unison without ever missing a beat. But they're not just drummers. They are, instead, masters of the craft.

Each sound translates into a different word. In essence, it's a language all in itself. Thus, the phrase "*the Talking Drums.*" It takes decades of rigorous study and practice under strict supervision by the preceding masters to acquire the knowledge of how all drum tones affect both the living and the spiritual entities. The drummers earn ascending titles depending on their education and achievements and hold expert knowledge of the spiritual realm, as well as the deities who dwell within it.

They must have proficiency in utilizing their skills in numerous rituals, such as marriages, deaths, calling upon entities, etc. Each spiritual entity is attracted to different drum tones, therefore, the drummers must have both the knowledge and skill set to call upon the desired entity or deity through varying sounds and tempos.

If you ever have the opportunity to attend an African spiritual ceremony, you'll see that, in most cases, the drummers are sitting behind the main platform. However, remember that they are the actual leaders, as well as the proverbial "rock stars" of these rituals and ceremonies!

Energy through sound can be transmitted vocally and output our desires, as well as call upon entities. As of ten years ago, the last of my elders had passed on. But, having spent over fifty years with *Santeros, Babalawos, Brujas,* and *Paleros,* never once did anyone ever engage in silent prayer, nor did they silently plead their magical petitions.

My mother would verbalize her prayers and magical petitions aloud. But my Aunt Isabel? She was another story. My aunt would literally scream them out. If she were in another room, it became difficult to ascertain whether she was praying, practicing magic, or engaged in an argument with another person!

My family attended and sponsored spiritual masses. The mass is called a *"Misa Espiritual,"* in which numerous practitioners gather to pray and summon entities. In a nutshell, they would smoke cigars (because both the odor and the smoke are pleasing to entities) while repetitiously praying aloud. The older ones would literally shout. These "very loud" behaviors usually resulted in successfully manifesting entities and their desired outcomes.

Verbalizing prayers and magical petitions serve two purposes. The first reason is because sound is energy that is being transmitted into the spiritual world. The second reason being, as my mother would say, "Nobody will hear you if you pray to yourself, but just make sure that you know what you're saying."

Precise Communication

Most people falter towards manifesting their desires due to faulty communication practices. Whether using verbal or written petitions, the communication must be brief, clear, direct, concise, and, of utmost importance, consistent.

As an example, if my desire was for John Doe to hire me at the Arabian Palace, my verbal petition would be: "John Doe will hire Miss Aida to work at the Arabian Palace." If this is a prayer that required an intercessor, my petition would be: "Please make John Doe hire Miss Aida to work at the Arabian Palace." The petition would be stated as it is every single time. It's brief, clear, direct, concise, and, if repeating the exact same petition more than once, it's consistent.

Never request what I like to call "a grocery list." For instance, the above petition could become that if it changed to: "John Doe will really like Miss Aida more than he likes anyone else, and he will hire Miss Aida immediately, and I will become his favorite employee, and he will give me promotions right away." My petition requested seven different things: that he likes me, prefers me over others, hires me, hires me immediately, I become his favorite employee, and get lots of promotions, and the promotions happen immediately. Let's examine why this grocery list won't work...

Remember that the intention of spellwork is to transmit as much energy as possible to a specific location or person. With that in mind, imagine having a water gun, and the water represents energy. If only petitioning for one goal, the gun will be set on a straight shot, and the target would be soaked by the water. If petitioning for two goals, the gun will have to be adjusted to spray two streams, lacking the strength of one stream, and becoming weaker. My hypothetical petition requested seven goals; therefore, the water gun must be set to a fine and weak mist that will miss my target altogether.

Changing the petition will also weaken the spell or the prayer. Do not ask for something and then change the verbiage. Be consistent to ensure that all the energy is reaching the target. My memory isn't the greatest, so, if you're like me, write out the petition to prepare for the event of forgetfulness.

Additionally, if using a written petition or inscribing a candle, the writing must be complementary to your verbal requests, as well as your demeanor.

Your Magic and Your Behaviors Must Complement Each Other

Magic alone does not manifest expeditiously or wondrously as it does in the movies. There have been countless of times that clients have ruined magical spells because they believed that spellwork alone would solve all their problems. Examples include:

- Steady work spells performed, yet the clients didn't actively seek employment.
- Students performing magic to pass examinations, but they never bothered to study.
- Attraction spells performed, but clients never left the home.
- Physiological healing spells performed, but clients never sought medical care.

What many fail to understand is that magic alone is not the one and only solution. Instead, it is simply a facilitator toward achieving one's desires. One must do the proverbial footwork. Your own behaviors can easily facilitate or ruin the spellwork. This is because the original energy output of a spell had a clear concise message. Remember that sound, emotions, and intentions also transmit energy. So, when our behaviors complement the magic, the spell is strengthened. But, when we speak, think, or act contrary to the intention of spellwork, we are, again, outputting energy with a different message. This can disperse the energies that were originally transmitted through spellwork and destroy your chances.

These contradictory behaviors are usually exhibited after attraction or love spells are performed. Arguing with, or becoming demanding of, the target will result in failed spellwork. Also, remember that we are all born with free will. It will override any magical spell if the target has had enough of bad behaviors.

Years ago, my own unintentional actions ruined my magic. My newly made attraction magical charm bag appeared to be too powerful. One day, after having showered and donned clean clothing, I briefly played with my German shepherd dog (GSD), Athena. She was menstruating and, therefore, emitting a horrific odor. Being nose blind to the smell, it didn't affect me.

With the magical charm bag in my pocket, I set off to the drugstore. A handsome Latin man approached me and initiated a conversation. As he spoke, it was apparent that he was also intelligent and charming. Convinced that my charm bag was working and that he would ask me on a date, he came a little closer to me. Then, suddenly, his facial expressions changed and he started slowly backing away, finally making a clear and fast escape. It was devastating. Familiar with the people at the register, I relayed the incident to them, then asked for truthfulness in telling me what was wrong. They glanced at each other, then looked at me and simultaneously replied: "You stink!"

My magic and behaviors were contradictory. That powerful charm bag was in direct competition with the dominating, noxious odor of a dog in heat. That handsome man, just like all of us, had a free will, and my bad behavior forced his free will to override my magic.

Always exhibit overt complementary behaviors while interacting with the target. However, there are other actions, as well as thoughts, that one must demonstrate prior to, during, and after undertaking the spellwork which will either facilitate or impede the energy output.

Attitudes that Will Make or Break the Spell

Determination

Magical spells ought not be performed for every single whim that one has. They are instead performed when there is no doubt whatsoever that there is an important need or desire which must be fulfilled. The fortitude of the need or desire must be an overpowering emotion that will not falter. When this happens, those intense emotions will output blasts of additional energy and help to tear down metaphysical obstacles.

If obstacles are obviously presented before, during, or after performing spellwork, there is no surrendering. Find other spells to accomplish your goals. In the mundane world, when people are determined to achieve a specific goal, they acquire numerous angles to prevail. In the end, the determined ones usually get what they want, because successful people try harder.

Never perform spells that are lackadaisical in nature or whimsical, as there is minimal energy output. Few will work, while most will not. It's usually a recipe for failure.

Patience

This is a virtue that most people lack, especially me, the Aries. But it's absolutely necessary to realize that, unlike the movies, magic does not manifest within minutes or overnight.

There are many internet entries stating that magic must manifest within three days, while others claim three months. The truth is that a magical spell may take up to two years to manifest. Always remember that our time frame is different than that of the spiritual world. Although my godmother in Santeria used to say "Our year in this world is about a week in the spiritual world," the Holy Bible says otherwise: "But, beloved, be not ignorant of this one thing, that one day is with the Lord as a thousand years, and a thousand years as one day" (2 Pet. 3.8).

So, if one thousand years is a day in the spiritual world, remember that the entities are, indeed, answering us pretty fast! If a spell isn't manifesting as quickly as you wish it to, or if events do not seem to be going your way, don't display frustration or anger, and do not concede. These are energies that will negate your original output. Instead, have patience and perform more or different types of spellwork.

If somebody else wins the job you wished to acquire, continue the spellwork, because it may not have been the right time for you. If the spell appears to not have worked at all, it may have been the spiritual world protecting you from some unforeseen problems. The same principle applies to romantic magic. Nevertheless, give the spellwork time to work. If working with entities, have faith in their abilities.

Persistence

Display resilience if actions or behaviors are not consistent with your desired outcomes. Repeat the spells and/or add more spells to ensure optimal energy output. Sometimes, completely different magical spells ought to be added to the mix.

If you had prayed to a saint, wait two months, then ask that entity to give you a specific sign if the answer will be "yes," and ask for a different sign if the answer is "no." If you've received neither, pray to a different saint. There's been numerous times that spellcasters for hire, especially those in the African diaspora practices, continued casting one spell after another toward their desired outcomes until they manifested. They won't stop performing magical spells until the target surrendered to their will. Be persistent, as are the experienced elders. In other words, be the energy that just won't go away. Remember the old adage: "Squeaky wheels get oiled."

Surrendering too soon displays a lack of confidence in yourself and your spiritual court assistants. Worse yet, surrendering after performing just one spell emits a crystal clear sign you lack determination. Always remember, it's all about energy output—the more, the better.

Think about how the slaves won their freedom. Archeologists have uncovered multiple remnants of spellwork on prominent figures of the antebellum period. However, those spells didn't work in a day, a month, or even a year. It took persistence on the part of the practitioners. It has always been my personal view that the Civil War was a result of the thousands of spells finally manifesting together.

Visualize your Desired Outcome

Creating a detailed mental image of your desired outcome and believing that image to be true is a different form of energy output. The power of the mind holds many wonders that we as humans are slowly beginning to discover. One such wonder includes manifesting your wishes.

Scientists are finally beginning to realize that visualization, or "mental rehearsal," of desired outcomes has proven to be successful in numerous documented cases. They have also professed that it can enhance motivation, prime your brain for success, and increase confidence.

Hundreds of alleged "recent discoveries" in the scientific communities parallel, or even impersonate, what metaphysical practitioners have known for eons. It is believed by millions that, centuries pre-dating the birth of Jesus Christ, there existed an island called Atlantis. It was a highly developed society. It is also believed that both scientists and metaphysical practitioners worked side-by-side in almost all matters. Hopefully, this marriage will occur again in the future.

Confidence

Even before initiating spellwork, it is imperative to believe that the spell is going to work. Do not begin to second-guess yourself, the spell itself, or any possible consequences that could happen. Those thoughts alone will not release the optimal amount of energy that is necessary to manifest your desires.

During and after performing spellwork, one of the biggest confidence hindrances is when we observe actions that seem to clearly behave in contrast to our desires. Instead of surrendering, continue with more spellwork. Don't allow anything to discourage you, as this will release opposing negative energies. My mother, a phenomenal Witch, taught me a valuable lesson about confidence in spellwork...

The Last Dog Story!

Twelve years ago, I was scheduled for surgery and had prepared to put my German shepherd dog, Asha, in a kennel. Kathrine F., a veterinary assistant and friend, desperately needed money. She begged me to instead pay her to care for Asha. Although she lived about sixty miles from me, Asha liked Kathrine and would be happy to stay with her. Because of her profession, I believed she knew dogs well and would be better able to safeguard my dog and provide lots of love.

She was granted permission to take my dog, but under two conditions: never remove Asha's collar and, if Kathrine had to leave her home, Asha had to be crated. When Kathrine brought Asha to her home, what's the first two things that she did? She removed Asha's collar and allowed her to roam free while she was out of the house.

Immediately after surgery and on doctor's orders to remain in bed for three days, Kathrine called to tell me that Asha had "escaped." Katherine was gone, Asha was roaming free, and her roommate's friend left the door opened. I immediately left my bed to try and find her. The temperature was frigid, there eighteen inches of snow outside, and Asha was lost in an unfamiliar neighborhood.

My mother initiated spellwork. For six days, the temperature continued to brutally decrease while my mother continued proclaiming that her spells are working. Believing that Mom was crazy and Asha was dead, I decided that the seventh day would be my final day of searching. Asha was found on that seventh day in the strangest place and under miraculous circumstances. She was emaciated, but alive and happy, and ultimately lived to be over twelve years old.

My mother's spellwork manifested, and she never once doubted the work. The most important lesson learned was to have confidence in the spellwork and never get discouraged, no matter the circumstances.

Mystery Succors Success

One of the biggest mistakes made, most often carried out by inexperienced practitioners, is to verbally and/or visually showcase spellwork. Respected elders of almost all metaphysical practices never say anything about spellwork and always keep the inquisitive afar. In fact, they rarely ever admit to being practitioners.

There's an old African parable that stresses the importance of silence. The story is about a hunter who accidentally stumbles upon a talking human skull. He asked the skull how it got there. The skull replied: "Talking brought me here." The hunter was so amazed that he quickly returned to the village and eagerly told everybody, including the king, of a skull that talks!

He led all the people back to the skull. The king asked the skull numerous questions, but the skull never answered. Infuriated, the king chops off the hunter's head. The villagers collected his body, but left his head behind. Later, the skull asks the hunter's head "How did you get here?" The hunter's head replied: "Talking brought me here."

When others know about your spellwork, they can either intentionally or unintentionally weaken or negate the work. Whether it's curiosity, ridicule, intrigue, gossip, or even disbelief in magic, they are all opposing influences that output negative energies. Never disclose your intentions to perform spellwork. When this happens, more often than not, your plans will suddenly face obstacles, including the loss of motivation to pursue the plan. My clients are also advised to keep their magical books and internet searches hidden from friends and family.

Do not allow anyone to see your spellwork or magical articles. Your pets are the exception and are free to see the spellwork. However, do not allow them to disrupt the spellwork, especially nosey dogs such as mine who have a desire to sniff and steal anything in sight. Cats are notorious for jumping on and slapping items off of altars.

When performing the spellwork, place bay leaves in the four corners of the room as they help to hide the spellwork. Some people also place the leaves on their altars. Wearing them in your shoes or socks can hide your identity from the prying eyes of psychics.

Magical symbols within charms, amulets, talismans, and jewelry emit vibrational energies. Showcasing the symbols or allowing others to touch them can impede those energies. The most common mistake is talking about the spellwork after it is performed. Keep everything secretive. Even if the spell is successful, keep quiet because, if future spellwork has to be performed, we don't want all inquisitive eyes on us. Suspicious minds yield negative thoughts.

These suggestions also apply to prayers. Your relationship with the entity for whom you are petitioning is a sacred bond, and not a party open to all. Of course, praise the entity, just do not disclose your petitions and pleas.

Try to become that mysterious practitioner who stands in the shadows watching and learning. Never allow anyone to suspect you and never let them see you coming!

Choose More than One Spell to Perform

It is my contention that performing one spell after another, or repeating the same spell, is akin to piling straws on a camel's back. Once there is enough weight on the camel's back, it will weaken and eventually break. The output of energy in spellwork ought to be transmitted at a constant pace in order for the message to flood the target and weaken the aura.

If the spellwork is for self-improvement or self-gain, that flooding of commands will affect your own aura in a positive manner. Others will sense the auric vibrations and will most likely respond to you favorably...

Be Observant of Timing

It is ideal to perform spellwork in accordance with the current moon phase and day of the week. However, if one must perform emergency spellwork, such as healing spells, waiting for the proper moon phase is not necessary. In any case, there are astronomical events in which spellwork ought to be avoided. These events include the following:

Mercury in Retrograde

Mercury is the planet that fosters communication. Three or four times a year, for about a three-week period, it will appear to be moving in the opposite direction as viewed from Earth. This period is known as "retrograde."

During retrograde, there are interferences in verbal communication, as well as computer and/or telephone glitches. These mishaps can result in confusion and arguments. There is also a breakdown in energy output, as evidenced by technological problems, resulting in confusion with spiritual messages.

However, it is perfectly acceptable to perform prayers or novenas to holy entities because they are not affected by any astronomical events.

Solar or Lunar Eclipses

A solar eclipse occurs when the Moon passes between the Sun and Earth, casting a shadow on Earth that either fully or partially blocks the Sun's light. A lunar eclipse occurs when the Sun, Earth, and Moon align so that the moon passes into Earth's shadow. In a total lunar eclipse, the entire Moon falls within the darkest part of Earth's shadow.

Most Hoodoo practitioners believe that, during a solar or lunar eclipse, the energies of both the Sun and the Moon are blocked. In ancient times, Witches didn't cast spells during an eclipse because they believed it causes discord.

Moon Phases

The Moon actually takes a little over 27.3 days to orbit the Earth. But, due to the Earth's involvement with supplementary activities, it causes the Moon to partake in a rest period. This rest period causes the Moon to take 29.5 days to cycle from new moon to new moon or full moon to full moon.

The Moon's 29.5-day cycle around the Earth happens in four primary and four intermediate stages. However, for the sake of ease in spellwork timing, we will explore the three most important phases that many Hoodoo practitioners observe: the waxing, full, and waning moon.

The Waxing Moon

This term is used to describe the apparent growth or thickening of the moon's shape from a new moon to a full moon. The duration of the waxing moon fluctuates monthly and varies from approximately thirteen to fifteen days. This is the ideal time to perform spellwork to increase, attract, or expand a situation or outcome. Amongst the most common spells performed during this phase are those to draw something or someone to you, increase a shortage of finances, love, companionship, notoriety, or knowledge. It is also a good time to perform attraction spells, favorable outcome spells, or improving a health matter.

The Full Moon

The full moon is the phase in which the Earth is located between the Sun and the Moon. When this happens, the lunar hemisphere that faces Earth appears fully illuminated, because it is opposite the Sun in its orbit around Earth. Therefore, the sunlit side is entirely visible from Earth.

Once or twice a year, the full moon will fall on the astrological sign of your personal moon sign. It is said that, on this first day of the full moon, if Mercury is not in retrograde and there are no lunar or solar eclipses, your chance of successful manifestation is optimal. This is your day, and you can perform any spell that you wish. The sky is the limit!

Many believe that the effect of the full moon produces inappropriate consequences on human emotions. Thus, the term "lunacy," deriving from the word "lunar," is used to describe intermittent insanity.

Although numerous academics proclaim that the full moon's effects on human emotions is merely a result of unfounded wives' tales, my own experiences as an emergency nurse have led me to a different conclusion. Having witnessed thousands of patients exhibiting bizarre behaviors and even more women experiencing false labor pains during full moon activity, it is my contention that there is, once again, documented proof to rebut the false accusations that all wives' tales are nonsensical.

It is a scientific fact that tides are higher when the Moon is full because, at that time, the gravity from the Moon and Sun are pulling together on the Earth in the same direction. Since 60% of the human body is water and the brain being composed of 73%, it is my belief that the full moon also produces a gravitational pull on our bodies, leading to temporary imbalances, thus causing unfavorable consequences.

Although we can see what appears to be a full moon for a period of two to three nights, and while most metaphysical practitioners claim that full moon activity lasts for three days, astronomers regard the Moon as full at a precise instant when the waxing phase ends and the waning phase begins. In other words, the waning moon begins shortly following the full moon. Therefore, my philosophy is that waning moon spellwork ought to begin the day succeeding the night of the full moon.

Since people are undergoing disruptions in their physiological wellbeing due to water imbalances during full moon activities, their auras have also been negatively affected, and their spiritual defenses are somewhat suppressed. Therefore, the waning moon immediately following the first night of the full moon is an optimal time to begin spellwork on your target.

The Waning Moon

This term is used to describe the apparent decreasing, or thinning, of the Moon's shape from a full moon to a new moon. Just as with the waxing moon phase, the duration of the waning moon fluctuates monthly and varies from approximately thirteen to fifteen days.

This is an ideal time to perform spellwork to decrease or banish unwanted conditions, situations, people, interpersonal relationships, and health problems. It is also an ideal time to perform break up, cursing, crossing, send away, and uncrossing spells.

Days of the Week

Each day of the week carries different magical energies. This is because the Sun, Moon, and planets are governed by the energies emitted by the sacred deity who rules over the individual celestial body. These deities, just like the saints, are assigned domains they oversee. Therefore, by beginning your spellwork on a specific day for a specific purpose, you are actually adding one more entity, the presiding deity of that specific day, to your spiritual court.

My first language was Spanish, and the names of the days in this language better helped me to remember the ruling planets. So, that will be shared with you too. Consider it to be a brief lesson in Spanish!

Sunday
The day of the Sun is ruled by the Christian God. In Spanish, the word for "Sunday" is *domingo,* which is derived from the Latin word *Dominicus,* meaning "The Day of The Lord." It is a day of masculine energy, strength, prayers, and God-centered rituals. Sunday is also a good day to perform spellwork on conditions pertaining to:

- Boys
- Energy
- Fatherhood
- Healing
- Heath
- Masculine issues
- Strength

Monday
The day of the Moon is ruled by the Christian Virgin Mary. In Spanish, "Monday" is called *lunes* from the word *Luna,* meaning "Moon." In the ancient Roman religion, Luna was the goddess and divine embodiment of the Moon, as well as the female complement to the Sun. In Catholic folklore, she was replaced by Mary, the mother of Jesus.

It is a day of feminine energy, emotions, intuition, and mysticism. Monday is also a good day to perform spellwork on conditions pertaining to:

- Divination
- Feminine issues
- Fertility
- Girls
- Motherhood
- Psychic gifts and visions

Tuesday
The day of Mars, named after the Roman god of war and courage. In Spanish, Tuesday is called *martes,* meaning "Mars."

It is a day of both physical and emotional strength, dynamic energy, revenge, courage, and power. Tuesday is also a good day to perform spellwork on conditions pertaining to:

- Athleticism
- Competition
- Conflict
- Confrontation
- Enemy work
- Military matters
- Victory
- War

Wednesday

The planet Mercury was named after the god of trade, communication, and messages. The Spanish word for "Wednesday" is *miercoles,* which was derived from the Latin words *diēs Mercuriī,* or "Day of Mercury."

Wednesday is a day for orators, public speakers, and entertainers, as well as to perform spellwork on conditions pertaining to:

- Communication
- Conflict resolution
- Financial negotiations
- Gambling
- Marketplace matters
- Speech improvement
- Stage fright
- Throat ailments

Thursday

This day belongs to Jupiter, who was also known as Jove, or Iuppiter. To the Romans, he was recognized as the god of the sky and thunder, as well as the king of kings and the father of the gods. In Spanish, "Thursday" is called *jueves,* which is derived from the Latin words *diēs Jovis,* meaning "Day of Jupiter."

Thursday is associated with abundance, prosperity, fairness, strength, and wealth. Thursday is a good day to perform spellwork on conditions pertaining to:

- Court cases
- Leadership
- Money
- Success
- Power
- Wealth

Friday

Venus, the goddess of erotic passion, beauty, fertility, and love, rules this day. In Spanish, "Friday" is called *viernes,* which derives its name from the Latin name of the goddess *Veneres.*

Something noteworthy is the fact that, due to the sexual matters associated with Venus, the term "venereal"—as in sexually transmitted diseases—is derived from her name!

Friday is associated with anything related to the improvement of physical appearances, as well as romantic or sexual matters. It is a good day to perform spellwork on conditions pertaining to:

- Attraction
- Beauty
- Fertility
- Love
- Lust
- Pregnancy spells
- Romance
- Seduction

Saturday

It is ruled by the god Saturn or Saturnus. Although Saturn was known to be the god of agriculture and abundance, he also ruled over the domains of death, destruction, dissolution, and war.

In English, "Saturday," or "Saturn-Day," is derived from the Latin words *diēs Saturni*, "the day of Saturn." The Spanish word for Saturday is *sabado*, which has no association with Saturnus, but instead honors the Hebrew Sabbath.

This day is associated with matters surrounding farming, including cultivation of the soil for the growing of crops, as well as petitioning for their abundance. It's also a good time for dismissing people or situations, as well as enemy warfare. Saturday is a good day to perform spellwork or conditions pertaining to:

- Banishing health problems, situations, or people
- Break up
- Enemies
- Harvest abundancy
- Hunger
- Imprisonment
- Uncrossing

Of interest is the input contributed by Jennifer K., one of my dear Facebook group followers. She told our group that Tuesday through Friday originated from Germanic and Nordic roots corresponding with their ancient, revered deities. Tuesday was Tyr's day, Wednesday was named after Woden, Thursday was Thor's day, and Friday was named after Freya.

Exceptions to Working with Days of the Week

When working with saints, you would not begin on the day of the week that corresponds with the condition for which you wish to manifest, or to transform. Instead, your petition will begin on the day of the week corresponding to the favored day of your chosen saint. But there is a way to do both...

My suggestion is to begin spellwork on the day containing the magical energies needed. Once the spell is either in motion or completed, petition a saint on their chosen day. That way, all the bases are covered!

We have amply explored the theoretical and behavioral aspects of magic. Now that you know the "hows" and "whys," it's time to make your physical preparations.

Cleansing

How many times have you encountered an object or an article of clothing that seemed to be lucky or unlucky? This is because various types of energies are everywhere and adhere to both people and objects. These diverse energies also adhere to the aura, or the protective shield, that surround all living organisms. Simple nuisances, such as a bad day at work, witnessing or engaging in a heated debate, and other annoyances, will attract negative energies that adhere to it. Some of those energies will also slough off, just as animals shed fur, and contaminate other people or anything in the surrounding environment.

If these lingering energies are not eradicated, they can interfere with your magic and may cause your spells to be obstructed, damaged, or even to go awry. Therefore, your body and your workspace ought to be cleansed before performing spellwork. The cleansing procedures are neither time consuming, nor complicated.

Cleansing your Workspace

Negative energies like to hide in piles of clutter, so ensure that your space is clutter-free. Also, try to keep your workspace clear from other unnecessary items to avoid energy contamination.

Prior to performing spellwork, cleanse as many areas as possible with a spiritual cleansing agent. If none is available, spray the area with either holy water, Florida Water, or a mixture of ½ tsp of sea salt to 1 cup of water. It is also prudent to do the same once the spell has been completed, especially if performing negative magic, as these energies linger.

Cleansing the Aura

Spiritual cleansing baths are intended to clear the aura of negative energies that have adhered to it. After regularly showering to remove the daily physical dirt and grime that we normally accumulate, taking a spiritual bath is highly advised.

If there are open sores or wounds on your body, or if you have an allergy to any of the mixtures listed below, do not bathe or shower with the solutions. To check for allergies, simply rub a little of the solution on a tiny surface of skin and look for reactions. If your skin displays redness, swelling, itching, or bumps, it's most likely an allergy or adverse reaction.

Bath 1: Holy Water Bath

1. Fill the bathtub with warm water.
2. Add 4 oz of holy water to the bathtub water and agitate the water to disperse.
3. While in the bathtub, pray Psalm 37 aloud to eradicate any negative energies.

Bath 2: Ammonia Bath

1. Fill the bathtub with warm water.
2. Add only 1 tbsp of ammonia to the bathtub water and agitate the water to disperse (remember: the adage "more is better" does *not* apply to ammonia. Do *not* increase the amount of ammonia, as it is a skin irritant).
3. While in the bathtub, pray Psalm 37 aloud to eradicate any negative energies.

Bath 3: Sea Salt Bath

1. Fill the bathtub with warm water.
2. Add ¼ cup of sea salt to the bathtub water and agitate the water to evenly disperse the salt.
3. While in the bathtub, pray Psalm 37 aloud to eradicate any negative energies.
4. Once you are ready to leave the bathtub, do not rinse yourself off with water. Instead, walk out of the bathtub and lightly blot yourself dry, then anoint the back of your neck and head with either protection oil, blessing oil, holy oil, or holy water for protection. Then don your clothing and remove the bathtub stopper to drain the water.

Casting a Protection Circle (Optional)

Although not a routine ritual in the Hoodoo tradition, some practitioners will cast a circle before performing spellwork. By using either sea salt or sulfur, a circle is created as a measure to protect both the practitioner and the altar from unwanted metaphysical influences.

Form a large circle round the altar by scattering the ingredient on the floor beginning in the East, then moving to the South, West, North, then back again to the East.

Once the circle has been laid down, you can either begin your spellwork or, if you wish to do so, call for additional entities to guard the cardinal directions, as well as to assist you.

Calling in the Corners (Optional)

This is the practice of facing each cardinal direction and calling in a particular entity for protection and assistance. There is an easy, fast, and safe way to do so. Let's first examine the improper ways of calling in the corners.

What to Avoid

In a popular movie, the verbiage was inappropriate. The Witches walked to the East and summoned "Guardians of the Watchtowers of the East," then walked to the South, doing the same, then to the West and, finally, summoned the "Guardians of the Watchtowers of the North." Please don't believe everything presented in movies.

First, there are no watchtowers in Hoodoo. Secondly, what are the names of these entities who sit atop these towers? Why do the towers even need to be guarded? Unfortunately, after this ridiculous movie was aired, we even see websites discussing the watchtowers as if they truly existed.

Sadly, in real life, there have also been hundreds, if not thousands, of people who have blindly called in *"Entities of the East"* and so on without ever addressing these unknown entities by their proper names. This is a dangerous practice, because there are lesser demons known as "cacodemons" who preside over directional domains. Cacodemons will consider this verbiage, as do the higher-ranking demons, as an invitation. Once a demon is invited in, it won't leave and will cause havoc in your life.

Calling in the Corners Safely

My preference is to call in archangels. There are four archangels who, amongst their other duties, also preside over the four cardinal directions:

St. Gabriel manages the East, St. Michael manages the South, St. Rafael manages the West, and St. Uriel manages the North. Once the protection circle is in place, you're ready to call in the corners. Some people will ring a bell prior to calling in each archangel. With or without a bell, it's a quick and easy ritual.

1. While inside the circle, stand to the foremost East side of the circle, facing East. You may ring your bell and/or bow, then say:

   "I respectfully call upon St. Gabriel to please protect me and to assist me with this spellwork of ___ (name the spell)."

2. While inside the circle, walk to the foremost South side of the circle, facing South. You may ring your bell and/or bow, then say:

   "I respectfully call upon St. Michael to please protect me and to assist me with this spellwork of ___ (name the spell)."

3. While inside the circle, walk to the foremost West side of the circle, facing West. You may ring your bell and/or bow, then say:

   "I respectfully call upon St. Rafael to please protect me and to assist me with this spellwork of ___ (name the spell)."

4. While inside the circle, walk to the foremost North side of the circle, facing North. You may ring your bell and/or bow, then say:

   "I respectfully call upon St. Uriel to please protect me and to assist me with this spellwork of ___ (name the spell)."

5. While inside the circle, walk back to the foremost East side of the circle. Either bow or ring your bell. You are now ready to perform your magic.

If the spellwork is active, you may leave the circle, but make a verbal announcement as to your intentions. You may want to say something such as: "I am leaving the circle now but will return within an hour (or whatever time you will return)." If you must get sleep, you might say: "I must get some sleep now and will return in the morning."

Once the spell is completed, it will be time to release the entities. This will be performed with reverence.

Releasing the Entities

Remember that the archangels are holy entities who serve God directly. In their presence, we must display humbleness and appreciation. Therefore, be very careful with your verbiage and avoid using any words that may appear to be arrogant. My suggestion is to never use verbiage such as "You're dismissed." Instead, avoid any questionable terminology that even remotely insinuates that you have control over their will. Below is my preferred method of releasing them:

1. While inside the circle, stand to the foremost East side of the circle, facing East. You may ring your bell and/or bow, then say:

   "St. Gabriel, this ritual has been completed. I humbly thank you for protecting me and assisting me with this spell. May God bless you. If you wish, go in peace."

2. While inside the circle, walk to the foremost South side of the circle, facing South. You may ring your bell and/or bow, then say:

   "St. Michael, this ritual has been completed. I humbly thank you for protecting me and assisting me with this spell. May God bless you. If you wish, go in peace."

3. While inside the circle, walk to the foremost West side of the circle, facing West. You may ring your bell and/or bow, then say:

   "St. Rafael, this ritual has been completed. I humbly thank you for protecting me and assisting me with this spell. May God bless you. If you wish, go in peace."

4. While inside the circle, walk to the foremost North side of the circle, facing North. You may ring your bell and/or bow, then say:

"St. Uriel, this ritual has been completed. I humbly thank you for protecting me and assisting me with this spell. May God bless you. If you wish, go in peace."

5. While inside the circle, walk back to the foremost East side of the circle. Either bow or ring your bell.

Closing the Circle

In other metaphysical practices, there are ritual behaviors to remove the circle once the spell is completed. My preference is to simply sweep away the salt or sulfur, then scatter it around the outside of my house or front door.

Write It All Down

Document every aspect of your spellwork. This includes who you had petitioned, what you said, every tool and ingredient used, what was written, the day of the week, and moon phase that the spell was performed under. This is very important, because our memories are not as good as we believe them to be.

Years ago, there was an unusually loud neighbor. He engaged in shooting off firecrackers, playing loud music, and had a dog that continuously barked. In a fit of anger, I grabbed as many ingredients as possible to create a powder that would banish him, while ensuring that the dog would not ingest anything harmful. After throwing it in his backyard and screaming, "You will move NOW!" he moved exactly one month later.

To this day, I have no idea what that banishing powder contained. Failing to document the ingredients of that powder is one of my failures as a responsible practitioner, as well as one of my biggest regrets. However, it was both a learning and a teaching opportunity.

If the spell is a failure, you will have the chance to examine what you may have done incorrectly. But, if the spell was successful, you could purchase a blank book and document it, along with other successful spellwork. This is the beginning of your personal "Book of Shadows," also known as a "Book of Spells," which is a book used by modern Witches for recording spells, rituals, magic recipes, and anything associated with their craft.

If you have read this chapter in its entirety and plan to adhere to the advice given, you are already on your way to becoming a masterful practitioner. You know the concepts, now the next step is for you to know your tools.

CHAPTER FIVE

THE TOOLS OF THE TRADE

"Give us the tools, and we will finish the job."
—Winston Churchill

The tools employed in spellwork can range from a few mineral grains to much larger objects. In most cases, the exact tools utilized are dependent upon the practitioner's location, accessibility to items, knowledge of the tool's magical properties, language, and cultural upbringing.

To date, there are 195 countries in the world and over 6,500 different spoken languages. When there are slight variances in magical practices from language to language, there will be a vast range of diversity in deity worship, theoretical approaches, behaviors, tools, and actions to perform in order to manifest one's desires.

There are, indeed, thousands of worshipped deities and countless ways to practice magic. The tens of thousands of tools used vary according to theoretical beliefs, the people's experiences with them, and whatever is available in their homeland.

Because Hoodoo is an evolving practice, additional tools are being introduced and implemented into the craft at a rapid pace, resulting in hundreds of new ways to perform magic. However, it would be impossible to list every single item utilized in the practice of this craft. Since we are discussing the traditional practice, only the most common tools will be explored.

Altars

An altar is simply an area designated as the space for which to perform a religious, spiritual, or magical ritual. It is not necessary to erect expensive altars, because all that really matters is that the space is regarded with respect and reverence. Remember that the old Hoodoo practitioners were initially slaves who kept their magical practices hidden from their owners. After emancipation, almost all remained impoverished people, so they had simple, uncluttered altars. Yet, their spells nevertheless worked!

Examples of common Hoodoo altars include:

- A bathtub
- A bureau
- A desk
- A dresser
- The floor
- The ground outside
- A nightstand
- A table
- The shower (first remove the shower curtains)

Do not create or place an altar in areas such as closets or anywhere that could generate a fire. Avoid locations close to traffic from family, friends, or pets. Exposing your spellwork to others could create curiosity, intrigue, and gossip, whereas animals are curious by nature and can inadvertently disassemble it. As previously stated (and worth mentioning again), always keep your spellwork hidden.

Altar cloths

Some Hoodoo practitioners will place a colored cloth on the altar that corresponds to the color of the candle. White, as a neutral color, can substitute for any color. My personal choice is to use a clean white cotton cloth. Readily available in most stores, these cloths are sold in packs of five or more and are often called "bar cloths" or "flour sack cloths."

Alcohol/Spirits

Wine

Some saints appreciate a glass of wine if they grant your petition. Expensive wines are not necessary, as a plain white or red table wine will suffice. Just place it on the altar alongside your other gratuitous offerings.

If a deceased loved one liked wine in life, it can also be offered to them on the altar or at their gravesite. However, if the person was an alcoholic, then it is inadvisable to offer any spirits.

Whiskey

The slaves and their descendants employed whiskey for several magical purposes. Whiskey was utilized to either cleanse an object for spellwork, to give life to a talisman (such as a magical charm bag), or as an offering to a particular entity. This practice still exists today.

The custom was most likely derived from Africa, because several of the African spiritual practices also use strong alcoholic spirits in their rituals. For example, in both Santeria and Palo, it is a common practice to instead use an alcoholic rum called *Aguardiente,* meaning "firewater," for the same purposes that Hoodoo practitioners use whiskey.

Amulets

Before discussing this topic, it is important to first answer one of the most common questions regarding the differences between an amulet, a charm, and a talisman. In his article entitled "Amulets, Talismans, & Charms," author Richard Webster summed it up perfectly. He clarifies that an amulet provides protection, a charm attracts good luck, and a talisman brings a particular benefit to its owner.

The word "amulet," arises from the Latin root word *amuletum,* meaning "an object that protects a person from trouble." Although this formal term was first introduced in a publication written by Pliny the Elder in AD 77–79, amulets have been utilized for preceding centuries by almost every culture around the world. They can protect the person by emitting specific defensive vibrations. Most amulets are worn by the bearer and may include minerals, gems, coins, pendants, rings, written words, and animal or plant parts.

Protection Against Demonic and Evil Entities

Having performed numerous spiritual eradications, detachments, and assisting with major exorcisms as well as performing minor ones, my methods were derived from trial and error. Due to these experiences, when called upon to diagnose a situation or eradicate malicious entities, four items are always on my person:

- **An Iron Cross:** Centuries ago, Muslims discovered that iron would repel dangerous djinn. These are entities that are either malicious, good, or apathetic to humankind. The malicious entities have an aversion to iron, specifically the magnetite within it. The cross adds extra protection, because it is a representation of a Christian religious event. Many welders will advertise their crosses as made of iron, but they are actually steel and do not contain magnetite. Therefore, ensure that you communicate with the seller and ask for clarification. Also, do not take a shortcut by wearing pure magnetite, because it can sometimes drain you of your energy, as it does to those nasty entities.
- **St. Benedict Medal:** St. Benedict of Nursia (Norcia) is venerated in the Catholic, Eastern Orthodox, Anglican Communion, and other Churches. He had performed an array of miracles, including warfare with the devil, and is frequently invoked against evil forces. His medal, according to the National Catholic Register, has the image of St. Benedict on the front side. However, on the other side, the medal itself has an important prayer, written in code, that is used in the Catholic Rite of Exorcism. More powerful is the Crucifix/St. Benedict combination, not only because of its exorcising properties, but also because the image of Christ's body is appalling to demonic and evil forces.
- **The Happy Death Crucifix:** Often used in exorcisms, this amulet combines a crucifix and a St. Benedict medal. It offers blessings from God, keeps evil away, and opens the doors when one finds blockages.

- **St. Michael the Archangel Medal:** Venerated in Christianity, Islam, and Judaism, St. Michael is a warrior who battles for righteousness in the name of God. His many victorious battles against the devil, evil forces, and injustices can be found in the Holy Bible. St. Michael is also the saint who led a teenage St. Joan of Arc into numerous victorious military battles. His image provides protection against evil forces, evil people, and injustices.

Other Amulets Offering Protection Against Malicious Entities

- **Religious or spiritual symbolism:** Images such as a crucifix or any other sacrament that contains a representation of protection.
- **Pentagram of Solomon:** Protects the wearer from curses and evil spirits.

Protection Against Other Forms of Threats

- **Anti-Evil Eye (Lucky Eye, All-Seeing Eye):** For many who know me, my perception of a compliment is akin to fingernails scratching across a chalkboard. In many cultures, including my own, compliments are feared to be sarcastic or insincere ways of delivering the jinx of the evil eye. Once a compliment is accepted by the recipient, it is viewed as allowing or inviting the jinx into one's life. It has been believed for over five thousand years, that the jinx of the evil eye, or "the eye," is delivered through a malevolent glare. The eye can also be delivered unintentionally through envy, jealousy, or gossip. The amulet to ward off the evil eye actually looks like an eye. Several cultures, including the Greeks and the Turks, are taught to affix the amulet to their inner clothing adjacent to the top of their left shoulder. Mine is always affixed at the top of my left bra strap.
- **Avoiding the law:** The Indian Head Cent is often utilized for the purpose of eluding capture by any law enforcement agency.

Protection For Pets

All my dogs have three important amulets on their collars. The first is a medal of St. Francis of Assisi, the patron saint of animals, to aid in protecting them. The second is St. Anthony, who can prevent our pets from being lost or ensure their speedy return home. In some Catholic spiritual stores, medals are available with the images of St. Francis on one side and St. Anthony on the other. The third is the anti-evil eye amulet because, as most pet owners know, many people either fear or dislike animals. Upon seeing a wandering animal, it will sometimes cause people to either intentionally or unintentionally deliver malevolent glares, thus jinxing our pets.

Animal and Insect Curios

Please do not inflict pain, suffering, torment, or death upon any living creature. Instead, seek their assistance in spellwork by respectfully asking them for their help. Trust me, they understand what is being said either through the tone of your voice, your demeanor, telepathy, or the actual spoken words. Speaking to them has never failed me. If it is already deceased, or if it's merely an animal part, give thanks to its spirit for sacrificing its life for you and ask for its assistance.

Below is a list of the most readily available zoological curios and their uses in spellwork:

Break-Up Work

- **Black cat and black dog hair:** These curios are joined together in break up work to make your targets fight like cats and dogs. Back in the old days, the Hoodoo practitioners would actually pull hair from their tails as they fought. However, for safety purposes, this method is highly inadvisable, because you will risk being attacked by either animal. Instead, you may obtain the hair of a black cat and black dog from any part of their body. Just ensure that the dog is not docile and that both animals are not companions or reside in the same abode. Otherwise, the desired fighting energy that's needed will not be acquired.
- **Termites:** Will eat away at a relationship.

Communication

- **Parrot feathers:** Because parrots tend to be hyper-verbose, their feathers are frequently used in spellwork aimed at improving shyness or enticing a target into conversation.

Cleansing (Spiritual)

- **Black hen feathers:** Used to brush away any negative energies attached to your aura.
- **Eggs:** Although a black hen's egg is preferable, the egg is used to absorb or "take on" the negative energies attached to the aura. The most common way to do this is to roll the egg over the entire body, starting from the top of the head and ending at the feet. The egg is then cracked to observe for discoloration, which indicates that the egg has performed its job. My preference is to crack it in the toilet, then, after observing the results, discard the egg by flushing it away.

Cursing and Crossing

- **Deer estrous:** Causes the target to be irritable.
- **Dog feces:** Usually smeared over a representation of the target to turn that person into a stinking mess.
- **Red ants:** Available for purchase in several spiritual stores, these dead ants are used in negative spellwork because they are spiteful creatures that bite.
- **Wasps:** Due to its aggressive and stinging nature, it can be used in almost any type of negative spellwork.

Gambling Luck

- **Alligator's claw:** Usually placed in a small flannel cloth bag while gambling.
- **Alligator's tooth:** Usually worn as a charm, such as in a necklace.

Good Luck

- **Chicken or turkey wishbone**: Scientifically called a "furcula" in its entirety, a wishbone is usually carried in a small flannel cloth bag.
- **Rabbit's foot**: I do not personally advocate for this charm. This is because, in the past, hundreds of thousands of rabbits had been needlessly killed by big commercial enterprises just to profit from their feet. However, if the animal is humanely killed for its edible meat, the foot can be salvaged, thus bringing good luck to those who carry it in their left pockets.

Love

- **Love birds' feathers:** For heterosexual relationships. The feathers must be taken from coupled birds. With a pink marker, write the name of the woman on the female's feather and the man's name on the male's feather. Then, bind the feathers together with pink thread.
- **Raccoon penis bone:** Used by men to obtain the love of another.

Protection

- **Pet's nail clippings:** In nature, nails serve many purposes, including offering protection to the animal. As a German shepherd dog (GSD) owner, my dogs are naturally protective of me. Because of their protective nature, their sturdy nails are great items to add to protection jars and mojo hands. Additionally, cats have dangerously razor-sharp nails that are utilized as the first line of both defense and attack maneuvers. Therefore, their nails can also be used in negative spells.
- **Egg shell powder (Cascarilla):** Most commonly sold in a solid consistency within cups, cascarilla is used for several purposes, including purification and adding extra power to positive spellwork. Using it as chalk, make the sign of the cross over the crown of your head for protection.

Reversing Spells

- **Crab shells or powder:** Because crabs have been known to walk backwards, it is a great ingredient to add to your "return to sender" spells.

Send-Away Spells

- **Ants:** Because brown ants are natural wanderers, take a very small piece of brown paper with the name of the person whom you wish to wander off. Anoint that paper with something that ants like to eat. Find an ant mound, tell them the situation, and ask the ants to make this person wander away. Gently place the paper next to the mound's entrance.
- **Pigeon feathers:** A popular send away spell in Santeria, pigeons are used because these birds love to frequently take flight. Write the name of the person whom you wish to send away on the feather, then, on a windy day, release it while exclaiming that the person will take flight and leave forever.

Uncrossing

- **Chicken foot:** Using its nails to scratch away crossed conditions, it is also hanged on walls, keychains, and car rear view mirrors for protection.

Brooms

Broom magic is popular amid several metaphysical practices. In fact, even today, marriage ceremonies in some practices involve the use of a broom. But, in the antebellum days, within Northern America, brooms sanctioned marriages amongst the slaves.

In his book *Slave Religions,* Dr. Raboteau said that the most frequent method of slave marriages was the custom of jumping over a broomstick, and relayed two of several variations of these ceremonies. In one variation, the bride-to-be would lay her broom in front of the groom-to-be. Then, he would lay his broom in front of her. While facing one another and holding hands, they would simultaneously cross over their designated broom. Once they did so, they were considered officially married.

In the second variation, a third party held the broom stick one foot off the ground. Then, the bride would jump over the broomstick backwards, followed by the groom. Once this act was completed by both people, they were declared husband and wife.

To this day, broom magic is utilized by Hoodoo practitioners for several purposes. Among the most popular application for brooms and/or broom straws magic include:

- Bringing good luck
- Causing bad luck
- Clearing crossed conditions
- Curing warts
- Making wishes
- Preventing a curse
- Sending enemies away
- Sending unwanted company away

Candles

Candles are utilized in magic to commence ceremonies or rituals, to honor or petition entities, represent deities, and energize spells. They also nourish entities by providing energy to them while affording open communication between the entity and the spiritual practitioner.

While simple oil lamps or plain candles were utilized for centuries, today's candles are available in all shapes, sizes, and colors. Exclusively shaped and colored candles have even been designed for specific spellwork, as will be explored in a subsequent chapter.

Charms

As stated earlier, a charm is simply an item that attracts good luck. There are two types of charms that attract good luck: items that had absorbed positive energies and items containing symbolisms that emit energetic vibrations to attract good luck.

Have you ever known anyone to have a personal lucky pen, a lucky coin, a lucky necklace, or a similar object? These items became lucky to the bearer because they had initially absorbed positive energies. When the owner interacts with the item, there is an exchange of positive energies, because the item slowly emits vibrations of good luck onto the recipient, then the recipient slowly emits the positive vibrations back into the original item. It becomes an even exchange of positive energies. However, if an unusually traumatic event occurs while the person is interacting with the lucky charm, that item reabsorbs negative energies. When this happens, it renders that personal lucky charm useless.

On the other hand, there are lucky charms that instead emit vibrational energies. Some carry symbolic images. These images emit energetic vibrations to attract either general good luck or luck in a specific genre. Others contain the energies that are emitted once they are worn by the bearer.

Lucky charms have been embraced by people all around the world since—or maybe even before—recorded history. Below are just a few of the most popular lucky charms:

- **Ankh:** Long life.
- **Buttons (Shiny):** General good luck.
- **Coins minted in your birth year:** General good luck.
- **Fish:** Fertility and money.
- **Four leaf clover:** General good luck.
- **Horseshoe:** General good luck.
- **Ladybug:** Good luck in prosperity and abundance.

Dirt and Pebbles

About fifteen years ago, my desire to study wild animal pack behavior led me to the Kalahari Desert in South Africa. Although it was an experience of a lifetime, the difficult atmospheric conditions, as well as perpetually fearing an attack by resident predatory creatures, made my desire to ever return to that desert slim to none.

Having made acquaintances with a few native South Africans, they urged me to bring the dirt of South Africa home with me to ensure my speedy return to them. Another chuckled and said, "And if you don't want to come back, you can use the dirt to send people you don't like far away from you." While the second option sounded more appealing, my baggage obviously contained heaps of dirt.

Numerous cultures never take dirt for granted as just being waste on the ground. As with everything created by nature, dirt also has a spirit. It absorbs the DNA, the blueprint for life, from waste products. That DNA allows dirt to have memory and personality. This is part of the reason that dirt and pebbles play an important role in several African magico-religious practices. For instance, some initiation rites include collecting dirt from numerous locations and later employed for specific purposes.

Dirt and its surrounding pebbles are powerful magical tools because they also absorb the energies of their surrounding areas. Due to DNA memory, those same energies are therefore emitted when displaced elsewhere. Additionally, my mother used to say that "kidnapped" dirt and pebbles long to return to their original habitat and, therefore, make excellent tools in send-away spells. She also said that if we release any "kidnapped" dirt, it will beg the wind to return it to its original home.

When the dirt is taken from its original "home," it acts as a talisman, attracting a benefit to the owner. But first ask its permission to use it; otherwise, it may long to return home. I always promise to return it from whence it came once my desire is manifested.

My followers are always encouraged to use their imagination and God-given ingenuity to create and affect their own ideas for spellwork. However, here are a few suggestions for the usage of dirt and pebbles:

- **Airport:** For travel spells, or to send someone away.
- **Bank:** To acquire a loan from the bank, or to improve a financial situation.
- **Cemetery (General):** For cursing or crossing spells.
- **Cemetery plot:** Plots belonging to specific people who will aid with specific spells.
- **Church:** For help from holy deities.
- **College or school:** To aid in academic achievement.
- **Courthouse:** For court case and legal spells.
- **Crossroads:** To open the roads.
- **Diet center:** To aid in weight loss.
- **Doctor's office:** For health purposes.
- **Financial loan building:** To obtain a loan.
- **Grocery store:** To prevent hunger.
- **Hospital:** For health purposes.

- **Land plot:** To acquire that land, to prevent others acquiring the land, or to move people out.
- **Law office:** To obtain the help of a specific lawyer.
- **Military base:** To conquer your enemy.
- **Pregnancy center:** To aid in fertility.
- **Veterinarian office:** For help with a pet's health needs.

Dolls

An effigy is an image or representation of something, especially a person. Although an effigy can be something as simple as a figural candle, the target's picture, or a toy doll, they are usually sculpted or modeled to represent the person or target for whom one wishes to magically influence.

The most common type of effigy is a doll. While the Hoodoo practitioners refer to them as doll babies, they are also called poppets in European practices and Voodoo dolls by others.

To my knowledge, based on my reviews of documented cases, the slaves most frequently sculpted their dolls with materials that were readily available to them, such as butter, twigs, or mud. Still, they were intelligent people and had obviously found an array of other materials from which to make their dolls. My Aunt Isabel would go as far as to sculpt cursing dolls out of dog feces. While avoiding the intensity engaged by my aunt, here are a few suggestions for sculpting materials:

- Bread or pizza dough
- Clay
- Cloth
- Corn husks
- Ground meat
- Papier-mâché
- Sticks
- Playdough
- Rope
- Yarn
- Wax

Herbs

Experts of the African traditional and diaspora practices believe that all plants, as well as minerals, have spirits. These seasoned practitioners of both the past and present are able to communicate with herbs, barks, leaves, and roots. Thus, acknowledging that life exist in all organisms is an essential core belief in the Hoodoo tradition.

In the practice of Santeria, the participants occasionally work with the deity Osian, who is a master herbalist. However, whether they work with or without a deity, the practitioners almost always implement fresh herbs that are usually still attached to their stems or bark. This is because an array of diverse and fresh plants was and still is readily available in the Caribbean Islands, as they are in Africa.

Additionally, the slaves in the Caribbean Islands were not as closely scrutinized as those brought to North America and therefore were better able to disguise their intentions with the multitude of available plants. Sadly, in North America, the slaves had to hide whatever herbs they may have found, and—in most cases—the plants eventually dried out. Amazingly, the experts were still able to communicate with the spirits of the dried-out plants and bring about the same results.

If a plant or root is fresh and still attached to its natural habitat, respectfully ask for its assistance in your spellwork. Explain that it will have to be removed from its home to assist you. Wait for a feeling of either consent or disapproval. If it consents, thank it then very gently detach it from its base. Handle it with care and always speak lovingly to it. Place the base of the plant in moist soil or water, for sustenance, until it is implemented into your spellwork.

If the root or plant is dried or has been extracted for a period of time, pray to God, as to awaken its spirit. Then, continue the rapport as you would with a live plant. My clients are instructed to begin this process with the following steps:

1. Respectfully hold the plant part in your hands for at least a minute.
2. With your mouth close to the plant part, pray Psalm 23 aloud, but do not close the prayer by declaring the word "Amen!"

3. Respectfully ask God to awaken the plant part and/or mineral and to bless it/them. Then, thank God for helping, declaring: "Amen!"
4. Continue to lovingly hold the plant part and/or mineral, tell it your situation, and respectfully ask it for its help. You are now ready to utilize it in spellwork.

Although a neophyte practitioner would not be able to readily engage in a two-way conversation with the aforementioned organisms, demonstrating respect is the first step toward communication. Plus, the plant will nevertheless understand you.

Once you have acquired long term experience with demonstrative respect, other plants will sense your integrity and desire for a two-way conversation. Eventually, they will comply.

Holy Bible

During the antebellum, the slaves replaced or syncretized the names of the African gods with several biblical figures. For example, as previously discussed, the Haitian Vodou Danbala/Damballa is also referred to as the biblical figure Moses. Additionally, thousands strongly believed that the biblical magical feats performed in Egypt were clear confirmations of Africa being the mother land of magic from the beginning of time.

Most Hoodoo practitioners of past and present believe that the Holy Bible is a spell book filled with formulas and spells to heal both physiological and emotional ailments. Additionally, there are magical recipes to create specific oils, incenses, and other wondrous formulas.

Moreover, it is also believed that the Book of Psalms is a book filled with magical incantations. These incantations were designed to alleviate or remedy any concerns or troubles that mankind may encounter.

Incantations

The spoken word is one of the most powerful magical tools that we possess. It is so powerful that, in millions of cases, simply speaking a petition numerous times a day every day will manifest our desires. Oftentimes, these words are expressed in the form of an incantation, which is a series of words believed to have a magical effect when spoken or sung.

Novena prayers to saints are a form of reciting incantations. When performing a novena, we are reciting a series of the same words for nine days in order to manifest our desires.

There are also magical incantations recited to awaken or summon an entity. It is a common practice with vastly experienced members of several African magico-religious and diaspora practices. However, because magical incantations are commonly spoken in languages other than our own native tongues, this practice can be dangerous. Never recite words in unknown languages, as you may inadvertently summon something evil. Additionally, do not take someone else's interpretation or blind faith of the meaning of those words. Research the words yourself and, if you feel uncomfortable, don't recite them.

Incense

Incense has been used in ritual practices since ancient times. The Holy Bible even tells us to burn incense. As a matter of fact, there are 121 passages about incense throughout eighteen books in the Bible. For example, in Exodus, God himself says "And thou shalt make an altar to burn incense upon..." (Ex. 30.1).

Many metaphysical practitioners believe that incense carry messages directly to our targets or to the spirit world. We believe that because spirits are attracted to its odor and smoke, and it is another form of summoning them to ask for their help. It is also another means of energy output. When we burn incense and pray and/or state our petitions aloud, we are outputting heaps of energy toward our desired goals.

Incense is available in a number of different forms.

Natural Resins

Burned on charcoal rounds, resins are actually the hardened sap of trees. Because they are reduced to smaller sizes comparable to a teardrop, they are oftentimes referred to as "incense tears."

One of my favorite resins to burn while reciting any Psalm in prayer to God is frankincense. This is because, since ancient times, it is widely believed that burning frankincense is another symbol of prayer directed at and ascending straight to God. Avoid using any powdered versions of frankincense, as it might be impure due to added chemicals.

Wood or Wood Chips

The chips are usually burned on charcoal. But, if a piece of wood is large enough, it can be burned alone.

Palo santo, or "Holy Wood," is one of my favorite woods. According to numerous spiritual practitioners, when palo santo is burned, the tree spirit in the wood is awakened and clears away negative energies and malevolent spirits.

The wood has also been found to be effective against the common cold and flu. Additionally, it is known to provide relief against stress, anxiety, and depression, as well as asthma.

Cones, Coils, and Joss Sticks

Although difficult to employ these forms of incense for extensive magical rituals, they are great to burn if one wishes to bring a certain condition or energy into the home. My personal preferences are beauty, success, money, good health, peaceful home, and uncrossing cones, coils, or sticks.

Herbs

Dried plants can be loosely or finely ground, and many botanical stores even sell herbs that are ground precisely into a powder. The ground herbs are placed on a lit charcoal round (with or without incense powder).

Powders

Incense powders are most often available already prepared to accommodate the conditions or desired effects that the practitioner wishes to achieve. Thus, they are called "condition incenses." They are usually self-igniting powders, but my penchant is to place the incense atop a burning charcoal round, then light the incense, to assure continuity in the burn.

When working with herbs and/or incense powders, my preference is to write out a small petition, with a pencil, on a very small torn piece of brown paper bag. Fold the paper and prepare a charcoal round. Light the charcoal round and place it in a fireproof censer. Wait until the round becomes hot, indicated by it turning a grey color. Place the petition paper atop the grey charcoal round, then immediately top the paper with the powder and/or herbs, and light that too.

Take the censer outside and, as the smoke rises, verbalize your commands several times. Once the contents have combusted and the charcoal round becomes cold, face the cardinal direction of East and allow the wind to take everything away.

If the incense is being utilized for negative spellwork, do the work outside. This is a precautionary measure to avoid harboring negative energies that are emitted by the smoke of the incense in your home. If it is impossible to light the incense outside, do so directly beside an open window.

Minerals/Rocks/Crystals

Why are rocks and crystals oftentimes referred to as minerals? Well, the answer is both simple and complex. A mineral is simply a naturally present element that is usually free flowing. A rock is simply two or more minerals bound together.

The explanation of a crystal becomes a little more complex. After minerals are exposed to heat, there is a cooling phase. During this phase, crystallites appear and form structures that are called crystals. Thus, a crystal refers to the minerals' observable crystallite structures.

As with roots and plant parts, it is a common belief that minerals, rocks, and crystals have spirits. In fact, some minerals even grow! In the year 2000, a cave filled with selenite crystals was discovered in Naica, Mexico. It became known as the "Cave of Crystals," and has been monitored by scientists ever since its discovery. The remarkable findings were that these crystals not only grow but are continuing to grow at an astonishing rate to mammoth sizes. Additionally, they are emitting clearly audible sounds.

Listed below are just a few of a vast number of minerals frequently utilized by Hoodoo practitioners:

Minerals

- **Alum (Aluminum sulfate or Potassium aluminum sulfate):** To padlock a target's body part.
- **Boric acid (Baron trioxide):** For jinxing, cursing, or crossing.
- **Epsom salts (Magnesium sulfate heptahydrate):** In a bath, it is used for spiritual cleansing.

- **Magnetic sand (Iron oxide):** Naturally magnetized sand used to feed lodestones.
- **Salt (Sodium chloride):** From protection and uncrossing to cursing, crossing, and send away spells, salt is a versatile spell ingredient.
- **Sulphur (Brimstone):** Similar in versatility to salt, it is employed for protection and uncrossing, as well as cursing and crossing spells.

Rocks

- **Lodestones (Magnetite):** Frequently referred to as crystals, they are in fact, rocks. Lodestones differ from simple magnetite because they are naturally magnetized by lightning. Because of their magnetic properties, lodestones are employed in general attraction spells.
- **River rocks (Granite, basalt, schist, etc.):** Depending on their location, they are formed by the prevalent minerals located in specific rivers. Because flowing water is soothing, these rocks have absorbed the rivers' positive energies and are utilized in healing work. In some African magico-religious and diaspora practices, it is believed that the rocks absorb the energies of the deities who dwell within the rivers.

Crystals

When selecting a crystal, always remember that real crystals never get warm when you touch them. This is because they do not retain heat. Test your crystal by holding it in your hand. If it retains the temperature of your hand, it is not real.

Although rocks are not cleansed, all crystals (with the exception of kyanite and citrine) ought to be ritually purified before usage. This can be done by simply smoking them with white sage or spraying them with either salt water, whiskey, or Florida Water. However, there is another extensive cleansing ritual that requires burying your crystals in sea salt for twenty-four hours, removing them, and rinsing with cold water. Then, smoke them with white sage. Repeat the process with new salt. Afterwards, lay them outside for twenty-four hours to absorb the energies of both the Sun and the Moon.

Because most crystals serve many purposes, it is also essential to program them after cleansing. This must be performed every time for each individual crystal. Simply ring a bell to awaken the crystal, hold it in your hands, and speak softly to it. Tell the crystal who you are, promise to take good care of it, then respectfully ask it to help you with your desire.

According to an article published by PhD student Alex Williams, there are over four thousand different types of crystals in the world. One of my favorite extensive encyclopedias on the topic is *Love is in the Earth: A Kaleidoscope of Crystals,* written by Melody. However, crystals were not popular in either the antebellum or immediate emancipation periods.

Nails, Needles, Pins

These items can be used in a plethora of ways, such as incorporating them into jar spells, jabbing them though pictures, binding an enemy, stopping gossip, or torturing a doll. No matter the method for which they are used, most everyone in the African magico-religious and diaspora practices possess nails, needles, and pins in their arsenal of tools.

Oils

Magical practitioners oftentimes utilize anointing oils for their candles and other tools. Even The Holy Bible speaks of anointing oils when God commands in Exodus: "Oil for the light, spices for anointing oil, and for sweet incense." (Ex. 25.6)

Top quality oils will contain either herbs, roots, minerals, and/or pure essential oils, which are actually liquidized plant extracts. Because we as Hoodoo practitioners believe that the aforementioned elements possess spirits, the oils therefore contain magical properties.

These magical oils are known as conjure oils, dressing oils, Hoodoo oils, prepared oils, anointing oils, and (the most confusing terminology of all) "condition" oils. So, allow me to explain this befuddling lingo.

The intention of the spellwork is also known as the spell's "condition," and the oil is designed to aid in achieving the specific desired results. For example, if one is performing a love spell, the condition is love and, therefore, the condition oil will have labels such as "Love,""Love Drawing," or similar classifications. Another example is a money condition oil that is designed to complement and aid with a money drawing spell and the like.

The terminologies differ regionally, but the purpose of the magical oils remain the same. However, there are numerous companies, as well as small businesses, who sell oils that do not contain any of the necessary ingredients to create a legitimate magical oil. Either ensure that the seller is reputable or make your own oils.

Personal Concerns/Taglocks

These are items that have been biologically connected to your target, most containing DNA (deoxyribonucleic acid) molecules, which are also referred to as the individual's personal "blueprint." Although other metaphysical practices refer to these items as "taglocks," Hoodoo practitioners call them "personal concerns" and believe that they contain an essence of the person's spirit.

Now, this isn't just a metaphysical belief. The theory of quantum entanglement is fundamental in physics, positing that, if two atoms previously attached to each other were separated, they would still be connected by an invisible umbilical cord. Thus, no matter how far apart they are from one another, the two atoms will forever be linked together. It never ceases to amaze me how science is slowly recognizing metaphysical beliefs. The scientists use different words, but the principles are the same.

Hair

There are about 100,000 hair follicles on each human being's scalp. Because the average person sheds about one hundred strands a day, it's one of the easiest personal concerns to obtain.

The early slaves had claimed that scalp hair is the best personal concern to work with because that hair was once closest to the brain than any other taglock. Therefore, if your target's scalp hair is in your possession, you can easier manipulate him/her because of the indirect connection to the brain, which controls emotional and body functions.

As relayed in the Book of Judges in the Bible, a man named Samson was granted herculean strength by God. He was told that his strength was in his hair, and, if it were ever to be cut, he would lose that strength. Sadly, Samson was betrayed by his wife, Delilah, who did indeed cut his hair while he slept. To make a long story short, he was weakened, captured by his enemies, and soon died.

Along with many old-timers, my ex-boyfriend—who was a scientist—claimed that the story of Samson and Delilah was simply a warning regarding what can happen if we relinquish our scalp hair to another. All of them said the same thing: "You are surrendering your power to another." So, convinced that the story was true, my ex always kept a meticulously clean hairbrush!

Other personal concerns/taglocks include:

- Blood
- Dandruff
- Ear wax
- Feces
- Fingernails
- Fingerprints
- Footprints
- Mucus
- Saliva
- Scabs
- Semen
- Skin cells
- Sweat
- Tears
- Teeth
- Toenails
- Vaginal secretions
- Urine

Adjuncts to Personal Concerns

Oftentimes, clients have asked me what to do if they are unable to attain a target's personal concern. Although they are weaker connections to the target, using as many adjuncts as possible may suffice. Adjuncts may include:

- **Your target's full birthname and birth date.**
- **Birth name of the target's mother:** This knowledge adds more power to any spell. So, for example, if your target's name is Jane

Doe and her mother's maiden name is "Mousey Moose," you would state: "Jane Doe, born 31 Feb. 1808, daughter of Mousey Moose."

- **A photograph of your target:** Ensure that the eyes are showing and looking directly at the camera. This is because the eyes are the windows to one's soul, and the practitioner can be better able to reach it. Use photo quality paper and not plain printer paper, as it is weak and of low quality, therefore, less effective.
- **Your target's signature:** Try to get an actual signature, as photocopies of signatures are extremely weak adjuncts and rarely work.
- **Your target's handwriting:** Again, photocopies are weak links and rarely work.

A Word of Caution

Oftentimes, neophyte practitioners will insert their own personal concern into spellwork. Never sacrifice your own blood unless you're an experienced, seasoned, and trained ceremonial magician.

Additionally, although urine is a personal concern used for domination, do not intermix your urine or saliva onto any negative spellwork. Yes, it's tempting to spit or urinate on a doll that was created for cursing or crossing, but that doll will inevitably absorb your DNA. It will result in the practitioner emitting negativity onto themselves.

Powders

For centuries, powders have been successfully used in spellwork by Hoodoo practitioners. They are effective in a multitude of purposes through deployment such as:

- **Blowing:** Placing the powder in your hands then blowing it at a target or toward the cardinal direction for which they reside can achieve a desired behavior.
- **Contact Magic:** Placing powder someplace where the targets will engage in either direct or indirect contact with it can also affect their behaviors.

- **Sprinkling:** Powders in or around the home can be used for purposes such as protection, uncrossing, etc. A great example of a protection powder is red brick dust, which is frequently deployed by sprinkling across doorways to guard against malicious human and spiritual intruders.
- **Wearing:** Dusting yourself or your clothing with a powder is commonly performed to attract someone or something to you.

Condition powders can be made by grinding herbs, plants, or minerals into a fine dust for use in spellwork. Back in the days of slavery, powders were made with naturally occurring ingredients.

Nowadays, many vendors sell condition powders that are mixed with talcum powder and are sometimes referred to as sachets. Sadly, its main ingredient is talc, a skin irritant formula comprised of magnesium, silicon, oxygen, and hydrogen. Worse yet, some companies add asbestos, a carcinogenic mineral, into their talcum powder. Most spiritual stores that make their own condition powders have replaced talc with cornstarch, which is a much safer component. Nevertheless, it is both wise and prudent to first inquire about the ingredients prior to purchasing a condition powder.

If your powder is made from purely ground herbs or plants, it is common to roll your candles onto them or to add them into your jar spells. However, if the powders contain cornstarch, it will not only prevent your candles from burning properly, it will also clump and/or rise to the top when deployed in jar spells.

Because condition powders are usually purchased, my policy is to simply avoid using any of them in jar or candle spells.

Roots

The root of a plant may or may not have similar powers as the rest of the plant. Therefore, it is necessary to study the properties that each part may hold. Nevertheless, various roots contain magical powers.

Root chips can be utilized in many formulas, such as oils. They can also be ground and used as powders, or the chips themselves can be incorporated into numerous types of spellwork. Whole roots, on the other hand, are usually carried as pocket pieces and act as talismans which attract particular benefits to its owner.

Almost every Hoodoo practitioner, author, or scholar of folklore knows the story of one root's power as relayed in his book: *Narrative of the Life of Frederick Douglass: An American Slave.* A slave master physically brutalized Douglass on a perpetual basis. One day, Douglass met up with an African slave who gave him a root to keep in his right pocket. The African promised that the root would prevent the slaver from ever harming him again. Alas, the slaver did indeed strike him again, but that root gave Douglass the courage and fortitude to fight back. After the slaver was beaten to a pulp, Douglass was never struck again.

What was that root? Douglass didn't know, but it is highly suspected by tens of thousands to be the High John the Conqueror. Practitioners suspect this because that root commands power and mastery.

An interesting side note to this story is that, when one wishes to attract or receive a particular benefit from a talisman, root, magical charm bag, or the like, it would be carried in the left pocket. Conversely, if we wish to release an attribute, as Douglass executed strength and power, the right pocket would be used.

Solutions

Colognes, juices, waters, and other solutions have been utilized in African diaspora traditions and religions for many decades. Solutions have been used in jar spells, floor washes, baths, or added to the rinse cycle when washing clothes. Depending on the metaphysical intention and the type of liquid used, there are numerous ways to employ them into magical spells.

Spritzing, sprinkling, splashing, or spraying are examples of how solutions are dispersed. When observing experienced magical practitioners, they do so in a ritualistic manner. However, this is not necessary for beginners. As a matter of fact, my nickname is "The Spray Bottle Queen," because it is my preferred method of deploying holy water, Florida Water, and different herbal waters when distributing the solution over large surface areas.

It is highly recommended to make your own herbal solutions, as most marketed ones contain alcohol which may ruin the magical properties of the herbs. Other solutions include:

- **Ammonia:** To eradicate malicious entities.
- **Bay rum:** Cleanses the aura.
- **Chinese wash:** Removes negative energies and draws in positive energies.
- **First rain of May:** Considered to be holy water.
- **Florida Water:** For spiritual cleansing.
- **Four thieves vinegar:** Protection from enemies. Also used for medicinal purposes.
- **Holy water:** For spiritual cleansing and protection.
- **Hot sauces:** For negative spellwork and sending people away.
- **Hoyt's cologne:** Brings good luck.
- **Hurricane water:** Rainwater collected during a hurricane is used to cause complete havoc to a person or to a relationship.
- **Kananga water:** Used for purification.
- **Kolonia 1800 (Natural):** Splashed on for good luck, as well as calming the nerves.
- **Lemon juice:** To sour a person's life or a relationship.
- **Milk, spoiled:** To spoil a situation, or a person's reputation.
- **Pine sol:** If a drop of pine essential oil is added to the bottle, it aids in removing negative energies. Also helps to attract money.
- **Rainwater:** If this rain is collected without having been exposed to a storm, it is considered pure. Metaphysical practitioners find this to be the perfect water as a substitute for tap water.
- **River water:** To wash away sins and cleanse the soul.
- **Rose water:** Used by Muslims in love work.
- **Sea Water:** Aids in healing physical pains when rubbed on the area. Also used for cleansing the altar.
- **Storm water:** Rainwater collected during a storm will cause turmoil to a person or to a relationship.
- **Vinegar:** To sour a person's life or a relationship.
- **War water:** To cause people to fight.
- **Whiskey:** Gives strength to magical charm bags, also used for cleansing magical tools.

Statues

In the 1973 box office hit movie "The Exorcist," a young girl is possessed by demons. This movie is based on a true story of a young man who soon became possessed after carelessly engaging in Ouija Board activities along with his aunt.

The boy's aunt soon died and, thereafter, the boy was taken over by demons. Along with the head exorcist, a team of priests and monks feverishly attempted to eradicate the malicious entities from the boy's body. After about six months, one of the team members placed a statue of St. Michael by the boy's bedside as they begged the Archangel for help. That statue, along with the prayers, finally banished the demons.

What makes a statue powerful? That power is emitted from the statue by the entity itself. In numerous African Traditional, Diaspora, and Derivative practices, an entity is ritually summoned and asked to live within statues, stones, masks, and other objects deemed sacred. If the entity agrees, it will place a bit of its essence into the object, thus technically residing in it. When the practitioner wishes to interact with the entity, they can readily do so by communicating with the occupied object.

Although non-initiates cannot engage in task-oriented summoning rituals, there is an alternative method by which to invite an entity to dwell within a statue. This is my preferred method:

1. Cleanse the statue with holy water and then allow it to air dry.

2. Anoint the crown of the statue's head with olive oil or holy oil.

3. Recite a prayer aloud specific to, or preferred by, the entity. Do not yet end the prayer with the word "Amen," as it closes the prayer.

4. In a respectful manner, introduce yourself by both your full birth name and present name, then announce your birth date. Tell the entity that the statue belongs to them and invite it to view the statue as its second home. Promise to offer fresh water and a lit white candle in front of the statue on a frequent basis. Thank the entity and close the communication with the word "Amen."

You are now obligated to offer candles and fresh water on a regular basis. This can be performed on either a weekly, bi-weekly, or monthly basis. Pray before the statue, then give your offerings. Failing to do so will cause the entity's essence to leave.

If dust is accumulated on the statue, tell the entity that you are going to cleanse it. Then, rinse it with holy water and re-anoint the crown of the statue's head with the oil.

Symbols

Magical symbols, such as sigils and seals, are emblematic representations of either a specific deity or the practitioner's desired outcome. Because they too emit vibrational energies and have been widely employed in magical practices for thousands of years, throughout the world.

In the African Diasporic Religion of Palo, which arises from the Kongo religion of the African Bakongo people, symbols are extensively used. In fact, it is believed that the souls of all human beings possess their own identification symbols, which is akin to a human's identifiable fingerprints. Once a person becomes an initiate of Palo, their personal symbol is disclosed to them. Another example is that of the practitioners of Vodou, who assign a specific symbol called a *veve* to each of their Deities.

Years after the antebellum, Hoodoo practitioners began to write their commands over appropriate symbols or seals listed in books such as *The Key of Solomon* and *The Sixth and Seventh Books of Moses*. This conduct may have indeed been derived from the magical practices of the Bakongo people.

Talismans

Unlike an amulet, which provides protection, a talisman is instead used to attract a particular benefit to its owner. Talismans contain religious or magical powers and can vary in sizes from extremely large objects down to pocket pieces.

Although the name itself originally derives from the ancient Greek word *telesma,* meaning "completion" or "religious rite," it has been speculated that they were actually first devised during the Stone Age. Talismans have been used in many civilizations throughout history, but the Muslim people were (and are still today) considered the world's foremost experts on the magical objects. As I mentioned in Chapter One, most black Muslim slaves brought their knowledge of crafting magical charms, amulets, and talismans to the Americas. These people were highly acclaimed for their abilities to craft magical objects that contained immense powers.

Talismans can be objects as modest as stones, bones, or plant roots. Others are simply symbols or written words that are blatantly visible or secretly encased. They can be made out of almost anything and appear as modest or elaborate as the bearer sees fit. Magical charm bags are often crafted to bring about a certain benefit to the owner. When they are crafted for this purpose, they are also considered to be talismans.

However, no matter the objects used, the experts do agree that they ought to be ritually cleansed and magically charged before use. Although there are many ways to cleanse and charge an object, here are my suggestions:

Cleansing a Magical Object

First and foremost, be sensitive to the vulnerability of the object. If a live plant is the talisman, don't cleanse it with anything harsh, such as purchased solutions containing alcohol, as the plant will be killed. My suggestion is to cleanse live plants with holy water. In fact, holy water is my preferred cleansing agent for any and all objects.

On inanimate items, whiskey, Florida Water, or a little sea salt dissolved into a glass of water are the most commonly used liquids for cleansing magical objects. A small spray bottle works well for dispersing the mixture.

Charging a Magical Object

Aside from magical charm bags which will be discussed in the succeeding chapter, this is one popular way of charging a magical object:

1. Cup your right hand with the palm side facing up. Then, cup your left hand and place it palm-side down over your right cupped hand. Hold this position for at least a minute.

2. Now, do the opposite by cupping your left hand with the palm-side facing up and place you cupped right hand over it. Hold this position for another minute.

3. Repeat steps one and two until you can feel the heat generating. Some magical practitioners will even visualize a growing ball of light between their hands as they do so.

4. Cup your right hand again and place your magical object in the palm of your hand, and cover it with your cupped left hand. Hold it in place for a few minutes.

5. While the magical object remains inside your cupped hands, slowly place your hands to your mouth and say: "By the power given to me by God, you are now activated to perform the magical duties of (State the responsibilities of the object)."

Although there are many more tools of the trade, this chapter explored the most commonly used instruments. As time goes on, you will develop expertise and discover and/or devise your own tools. It just takes practice and patience.

Next, we will explore some of my favorite and most successful magical formulas.

CHAPTER SIX

MAGICAL FORMULARY

There is an abundance of metaphysical stores from which we can buy top quality products needed for spellwork. Conversely, there are probably an equal number of stores that do not sell legitimate items. For instance, I once purchased black cat hair advertised as being legitimate and combed from the seller's pet black cat. To my dismay, it was instead a synthetic material pulled from a toy animal. Another example was an online vendor who sold potting soil but advertised it as being graveyard dirt. There are many more distressing stories of fraudulent products being sold.

We must always carefully research the vendor's credentials. Before purchasing anything, ask questions about the products. Where were the products manufactured? Also, ensure that there is a refund guarantee if the product is not genuine. Another option is to make your own products. Remember that in the days of the antebellum, the slaves did not have the luxury of purchasing products. They instead successfully crafted their own.

This chapter contains many of my favorite formulas, but don't limit yourself to just mine. As you become more adept as a Hoodoo practitioner, you will be better able to create your own magical recipes. When doing so, remember to never intermix metaphysical craft items because the purpose of one magical organic or inorganic element in one craft may represent something entirely different to another.

Baths

Ask yourself this question prior to taking any type of magical baths and/or performing spellwork: "If you haven't bathed in a year and smelled bad, then donned perfume, how would you smell?" Of course, you would either still smell bad, or perhaps even worse.

On a daily basis, we all attract negative spiritual energies that attach themselves to us. When this happens, they soil the aura, our own personal energy field. We want our auras to be clean, bright, and healthy. Therefore, prior to performing spellwork, it is important to first perform a spiritual cleansing bath to cleanse the aura. Otherwise, those negative energies clinging to us will impede the steady output flow of desired energies.

Spiritual cleansing is especially important if engaging in spellwork for self-improvement or to attract someone or something to you. Even if the spell is as simple as applying oils or powders to oneself, your aura must be clean, or else those products will not work. In other words, if your underlying spiritual odor is bad, the products are not going to emit energies to make you look or smell good.

Similar principles apply when engaging in other types of magical baths. We must first shower to remove physical dirt or grime attached to our bodies prior to occupying a bathtub containing magical properties. Although showering with any soap or body wash will suffice, my personal choice is sulfur or rue soap, because they also removes negative energies.

Academic Achievement Bath

In the African Diaspora Religion of Santeria, this bath is originally intended to seek help from the Orisha, or deity, Obatala. He is a phenomenal Orisha, as are the others. After having performed this bath once a week for a month while in graduate school, I had attained my Masters of Science with a 4.0 grade point average.

Since one syncretism of Obatala is Jesus Christ, the Christian Son of God, this bath is just as effective when petitioning and praying to Jesus rather than to Obatala.

Ingredients:

- 1 carton of fresh goat's milk
- A splash of Florida Water
- At least ¼ tsp (or more) of cascarilla (eggshell powder)
- 2 handfuls of fresh, white carnations or white roses (remove stems)
- 1 tealight or four-inch taper candle white candle

Instructions:

1. Fill a bathtub with a comfortable water temperature. Pour the go-at's milk into the water. Now, recheck the water and readjust the temperature if it's not warm enough for you. Add the Florida Water, cascarilla, and the flowers last.

2. Light the candle and place it at the front of the bathtub. Enter the bathtub and relax. At convenient intervals, immerse your entire body into the water. Do this at least three times. Then, recite this prayer aloud:

"O Lord Jesus, King of kings and the Lord of Lords,
the hour and time have come for me to show how much I have learned
and the effort I've put into my studies. Mighty Lord, I ask that you
give me clarity of mind and good memory to re-member all I've read.
I rebuke any spirit of confusion or forgetfulness today in my exam hall.
I also ask for guidance. May no evil befall me during this period;
I cover myself and my steps with the blood of Jesus.
(Ask your request here)
Thank you, Lord, for giving me the grace and confidence I need,
for I know you're with me always.
AMEN."

3. Once the bath is completed, step out of the bathtub, blot yourself dry with a clean towel, and don clothing. Gather the flowers and place them outside your front door. Drain bath water.

Attraction Shower

The herb basil serves many purposes in the African Diaspora Religions and Traditions. For instance, the Gullah people of the Carolinas depend on this herb for protection. In fact, the old Hoodoo saying "Evil cannot walk where basil has been" clearly illustrates the protection properties of basil. However, this herb is also widely used in both romantic attraction and love spells.

Although the effects of this spell only last for two days, my mother always prescribed this wash to young single people prior to attending any event where they may meet potential suitors. It perpetually yielded great success stories. I've used it myself on numerous occasions and have attracted many courters. Therefore, this spell is dedicated, in loving memory, to my wonderful mother, Kiriaki Catel:

Ingredients:

- 2 handfuls of fresh Basil (Ocimum basilicum)
- ½ cup Florida Water
- A large pot of tap water

Instructions:

1. Boil the pot of water, then remove the pot from the stove. Immediately add the basil leaves and let them steep in the hot water. Once the water is at a lukewarm temperature, add the Florida Water and stir the mixture with a wooden spoon. Do not remove the basil.

2. Shower with soap and water, then rinse off. Immediately take the pot and pour the entire mixture over your head. Exit the shower and, with a towel, blot your hair. Allow your body to air dry. No prayers are necessary.

3. Gather the basil leaves, take them outside, then respectfully place them on the ground. This is performed to symbolically represent that the leaves are being returned to the ground from whence they came.

Forgiveness for Sins Bath
Although it is highly recommended to take this bath after having performed negative spellwork, it is also suggested to do so after one has sinned. The only herb needed is hyssop, a spiritual purifying agent. The Psalm recited during this bath actually mentions the herb.

Depending on the nature of the sin or the need for spiritual forgiveness, take one bath daily around the same time each day for as long as you feel is necessary. However, according to the Holy Bible, if one is especially stained, "And when he that hath an issue is cleansed of his issue; then he shall number to himself seven days for his cleansing, and wash his clothes, and bathe his flesh in running water, and shall be clean" (Lev. 15.13).

Ingredients:
- 1 tsp of extra virgin olive oil
- 2 tbsp dried hyssop *(Hyssopus officinalis)*
- A pot filled with about one quart of water

Instructions:
1. Boil the pot of water, then remove the pot from the stove. Immediately add the hyssop and allow it to steep in the hot water for nine minutes.

2. In the meantime, fill a bathtub with a comfortable water temperature. Add the olive oil.

3. After the hyssop has finished steeping, strain the herb and put it aside. Add the herbal tea water to the bath.

4. Enter the bathtub and relax. Begin to recite Psalm 51 aloud and, at convenient intervals between prayer lines, immerse your entire body into the water. The immersion ought to be performed between nine and thirteen times.

5. Once the bath is completed, step out of the bathtub, blot yourself dry with a clean towel, and don clothing. Drain bath water. Take the hyssop outside and respectfully place it on the ground to symbolically represent that it is being returned to the ground from whence it came.

Money Bath

This spell was given to me almost fifty years ago by an old African American woman. Traditionally, it is performed on New Year's Eve, but it can also be performed any time during the year, preferably on a Thursday during a waxing moon. Her version solely involved bathing with coins; however, my version also includes money-drawing herbs. Therefore, the instructional steps for herbal preparation is optional.

Ingredients:

- 1 tsp dried alfalfa *(Medicago sativa)*
- 1 tsp dried fumitory herb *(Fumaria fungosa, Fumaria spp.)*
- 2 rolls of quarters or more
- 2 rolls of dimes or more
- 2 rolls of nickels or more

(If you live in a country outside of the United States, use enough silver-colored coins to scatter evenly inside your bathtub.)

Instructions:

1. Boil a pot of water. Once the water is bubbling hot, empty the rolls of coins into the water and boil for at least ten minutes to rid them of any germs. Strain the coins and place them aside. Do not touch the coins until they have cooled off.

2. In a clean pot, add one quart of water and boil. Once the water has boiled, remove the pot from the heat and add the herbs. Allow them to steep in the hot water for five minutes.

3. In the meantime, fill a bathtub with a comfortable water temperature. Add the coins and scatter them around the bathtub. After the herbs have finished steeping, strain the herbs and put them aside. Add the herbal tea water to the bath.

4. Enter the bathtub and relax. Begin to recite Psalm 23 aloud and ask for money to come to you. Recite this Psalm at least three times. At convenient intervals, immerse your entire body into the water. The immersion ought to be performed five times.

5. Once the bath is completed, step out of the bathtub, blot yourself dry with a clean towel, and don clothing. Remove the coins and place them on a towel to dry. Drain the bath water. Take the herbs outside then respectfully place them on the ground to symbolically represent that they are being returned to the ground from whence it came.

The Bath Coins
You may spend the money or use the coins to create a money jar spell. If you chose to perform a money jar spell, it will enhance your chances of attracting money.

Ingredients:
- The coins used for the money bath spell.
- 1 small glass jar with a metal lid
- 1 small picture of yourself, with eyes showing, on photo quality paper.
- 1 four-inch white or green taper candle.
- Olive oil

Instructions:
1. Once the coins have completely dried, place half of them inside the jar. Insert your picture atop the coins. Then, place the remaining coins over your picture and ensure that it is completely surrounded by money.

2. On Thursdays during the waxing moon, perform a candle spell. With a pencil, inscribe the taper candle with the words "Money come to me." Anoint the candle with extra-virgin olive oil. Place the candle atop the lid and light it. Pray Psalm 23 and ask for money to come to you.

Dolls

Before discussing the crafting of dolls, let's first examine the terminologies associated with them. A fetish is a term most commonly used to describe an object, such as a doll, that is believed to contain magical powers or is inhabited by an entity possessing magical powers.

If the fetish is inhabited by a malevolent entity; those powers can be harmful. However, if it is inhabited by a benevolent spirit, the fetish could protect or aid its owner.

On the other hand, dolls used as effigies, most commonly referred to as "doll babies" by Hoodoo practitioners, are crafted to represent people or animals. After inserting a personal concern of the target into a doll, it is believed to then contain an essence of the target's spirit, linking them together. Because of this, spells can be cast upon the target through imitation magic, a term used to define mimicking the desired results.

Thousands of people even craft dolls of themselves for favorable desired results, such as healing or protection, while others craft effigies of their pets and loved ones for the same reasons. In the days of slavery, dolls were most commonly created for the purposes of either protection from danger or to control or harm their cruel slave owners.

Listed below are several ways to craft a doll. However, before crafting any doll, please keep three important details in mind:

- **Never bake any doll to harden it.** What happens to raw meat after it's been baked? It transforms into a different texture and appears, smells, and tastes different. This is because the heat of the oven changed the molecular structure of that meat. It is no longer raw, but instead cooked. The molecular composition may also change. Thus, baking your dolls will also change the structures of the personal concerns, and it will no longer be an essence of your target. The best option is to lay the dolls on paper towels to absorb the moisture until they are completely dry.

- **Do not place a doll made of clay, dough, or papier-mâché outside in the hot sun to dry.** The extreme heat of the sun will cause cracks or even breakage to the doll.

- **Never worry about the appearance of your artistry.** Even though numerous magical practitioners make aesthetically stunning dolls; it doesn't matter what they look like. If the doll is crafted properly, it will work in spite of its appearance.

Crafting a Clay Doll Baby

Ingredients:

- 1 package of air-drying clay
- 1 roll of paper towels
- A vat of warm water
- A pencil
- Petition papers
- Personal concerns of your target
- Photograph of your target (if available) with the eyes showing
- Other ingredients that will assist in achieving your goals, such as herbs, minerals, root chips, oils, and/or powders

Instructions:

1. Divide the packet of clay into three sections: one for the back torso, one for the front torso, one for the extremities—legs, arms, penis (if male), and head. Place these sections into warm water to prevent rapid drying.

2. Place layers of paper towel on a flat surface to absorb the moisture of the clay that was absorbed from the warm water. Ensure that each section of the clay is molded over fresh paper towels.

3. Remove one section of the clay from the water to make the back portion of the torso. This will be the "foundation" of the doll. Knead it flat until there is enough clay surface to contain the personal concerns and the optional ingredients. With your pencil, inscribe the target's name and birthdate into the clay.

4. With the second section of the clay, mold out the head and four limbs. If the target is male, also construct the penis. Press the limbs, head, and (if applicable) penis, into the foundation clay piece. Next, set the personal concerns, petition papers, name papers, photograph, and optional ingredients over the foundation portion of the doll.

5. Knead the last section of the clay to make the top torso portion and ensure that this piece is just slightly smaller than the bottom portion. Also inscribe the targets name and birthdate into this portion. Then, lay it over the foundational clay to completely cover the limbs and ingredients.

6. Fold the foundation portion up and over the top section and mold the entire doll until there are no visible seams. If desired, also inscribe the target's name and birth date over the top portion of the torso. Once this is accomplished, if the target is a female, you may insert your pencil between its leg to form a vaginal opening. Using the tip of your pencil. etch in the eyes, nose, mouth, and any other desired features.

7. The drying period becomes a little time consuming. It does require that the doll rest on daily fresh layers of paper towels and be turned at least once a day until it is completely dry.

Crafting a Cloth Doll Baby

1. Acquire a large piece of white cloth, as it is a neutral color. However, the color of the cloth can coincide with the magical purpose, such as pink for love, green for money, etc. Also, if using an unwashed article of clothing that the target has worn, then the color is not as relevant, because it contains taglocks, most commonly being dried skin cells. Ensure that the side of the cloth containing the taglocks faces inward.

2. Patterns for dolls can be found online, and they simply resemble the image of a gingerbread cookie man. Because of their simplicity, they can be hand-sewn. Sew one side closed and work with the open side.

3. Stuff the doll with as many taglocks as possible. Add one or more petition papers, small pictures of the target, and name papers. Next, add optional ingredients that will assist in your desired goals. Then, sew the doll shut.

Crafting a Dough Doll Baby

Working with dough can become a little challenging because of its inconsistent, pasty, and adhesive nature. Therefore, the best option is to create it rapidly by using just one large piece and one small piece of dough, any kind.

Instructions:

1. On a scantily floured surface, mold the image of the target's entire body with the large portion of dough. With the convex side of a small, floured cookie scoop, push into the belly of the formed body to create a small well. Immediately fill the well with a name paper, petition paper, and any taglock that you may have.

2. Take the small piece of dough, immerse it in water to regain its adhesiveness, then use it to cover the contents. Ensure that the top piece of dough adheres to the body of the doll.

3. Allow the doll to air dry on a flat surface.

Crafting a Ground Meat Doll Baby

This type of doll is constructed to inflict harm to another by either laying it outside to rot or burning it to a crisp. Unlike baking personal concerns and changing the molecular structure, rapid burning of taglocks is akin to destroying the target.

Simply mold the meat into the image of the target's entire body. With your fingers, push into the belly of the formed body to create a small well and fill it with a name paper and/or the target's taglock. Cover the contents with more meat. With a pencil, inscribe the target's name and birthdate into the meat.

Converting a Toy into A Doll Baby

Unless a plastic doll contains an outlet to insert items in order to create a link between the target and the toy, it becomes a difficult task by which to achieve your desired results. It can be done, but it is rarely successful for neophytes. Therefore, my preference in toy selections are either cloth dolls or stuffed animals.

It doesn't matter what the stuffed animal looks like, but it ought to have your own psychological representation of the target. For example, in my opinion, teddy bears are great toys for use in love work. Conversely, monkeys, donkeys, and snakes are best for negative spellwork. I once casted negative spellwork using a toy stuffed horse on an evil woman with an abnormally long face, as well as unusually large yellowing teeth.

Simply slit one side of the toy open and remove a portion of the stuffing from the head and torso, leaving the limbs as they are. Stuff the head with a picture of the target and any other desired ingredients. As with the cloth doll, stuff the torso of the toy with as many taglocks as possible. Add petition papers, small pictures of the target, and name papers. Next, add optional ingredients that will assist in your desired goals. Then, sew the doll shut.

An easier option for filling the torso of the body is to insert all items into a small white crew sock or baby sock. Then, place the sock into the torso section of the doll and sew the doll shut.

Baptizing and Naming the Doll

Baptizing and naming an effigy is performed to awaken the contained essence of the target's spirit via taglocks into the effigy. My preferred method is similar to that of the Catholic priests, anointing the second and middle fingers with holy water or Florida Water. Then, with those two fingers, make the sign of the cross over the crown of its head while stating aloud: "I baptize you in the name of the Father, of the Son, and of the Holy Spirit, Amen."

If your effigy is firm, hold it up toward the ceiling or sky with both of your hands. Imagine volts of electricity running from your shoulders to your arms and into the image while stating aloud: "And I name you (target's name)." Repeat the target's name for a total of nine times, screaming the name on the ninth time. If the effigy is limber and made from substances such as ground meat or mud, instead place your hands over it while naming and baptizing the doll.

Herbal and Root Chip Blends

We have already explored the fact that all plants and roots have spirits who are able to communicate with the herbalist. However, the communication process between man and plant cannot be fully achieved overnight. Just as with any acquired skill, it takes time, patience, practice, determination, and commitment to become a proficient communicator.

As formerly discussed, the first step toward acquiring this skill is to demonstrate respect both verbally and through your actions. Follow the instructional steps in Chapter Five to begin your rapport with living or dried plant parts.

Plant parts are utilized in a vast array of spellwork. For example, in several African magico-religions and their diaspora, entire branches are used to dispel negativity from an affected person. Plant parts are also included in an immense range of magical formulas. Listed below are examples of their common usages:

- **Amulets, talismans, and mojo bags:** Dried plants are oftentimes added to these objects to either introduce or enhance their magical powers.
- **Baths:** Although whole fresh herbs and roots can be added directly to baths, in most cases dried herbs are instead used. Simply steep the herbs and/or roots in water, then strain them, keeping the water. Place the strained plants aside and add the herbal tea into the bath water.
- **Incense**: Finely chopped or ground dried plant parts or root chips can be placed directly on charcoal discs. More often than not, dried herbs are mixed with plain incense powder or resins to maintain combustion stability.
- **Natural state:** There is a plethora of usages for dried herbs, roots, and root chips used alone or with other varieties in their natural state. They can be carried on the person, placed in a wallet, in dresser drawers, pillows, or sprinkled in or around properties for various purposes.
- **Oils:** A good condition oil will contain an essential oil, which is the concentrated extract of a plant. However, if additional dried herbs are added, the oil's magical powers will heighten. In most cases, three to four dried plant parts are added to a good condition oil.

- **Powders:** Finely ground plant parts can be used alone as a powder. They can also be added to cornstarch to expand the consistency or added to an already existing condition sachet or powder.
- **Sprays and washes:** As with the instructions for baths, simply steep the herbs and/or roots in water then strain them but keep the water. Place the strained plants aside and add the water to either a spray bottle or use the water for either a hand, wall, or floor wash.
- **Vapor:** Simmering fresh or dried herbs in a pot of water is not only used as another form of delivering magical intentions, but they can also be used as air fresheners or serve medicinal purposes. Eucalyptus, for example, is an herb used for spiritual eradiation. Simmered in a pot of water it will also deliver a refreshing scent throughout the house while assisting to open airway passages.

Listed below are several of my successful herbal blends. A comprehensive exploration. of herbs and roots can be found in the book *Hoodoo Herb and Root Magic* by Catherine Yronwode. Unless otherwise noted, use equal amounts of each ingredient:

Banishing People or Situations

- Asofoetida (*Ferula assa-foetida*)
- Red pepper (*Capsicum annum*)
- Sulphur powder (Brimstone)

Blessings

- Angelica root (*Angelica archangelica, spp.*)
- Cascara sagrada (*Frangula purshiana*)
- Yerba santa (*Eriodictyon spp. Benth*)

Control and Domination

- Calamus root (*Acorus calamus*)
- Knot weed (*Polygonum arenastrum, Polygonum aviculare*)
- Licorice root (*Glycyrrhiza glabra, Glycyrrhiza spp.*)

Love

- Cubeb berries (*Piper cubeba*)
- Damiana (*Turnera aphrodisiaca*)
- Lovage root (*Levisticum officinale, Ligusticum Levisticum, Ligusticum spp.*)
- Red rose petals (*Rosa spp.*)

Lust

This is one of my favorite biblical passages. It's about King Solomon's discussion on adultery. After all, the King had over one thousand wives and concubines, so he ought to know what he's talking about! This passage below is a little racy, but who are we to argue with the Bible? Proverbs 7.17–18 reads: "I have perfumed my bed with myrrh, aloes, and cinnamon. Come, let us take our fill of love until the morning: let us solace ourselves with loves."

- Aloes (*Aloe vera l.*)
- Ceylon cinnamon (*Cinnamomum zeylanicum*)
- Myrrh (*Commiphora abyssinica*)

Money

- Alfalfa (*Medicago sativa*)
- Allspice (*Eugenia pimento, Pimento officinalis*)
- Bayberry bark (*Myrica cerifera*)
- Cinnamon chips (*Cinnamomum aromaticum, Cinamomum spp.*)
- Earth smoke/fumitory (*Fumaria fungosa, Fumaria officinalis, Fumaria spp.*)

Peace With God

- Olive leaves (*Olea europaea L.*)
- Rue *(Ruta graveolens)*—Note: Please do not use rue if pregnant, as it is an abortifacient and can cause a miscarriage.

Protection

- Agrimony (*Agrimonia eupatoria, Agrimonia grypsosepala*)
- Alder (*Abus glutinosa, Albus spp.*)
- Basil (*Ocimum basilicum, Ocimum spp.*)
- Blue cohosh (*Caulophyllum thalictroides*)
- Eucalyptus (*Eucalytus spp.*)
- Rue (*Ruta graveolens*)

Reconciliation

- Balm of gilead buds (*Commiphora opobalsamum, Commiphora gileadens*)

- Basil (*Ocimum basilicum, Ocimum spp.*)
- Forget-me-not (*Myosotis spp.*)
- Passion flower (*Passifora incarnata*)
- Primrose (*Primula officinalis, Primula spp.*)

Road Opener

- Abre camino (*Koanophyllon villosum*)
- Cinquefoil (*Potentila anserina, Potentila, spp.*)
- Lemon grass (*Andropogon citratus, Cymbopogon citratus*)
- Masterwort (*Imperatoria ostruthium*)

Success

- Cinquefoil (*Potentila anserina, Potentila, spp.*)
- Grains of paradise *(Amomum granum-paradisi, Ampelopsis grana-paradisi)*
- Gravel root (*Eupatorium purpureum*)
- Masterwort (*Imperatoria ostruthium*)
- Solomon's seal (*Convallaria polygonatum, Polygonatum biflora*)

Incense

We know that incense has been implemented in spiritual practices for over four thousand years, from some of the earliest times of recoded history. The Canaanites, who were neighbors of the Hebrews, had left various incense stands, altars, censers, and spoons in city levels dated all the way back to the second millennium BC. It was also employed in worship by the early Egyptians, Hebrews, Babylonians, Assyrians, and Arabians around that same period.

In ancient times, incense was primarily burned as an act of worship. Nowadays, incense is marketed for various purposes. Depending on the type of incense used, there are three different ways to disperse its smoke.

If the intention is to send a message or to draw something to you from the outside, such as money, a romantic partner, happiness, etc., then the smoke must be dispersed to the outside world. Either burn the incense outside or near an open window.

When the intention is to keep desired energies with you, such as beauty, good health, or a lover, then the smoke ought to remain inside your abode.

If a malicious entity has entered your home, then the incense is used as if it were tear gas. One would close all the windows and doors and light the incense until the room is consumed with smoke. This will suffocate the entity, and it will look for an escape route. Then, open only one door or window and order it to leave. Wait about five minutes and slam the door or window shut to ensure that it doesn't return once the smoke has dissipated.

Reconciliation

Years ago, the man of my interest lived in Greece half of the year and the other half in Florida. While he was back in Greece, we began to argue incessantly until it was mutually decided to terminate our relationship. Thereafter, he ceased calling me.

A few weeks later, I began to miss him terribly. Because we were continents away, it was doubtful that any spell would soften his heart from such a distance. Then, a Wiccan friend suggested an incense spell, along with an incantation, to perform.

Having been a little hesitant to recite an incantation containing a European tone, it was obvious that there was nothing to lose in doing so. After performing the spell for seven consecutive days, he called, apologized for his behaviors, and returned to me, all within a week. Thereafter, this spell was suggested to a few of my clients, and it worked for them too. It's simple yet effective.

Reconciliation Incense

For each day of the week, you will need:

- 1 charcoal round
- A censer
- A long match or long lighter
- A very small piece of torn piece from a brown paper bag
- A pencil
- A censer
- ½ tsp of orris root powder
- ½ tsp of dried passion flower

Instructions:

1. With your pencil, write the birth name and birth date of your target. Turn the paper to the right and cross the information by writing your birthname and birthdate over the target's information. Repeat these same steps on the other side of the paper. Fold the paper toward you, turn it to the right and fold it again toward you.

2. Light the concave portion of the charcoal round and place it in the censer. Once the charcoal turns grey, place your folded paper on it. Next, place the herbs over the paper.

3. Because a message is being sent to someone far away, the smoke must be dispersed outside. As the smoke from the herbs begin to waft, start reciting your incantation aloud for a total of seven consecutive times:

   "(Target's name),
   peace and love I send to thee.
   No longer angry shall you be.
   Forgive me and return to me.
   As my will so mote it be."

4. Stay with the incense until the paper and herbs have been completely consumed by the heat of the charcoal round. Once the charcoal has cooled and later reduced to ashes, face East on a windy day and allow the air to take the remains away.

Spiritual Eradications

The Holy Bible introduces us to incense in the Book of Exodus. It occurs when God gave Moses and Aaron a divine command to burn incense as an act of holy worship. Throughout the Bible, we see various types of incense being burned, primarily for worship or atonement of sins.

However, later in the Bible, instructions are provided on what to burn as an incense if one is plagued by a malicious entity: "As for the fish's heart and liver, if you burn them to make smoke in the presence of a man or a woman who is afflicted by a demon or evil spirit, any affliction will flee and never return…" (Tob. 8.6).

As a substitute for burning fish parts, my favorite incense for this same purpose is a phenomenal product manufactured by Zambala...

Tibetan Purging Incense Powder
The formulation of this incense is under the supervision of a religious master who is also the national level incense maker of Tibet. Following its composition, the incense is then subsequently blessed for forty-nine consecutive days in a grand prayer ceremony, empowering it to:

- Subdue demons
- Remove spiritual impurities
- Protect from harm
- Remove obstacles.
- Alleviate negative karma

Instructions
Use this incense as if it were a spiritual tear gas, as discussed earlier in this section. This is a self-igniting incense therefore, charcoal rounds are not needed. Place the incense into a censer, light the incense, and, with the smoke, spiritually fumigate each room individually.

Uncrossing
Oftentimes, people refer to being cursed or jinxed by another as having a "crossed condition" or "being crossed." This is technically correct. However, the more elaborate explanation of having a crossed condition is when loads of negative energies are weighing down the aura, our spiritual protective shield, causing numerous problems in one's life. The negative energies then attract more of the same. An overload of negative energies can ultimately cause tears or holes in the aura. When this happens, it will wreak havoc in one's life. Some of the symptoms of a crossed condition may include:

- **Accidents:** Numerous accidents may be attributed to a crossed condition.
- **Avoidance:** People will suddenly begin to sidestep or shun you.
- **Apathy:** People are suddenly unemotional toward your misfortunes.

- **Bad luck:** There is an ongoing run of bad luck.
- **Dismissal:** People no longer value your input or opinions.
- **Difficulty sleeping:** A sudden onset of sleep deprivation.
- **Emotional variances:** Undesirable feelings such as depression, anxiety, fear, restlessness, or even feelings of impending doom.
- **Exhaustion:** Fatigue and exhaustion are present with undue causes.
- **Financial difficulties:** There can be sudden, and ongoing, financial losses with the inability to recuperate or recover from the damage.
- **Health problems:** Usually deteriorating in nature while physicians are unable to diagnose the illness or its cause.
- **Nightmares:** Ongoing nightmares are oftentimes present.
- **Roadblocks:** The inability to achieve any goal due to ongoing obstacles.

There are numerous techniques to rid oneself of negative energies. In fact, my book *Hoodoo Cleansing and Protection Magic* provides both a complete understanding of crossed conditions and how to eradicate them. One such technique of eliminating surrounding unwelcomed energies is to disperse uncrossing incense throughout your home and keep the fumes of the incense within the dwelling.

Uncrossing Incense

This recipe provides enough incense to ignite for numerous days.

Ingredients

- 1 small square of camphor, crushed
- 2 Frankincense resin tears, crushed
- 2 Myrrh resin tears, crushed
- 2 tsp dried Rue (Ruta graveolens)
- 2 tsp dried eucalyptus (Eucalyptus spp.)
- 2 tsp dried boldo leaves (Boldoa fragrans, Peumus boldoa)
- A censer
- Charcoal rounds
- A feather or hand fan

Instructions
Mix all the ingredients together. Light the concave portion of the charcoal round and place it in the censer. Once the charcoal turns grey, place about ½ tsp of your mixture onto the charcoal. With a feather or a hand fan, walk around your dwelling while fanning the smoke into each room.

Magical Charm Bags

The Mojo Bags
Through archaeological discoveries, we know that the early Egyptians used charms, talismans, and amulets as early as 3000 BC. They did so for numerous magical purposes, such as protection, fertility, love, prosperity, etc. Because magical charm bags are most often created as either an amulet for protection or a talisman to draw a particular benefit to its owner, inserting the objects into bags could have been practiced during the same time period.

Nevertheless, we factually know that magical charm bags have existed for hundreds of years throughout the world. Today, they are popularly used among the Romani, Muslims, Neopagans, modern Witches, Shamans, Latinos, and members of the various branches, if not all of the African spiritual practices.

In metaphysical practices unrelated to Hoodoo, a charm bag is known by names such as "Putsi Bag," "Sorcerer's Hand," "Spell Bag," "Medicine Bag," "Magic Bag," and others. In the Hoodoo tradition, the bag is referred to by several terms such as: "Hand," "Lucky Hand," "Conjure Hand," "Conjure Bag," "Trick-or-tricken Bag," "Root Bag," "Juju Bag," "Jomo," "Toby," "Oanga," and "Gris-Gris" (pronounced "gree-gree"). However, the most popular and common name among Hoodoo practitioners is either the mojo bag or mojo hand. Therefore, from here, the charm bag will be referred to by the Hoodoo terms.

Mojo bags may contain herbs, roots, minerals, symbols, petition papers, name papers, personal concerns, pictures, crystals, stones, rocks, animal parts, dirt, charms, and/or objects representing your desired goals. Do not include all aforementioned objects into one bag, as it would become too bulky. Instead, just add the most important items in relatively moderate quantities.

The bag itself is traditionally made of red flannel, it has drawstrings, and measures around 3" (W) x 4" (L). However, the magical items can also be contained within metal containers, leather bags, cotton bags, or muslin bags. Although red is preferred, the bag can be of a different color, usually coordinating with the condition, such as green for money, pink for attraction, etc. Color coordination to conditions will be explored in a subsequent chapter.

Before sharing recipes for some of my favorite mojo hands, it is imperative to first become familiar with the process of constructing a successful and powerful hand. Additionally, there are a few basic principles that must be practiced to ensure that the bag remains active.

Constructing your Mojo Bag

There are diverse styles of constructing a mojo bag. Therefore, variations to my personal preferences may exist. These variants are normal because, as we have already discussed, Hoodoo is a divergent metaphysical practice. Just keep in mind that the powers within a mojo bag not only depend on the ingredients, but upon the fortitude of the practitioner.

1. First cleanse inorganic items with Florida Water, holy water, whiskey, or a mixture of a little sea salt in water. Then, insert all of the ingredients into the bag.

2. Place your lips into the open bag and pray Psalm 23 aloud. Before closing the prayer, ask God to awaken the spirits of the plants, minerals, and/or animals, to bless them and thank them for their help.

3. Close the prayer with the word "Amen," then tell the spirits who you are and let them know that they are in a bag. Also, let them know what it is that you wish to accomplish.

4. Promise them that you will take care of them. Some people even give their bag a name.

5. State aloud: "I am now activating this mojo hand." Old timers believe that saliva is an activator. So, lightly and respectfully release a little of your saliva into the bag.

6. The drawstrings ought to be tied at least three times. Each time a tie is made, state your petition aloud.

7. Because herbs and powders tend to fall out, it is wise to sew the bag shut. Simply hand sew the bag closed with either white thread or a color that matches the bag.

8. Now, anoint the bag. Many slaves said that whiskey gives the bag strength. They anointed the bag with whiskey by either spritzing it onto the bag from their mouths or anointing it in a five-spot. Nowadays, many practitioners use a condition oil to anoint the bag in a five-spot fashion.

9. The five-spot anointing ritual consists of dabbing the oil with your finger starting top left, to top right, to bottom right, then bottom left, and finally one dab in the middle.

10. Hold the bag in both hands to charge it, as previously explained in the amulet section.

11. For the first seven days, anoint the bag every day. Thereafter, it will only need anointing once a week.

12. The bag also ought to be kept close to your skin for the first seven days. Pinning it to the inside of your clothing is the most common method.

Maintenance of your Mojo Bag

- After the first week of construction, try to keep the mojo bag as close to you as possible. Pockets and bras are preferable locations.

- Anoint your bag at least once and week and talk to it. Remember, it is important to establish a personal relationship with your magical items.

- Your mojo hand will become inactive if another person sees or touches it. When this happens, keep any personal concerns, whole roots, stones, or inorganic items. Respectfully dispose of the rest of the items, including the bag, and start all over again.

- Although your pets may see and/or smell your mojo bag, do not allow them to interact with it. Pets like to chew and/or disassemble things.

- The mojo bag usually loses its power anywhere between eight months to a year.

- If the bag begins to fray before eight months, my preference is to put the existing bag into a new empty bag.

- If the mojo bag loses its power through old age, either renew or bury it. Renewal entails replacing the herbs, papers, and pictures, then repeating the steps as if it were a new mojo hand. There are a couple of choices for burying the bag. If it is to draw something to you, either bury it in your front yard or near a tree. If the bag was designed to keep something or someone with you, bury it in the back yard or in a potted plant that is placed furthest from your front door.

You are now ready to construct your mojo hands. Although others may disagree with my belief, it is my contention that a single mojo hand ought not have numerous intentions. A multi-purpose mojo hand weakens its powers.

Also, remember that if you are wearing the mojo hand or any talismans inside your pocket, the direction makes a difference. Place the mojo hand in your left pocket if you wish to attract a particular benefit. Use the right pocket if you wish to emit a specific vibration, such as power, strength, etc.

See the herbal and root chips blends section for your plant selections.

Attraction Mojo Hand

- 1 small Rose Quartz crystal
- 1 small Lodestone
- ½ tsp of magnetic sand to feed the lodestone
- 1 raccoon penis bone
- 1 picture of yourself with eyes showing

- A petition paper stating your desires
- Love or attraction plant parts

Communication Mojo Hand

This mojo hand is used to enhance communication abilities. It is especially useful to have on hand when Mercury, the planet of communication, is in retrograde. When this happens, most forms of communication, including technical modes, can go awry.

My preference is to use a yellow bag. In Hoodoo, it represents the color of enhanced communication. To avoid a bulky bag, use smaller crystals.

- **Aquamarine:** Fosters clear communication
- **Emerald:** Smooths communication
- **Blue lace agate:** Improves communication
- **Amazonite:** Harmonizes communication
- **Fluorite (any color):** Also improves communication
- If desired, also include about 1 tbsp of the herb deer's tongue/ vanilla leaf (Liatris odoratissima, Trilisa odorata)

Money Mojo Hand

- 1 small Pyrite crystal
- 1 small Lodestone
- ½ tsp of magnetic sand to feed the lodestone
- Money plant parts
- 1 picture of yourself with eyes showing
- A petition paper stating your desires

Protection Mojo Hand

My German shepherd dogs (GSDs) are trained in a sport called "Schutzund." It is a German word that is roughly translated to mean: "Protection Dog." Because nail clippings of aggressive animals are used in Hoodoo to attack anything that is a threat, my dogs' nail clippings are also included in protection amulets, not because my dogs are aggressive, but because they are trained to protect me. If your pet loves and protects you, by all means, include their nail clippings in your mojo bag!

- 1 small Jet crystal (also called an "Azabache")
- 1 St. Benedict medal
- Protection plant parts

- 1 picture of yourself with eyes showing
- A petition paper stating your desires

Road Opener Mojo Hand

- 1 small key
- 1 St. Peter medal
- 1 tsp of dirt from the middle of a crossroad
- Road opener plant parts
- 1 picture of yourself with eyes showing
- A petition paper stating your desires

Whole Roots as Mojo Hands

Single whole roots can be carried as pocket pieces or placed in a bag. I like to keep them in a bag because it becomes more difficult to misplace them. Additionally, the bag provides safety for the spirit of the root. Think of the bag as a security blanket for your new friend.

Follow the same construction and maintenance guidelines as if there were numerous items in the bag. Here are a few of my favorite whole roots:

High John the Conqueror Root

Controversy exists as to how this root acquired its name. Most experts believe that the High John the Conqueror Root (Bindweed, Jalap, King of the Woods, King Root, Man Root, Man of the Earth) was named after one particular slave who was an African prince. Others believe that it was named in honor of all the African princes who were captured and enslaved. Nevertheless, it is a powerful root. It commands self-confidence, power, personal mastery, and physical and emotional strength. The root will also help men to attract women.

Master Root

This is one of my very favorite roots. Master root (*Imperatoria ostruthium*) helps one to gain strength, power, success, and respect from others. Used in oils such as "Crown of Success," it helps one to achieve mastery in any skill one wishes to pursue. It is most useful in most academic milieus.

Orris Root/Queen Elizabeth Root

Most often utilized by women and gay men, Orris root (*Iris florentina, Iris germanica*), is carried to attract men. It is said that this root can not only draw lustful attention from a man but even entice him into a marriage proposal.

Nails

Both rusted and coffin nails are commonly used in destruction, break-up, or enemy spellwork.

How to Rust Nails

There are a couple of ways to rust nails. The first is to place uncoated nails in vinegar until they rust. The second method is to boil uncoated nails in water, drain them (but do not blot them dry), and then set them out in the sun. Repeat this process for a few days. On the last day, save the rusted water to include in your War Water recipe.

How to Make Coffin Nails

Authentic coffin nails were commonly used in the past to seal pine boxes containing corpses. Decades ago, many of the old pine boxes were not properly contained in the ground. They would float to the surface, making it easier to obtain the nails. However, in modern times, coffin nails are difficult to obtain, because caskets now either have hinges that create seals or simply click shut.

If you are fortunate enough to find an authentic dealer of used coffin nails, they can be extremely expensive. Twenty years ago, I had a friend who frequented old graveyards immediately following rainstorms to obtain nails from caskets that floated to the surface. At that time, she charged a hundred dollars per nail.

As a substitute for authentic coffin nails, two of the most common methods employed are to either bury your rusted nails in a cemetery for nine to thirteen days or store your rusty nails in a bag containing graveyard dirt. If you chose the latter method, ensure that the nails have been placed in the graveyard dirt for at least nine to thirteen days.

Oils

Top quality oils will contain either herbs, roots, minerals, and/or pure essential oils. In most of my formulas, other than those containing mineral oil, a drop or two of an essential oil is added into the carrier oil.

Typical carrier oils are as follows:

- **Almond oil:** The most widely employed of the carrier oils that contain plant parts. This oil will require a preservative of Vitamin E oil.
- **Jojoba oil:** Also employed when using plant parts and requires a Vitamin E preservative.
- **Mineral oil:** Most commonly used when contents contain solely minerals such as Lodestone oil. This oil does not require a preservative.
- **Olive oil:** Due to its odor, most Hoodoo practitioners only use this product to formulate holy oil.
- **Grapeseed oil:** In numerous metaphysical practices, grapes represent abundance. Therefore, this is my preferred carrier oil in money drawing formulas. It also requires a preservative of Vitamin E oil.

Anything containing an alcohol base could impede the strength of the spirits within the plant parts or minerals. Therefore, avoid adding anything artificial to your condition oils, such as perfumes, colognes, toilet water, or fragrant oils.

Many companies will add a coloring agent to their condition oils. Although soap dye is highly recommended, I have found that it does not disperse evenly throughout the carrier oil. My preferred coloring agent is candle wax dye. Just add one or two drops to one ounce of carrier oil.

To create your oil, combine the essential oil, candle wax dye, Vitamin E oil, and the carrier oil. Mix well, then set aside. Insert your plant parts and/or minerals into a one-ounce bottle. Now, add the carrier oil that contains the other ingredients into the bottle. Cap the bottle and shake well.

Remove the cap and pray Psalm 23 over your condition oil. Then recap the bottle. Keep the oil in a cool dark area for a week and shake daily.

Attraction Oil

- 1 drop of rose essential oil
- A pinch of attraction plant parts/minerals
- 1 drop of Vitamin E oil
- 1 oz of almond oil

Control and Domination Oil

- 1 drop of calamus essential oil
- A pinch of control and domination plant parts
- 1 drop pf Vitamin E oil
- 1 oz of almond oil

Lodestone Oil

- 3 lodestone pebbles
- A pinch of magnetic sand
- 1 oz of mineral oil

Magnet Oil

- 3 large magnets
- 4 oz of mineral oil

Money Drawing Oil

- 1 drop of cinnamon essential oil
- A pinch of money drawing plants parts/minerals
- 1 crystal pyrite pebble
- 1 drop Vitamin E oil
- 1 oz of grapeseed oil

Psychic Vision Oil

- 5 drops of pure anise oil (available in almost all grocery stores)
- 1 drop of Vitamin E oil
- 1 oz almond oil

Protection Oil

- 1 drop of black pepper essential oil
- A pinch of protection plant parts/minerals
- 1 drop of Vitamin E oil
- 1 oz of almond oil

Road Opener Oil

- 1 drop of lemongrass essential oil
- A pinch of road opener plant parts
- A pinch of dirt from the crossroads

- 1 drop of Vitamin E oil
- 1 oz of almond oil

Rue Oil

- 1 drop of rue essential oil
- A pinch of dried rue herb (Avoid rue if pregnant as it is an abortifacient)
- 1 drop of Vitamin E oil
- 1 oz of almond oil

Stop Gossip Oil

- 1 drop of clove essential oil
- ¼ tsp powdered alum (*Aluminum Sulphate*)
- A pinch of chia seeds (*Salvia hispanica*)
- 1 drop Vitamin E oil
- 1 oz of almond oil

A Word About Holy Oil

In the Book of Exodus, God gave Moses the recipe for holy oil (Ex. 30.22–25). The ingredients are olive oil, ceylon cinnamon, cassia cinnamon, Myrrh, and one unknown element. However, the measurements call for about 1.5 gallons of olive oil, 12.5 lbs. of myrrh, 6.5 lbs. of ceylon cinnamon, and 12.5 lbs. of cassia cinnamon. Now, that's a lot of holy oil!

Nevertheless, many Hoodoo practitioners utilize this recipe as a guideline for making the oil. They incorporate the cinnamons and myrrh into extra-virgin olive oil (preferably the brands imported from Israel) in much smaller amounts. When formulated properly, the blend will have a subtle odor of cinnamon. If it is improperly prepared, there will be an overwhelming scent of either cinnamon or olive oil. Avoid manufactured products labeled as "Holy Oil" that instead contain a carrier other than olive oil.

Powders

Grinding ingredients into a fine powder requires tools. Depending on the resilience of the component, there are different types of tools designed to reduce even the strongest elements into a powdered state. They include, but are not limited to:

- Coffee grinders
- Mortar and pestles
- Cheese graters
- Hammers

Use prudence when selecting a grinding tool. Placing lightweight herbs into a coffee grinder will not only fail to grind the herbs, but it will also create a mess. On the other hand, hard, resilient objects could destroy simple tools, such as a cheese grater.

Being overly cautious and recognizing safety protocols is a main priority. My advice is to wear protective gloves when working with hard objects and sharp tools. Additionally, safety goggles ought to be worn in order to prevent any stray airborne fragments from entering the eyes.

Also, ensure that all elements being converted into powders are completely dry. Any moisture will cause the powder to clump and/or produce mold, rendering all of your efforts and hard work worthless.

Anger Powder

This powder is used to provoke anger onto the target(s). Just mix equal amounts of:

- Volcanic ash
- Cayenne pepper

Banishing Powder

Banishing formulas are designed to gently send a person or a bad situation away.

- 4 parts asfoetida
- 1 part ground black pepper
- 1 part salt

Eggshell Powder (Cascarilla)

This powder is widely used in the African Diaspora Religions for numerous purposes. For example, it is sprinkled into spiritual baths for extra blessings, purification, power, and protection. Because it is pleasing to certain deities, it is included in almost all rituals. As a chalk, it is used to draw spiritual symbols or mark an area of the human body before one can receive a ritual object.

Whenever you crack eggs, gently remove the soft inner membrane and keep the shells. Once you've collected about fifteen shells, lay them out in the sun for a few days to dry. Other practitioners will instead preheat the oven to 350°F, then bake them for about nine minutes, or until they are brittle enough for grinding.

Whichever method is used, once dried, insert the dried shells into a coffee grinder and grind them until you have a fine powder. Remove any remaining larger pieces.

Eggshell Chalk

Take 1 tbsp of the eggshell powder and mix it with 1 tsp white flour and 1 tsp of hot water until it becomes a thick paste. Lightly flour your hands and shape the paste into small chalk sticks, then place them on a lightly floured paper towel. Set the sticks outside to lay out in the sun. While outside, turn them twice daily until completely dried, which may take anywhere from three to five days. They may take on odd shapes, but the aesthetic appearance of the cascarilla does not matter.

Attraction Powders

The root chips named in the formulas below ought to be placed in a coffee grinder in order to convert them into powders. The integration of your own personal concerns into the powder will enhance your target's desire to be with only you.

My clients are advised to shave either their arms, legs, or other parts of their bodies where short hair stubs are growing with a clean, dry razor. Then, incorporate the personal concerns into the powder. Lightly sprinkle the powder someplace where the target will either directly or indirectly interact with it.

Attract a Man Powder

- 4 parts orris root powder (ground from root chips)
- 1 part of your hair stubs

Attract a Woman Powder

- 4 parts John the Conqueror Powder (ground from root chips)
- 1 part of your hair stubs

Goofer Dust

Derived from the Kilongo word *kufwa,* meaning "to die," this is a cursing and crossing powder. The original formula, derived from Africa, contained toxic poisons. As time passed, the recipes have been modified and vary from one practitioner to another. This is my personal recipe mix:

- 1 part powdered snake sheds or snakeskin
- 1 part gunpowder
- 1 part black salt
- 1 part cayenne pepper
- 3 parts graveyard dirt
- If desired, powdered dog feces and/or rat feces to the mixture

Gunpowder

It aids in the swiftness of numerous spells, especially to drive people away. My godparents in Palo would draw symbols with the gunpowder, then light it to expediate certain spells. Many Hoodoo practitioners will sprinkle just about one-sixteenth of a tsp of this powder into their spellwork.

- 74.8% Saltpeter (potassium nitrate)
- 13.3% Charcoal powder (carbon)
- 11.9% Sulfur powder (brimstone)

Hot Foot Powder

Hot foot products are designed to send people away and are much harsher than any of the banishing formulas. The powder can be positioned in a place where the target will either have direct or indirect contact with it.

- 5 tsp of cayenne pepper (*Capsicum frutescens*)
- 1 tsp of salt (*sodium chloride*)
- 1 tsp of black pepper (*Piper nigrum*)
- 1 tsp of dirt from a railroad track
- ⅛ tsp of gunpowder (potassium nitrate, carbon, brimstone)

Protection Against Enemies and Negative Entities

"The Skeleton Key" was a phenomenal movie about Hoodoo/Conjure. Although the script writers exaggerated the realities into far-fetched fantasy, they did get quite a few facts correct.

One of the factual scenes is when the victim was chased by an evil being. She successfully made a line across the doorway with red brick dust to prevent the evil person from entering the room. Hoodoo practitioners know that red brick dust wards off enemies and negative entities. Mixed with salt, it provides additional protection. Lines are made with the powder across any entrances, such as windowsills and doorways.

Red brick dust can be purchased in most spiritual stores. If you plan to make your own, a strong microplane grater tool is needed to scrape the brick into a fine powder. For protection, mix equal amounts of:

- Red brick dust (a combination of silica, alumina, iron oxide, magnesia, and lime)
- Salt (sodium chloride)

Purifying Cursed Objects or Areas

Many times, people will find cursed objects on their doorsteps, cars, or other areas for which the person has to physically touch. Just spray holy water on the object and pick it up with gloves. Then, sprinkle the contaminated area with the powder. Mix equal amounts of:

- Sulfur powder (brimstone)
- Salt (sodium chloride)

Reversing Bad Luck or a Curse

This powder can be used in altar work, carried in a muslin bag, or sprinkled around the outside of your home. The herb can be pulverized with a mortar and pestle, while the crab shell ought to be pulverized in a coffee grinder. Mix equal amounts of:

- Crab shell powder
- Agrimony powder (*Agrimonia eupatoria, Agrimonia gryposepala*)

Solutions

Plant and Mineral Solutions

For herbal waters, simply choose your desired herbs, plant parts, and/or minerals to make your solution. Although one herb is satisfactory for ritual purposes (such as hyssop being the only herb employed for the forgiveness of sins), there are other methods for determining the amount of herbs to be used. Old Hoodoo practitioners believe that there ought to be either three, five, seven, nine, or thirteen herbs in your solution. Additionally, a drop of essential oil can act as a substitution for an herb because it is a pure plant extract.

Another ritualistic belief is that the steeping time of the herbs ought to coincide with the amount of herbs employed. For example, if using three herbs, boil about a quart of water. Once the water starts to bubble, remove the pan from the stove. Immerse the herbs into the water, either freely or in a cotton muslin bag, and allow them to steep for three minutes, which coincides with the number of herbs in the water. Then, either strain the herbs if they were free flowing, or remove the muslin bag. Remember to respectfully return the plants to the ground from whence they came.

Your solution can be used to spritz, spray, or sprinkle on or around desired areas. It can be introduced to the rinse cycle of your washing machine or added to baths, floor washes, spray bottles, etc. Always ensure that there are no plant parts in your bath water or spray bottles because they clog passageways. If purchasing bath crystals, they ought to be treated as if they were herbs, because many do contain clogging plant parts. If unsure about the number of herbs in bath crystals, the minimal steeping time is three minutes.

Other Homemade Solutions

To end this chapter, allow me to provide you with a couple of popular old-time recipes.

War Water

This water is used to cause conflict between people and to move enemies away. Back in the olden days, the practitioners would put war water in a small glass bottle and smash it at their enemies' doorsteps. Nowadays, this act is virtually impossible to perform because of the extensive usage of video cameras. Nevertheless, one can pour the water someplace where the target would have either direct or indirect contact with it. War water can also be used in jar spells and other altar spellwork.

- 16 oz of rainwater collected from a violent storm
- Hair from both a black dog and a black cat that do not live together
- ½ cup of Spanish moss

- 2 tbsp of magnetic sand
- ½ cup of white vinegar
- 13 rusty nails
- Pieces of broken glass
- ½ tsp of asofoetida

Place everything in a glass bottle. Do not release your saliva into this solution! Seal tightly with the cap and shake every day for two weeks. Thereafter, keep refrigerated. The shelf life is virtually everlasting.

Peace Water

The two ingredients must be mixed well and sprinkled around the house. Do not put this solution into a spray bottle because the sugar will clog the nozzle and dip tube.

- ½ cup holy water
- ¼ tsp sugar

CHAPTER SEVEN

MAGICAL SPELLS AND RITUALS

By now, you ought to have the basic knowledge to understand the intricacies surrounding both the art and science of magical processes. If you implement the information provided in the preceding chapters, your chances of successfully manifesting your desires will greatly improve.

The most common reason that tens of thousands of people fail to achieve their goals—even though they performed their spells exactly as prescribed—is because they violated one or more of the constructive tenets of nearly all metaphysical practices.

Although these tenets have been previously discussed in greater detail, it is essential to be reminded of these principles in order to avoid disappointments:

- **Keep quiet.** Do not tell anybody about your spellwork.
- **Behaviors and magic MUST complement each other.** If you are performing negative spellwork on a target, you must be cunning. If you are performing positive magic, do not behave contrary to the purpose of your spellwork.
- **Have faith.** Show confidence in both yourself and the members of your spiritual court.
- **Be patient.** Remember that spellwork may take up to two years to manifest.

Now that you possess a firm grasp of how to become a formidable spellcaster, it's time for the spellwork...

Animal (Pet) Magic

Having owned animals for over fifty years, the spells below have been successfully utilized for about the same amount of time.

Bonding with your Pet

Whenever you cut yourself, allow your pet to ingest some of your blood. Do not use menstrual blood for this purpose, as it will produce undesirable results.

Enhancing Two-Way Communication with your Pet

Keep the crystal leopardite jasper, also known as leopard skin jasper (silicon dioxide), in your right pocket. You would be amazed at how this crystal enhances communication.

Evil Eye Overthrow

When people dislike animals, they usually (either intentionally or unintentionally) deliver the evil eye. This happens often to my pets because they are German shepherds, which is a breed that oftentimes intimidates others. Simply state that all magic is eradicated from your pet and spit on it three times.

Healing your Pet

Gather a picture of your pet, its fur, feathers, and/or skin cells, and the herb Althea (*Althea spp.*). Make a clay doll in the image of your pet and insert these items into the doll. Once the doll has dried, anoint it with olive oil while baptizing it. Place it on an altar with a five or seven-day glass encased candle dedicated to St. Francis of Assisi, the patron saint of animals. Do not extinguish the candle. Recite the following prayer at least once a day while pleading for your pet's good health to return.

Prayer to St. Francis of Assisi

"O heavenly St. Francis, patron of all animals,
your protection for them is so great, so prompt, and so strong.
Please assist (name of pet) with your powerful intercession.
Through your prayer, may they obtain God's healing powers.
May their suffering be taken away and their health restored

(state your petition here)
St. Francis, please help my pet. AMEN!"

Protection Amulets

Each of my dogs have three amulets on their collars for protection from their own wandering curiosities, from other animals, and from harmful people.

- **St. Anthony medal:** To prevent pets from getting lost.
- **St. Francis of Assisi medal:** For protection from harm.
- **Anti-Evil eye:** To avert the evil eye from animal haters.

Attraction Magic

These spells were not necessarily designed for romantic attraction. Rather, they were conceived through decades of practice by thousands to attract positive attention.

Attractive Appearance

Wash your face every day with the morning dew. This is not only a Hoodoo spell, but it is also practiced in Cuba and other Latin countries.

Attractive Disposition

Place a picture with your eyes showing in a jar of sugar to completely immerse the picture within the sugar. Cap the jar and shake daily. The sugar will assist in making you appear sweet to others.

Attractive Handshake

Thirty minutes before an important encounter with another, lightly spritz your hands with rose water and rub your hands together. When you meet the person, shake their hand. That handshake will be pleasing to your target.

Attracting Visitors to your Home

Place a rose quartz crystal, a handful of the herb forget-me-not (*Myosotis spp.*), and seven cloves (*Syzygium aromaticus*) in a cotton muslin bag. If you live in a house, bury the bag outside your entranceway. If you live in an apartment, hang it over your front door.

Sweet Talk

This is a great spell to perform for job interviews, romantic pursuits, or any other important verbal encounters with people. Before speaking, place 1 tbsp of honey in your mouth, then swish and swallow. Your words will sound sweet to others. The spell will be broken once anything else enters your mouth, including water.

Bible Magic

Bibliomancy is the art of predicting future events by interpreting randomly chosen passages from a book, especially the Holy Bible. Although this subject is too entailing to explore here, numerous instructional books on the topic are available.

However, incorporating the physical book for specific magical purposes is also a common Hoodoo practice. Here are just a handful of examples:

- **Assisting the deceased:** Place the deceased person's prayer card within pages on the Holy Bible. It will help the soul to rest in peace.

- **Causing bad luck:** Lose a Holy Bible and it will cause bad luck. Stealing another person's Bible will bring the thief or their family bad luck.

- **Deterring negativity in your home:** Proudly displaying your Holy Bible within your abode will oftentimes scare away bad entities. It is also said that because the Bible emits bright energies, it will also dissuade the negative ones.

- **Preventing nightmares:** Sleeping with a Holy Bible inside your pillowcase will prevent nightmares.

- **Preventing spiritual attacks while sleeping:** Open the Holy Bible to Psalm 121. This psalm protects people from malicious entities, especially when they are sleeping. It does not matter if the psalm is written on one page or on two. Hold the Bible in both hands and bend it backwards to crack the spine and keep it open to that page.

Repeling Negative Entities
An array of uses for scissors in spiritual practices have been practiced for years. One function of scissors is to repel negative entities. Open your scissors so that the blades are far apart. With the blades of the scissor facing upward, place the opened scissors atop the two pages of the Bible, so that one blade and one handle of the scissors is over each page. Position the Bible under your bed, closer to your head is positioned, and keep it there permanently.

Binding Magic

Binding spells are employed to metaphysically restrict or restrain predators from antagonistic intentions, behaviors, or speech destined to financially, emotionally, or physically hurt an innocent victim. These predators include gossipers, abusers, con artists, scammers, liars, thieves, narcissists, sociopaths, and psychopaths.

There are also prayers that assist with spellwork, which will be provided in the last chapter. While both Psalms 94 and 140 are designed to bind enemies, Psalms 12 and 120 help to stop gossip.

Doll Binding
Create a small doll representing your target and fill it with a name paper, petition paper, personal concerns (if you have them), and a picture of your target with eyes showing. The rest of the entire stuffing will consist of knotweed (*Polygonum arenastrum*), which is a powerful binding herb. Name and baptize the doll.

Mix a generous amount of more knotweed with the water that will be used in this spell. Fill an oblong plastic container (that has a lid) one quarter-full of knotweed water. Place your doll in the water and place the container in the freezer. Once the water has frozen, the doll will float to the top, but remain stationary. Pour more knotweed water over the doll and ice to completely cover the doll and place the lid on the container. Return the container to the freezer.

Mirror Box Binding Spell

The main objective of this spell is that whatever the target is will bounce right back to them. So, if this is a good person, no harm will manifest. But if the target is of an evil nature, those monstrosities will bounce right back onto that person. The freezer will ensure that the target will be bound to their own wrongdoings.

You will need six small two-inch or four-inch mirrors and duct tape. Do not catch your gaze with the mirrors. With two strips of duct tape sticky side up, make a cross on a flat surface to form the foundation. Lay one mirror shiny side up in the middle of the cross of the tape. From there, lay one mirror shiny side up at each side of the first mirror. Bring each mirror up, along with the duct tape, until five sides are formed. Place a picture of the target with eyes showing inside the box and command: "Whatever you are will bounce back to you and stay with you." Complete the box by topping it off with the last mirror.

Then, wrap a generous amount of duct tape all around the box, ensuring that no cracks are visible. Finally, set the mirror in the freezer.

Twining Vine Binding

Any type of natural twining vines also possess binding powers. My personal ever-persistent battle is that of the hedge bindweed species of morning glory (*Calystegia sepium*) that spread via long, creeping, and grasping stem vines. They grow faster than I can cut them down. However, they do serve a terrific metaphysical purpose.

Ask the plant for its assistance in what you wish for it to do. Take a generous amount of the vines by the roots and wrap them around a picture of your target with eyes showing. Place everything in a large jar and add enough water to the roots for the plant to grow. Before placing a lid on the jar, poke several small air holes into it in order for the plant to breathe. Then, cap the jar. If you continue to provide the plant water, it will continue to wrap itself around the target as it grows.

Gossip Dissipation

Purchase a medium-sized whole fish. Thank the fish for sacrificing its life for you and ask it to help you in what you wish for it to do.

Insert pieces of alum (*Aluminum sulphate*), either powdered or chunks, into its mouth. Then, sew the mouth shut. Make an incision into its body and add a name paper, a petition paper, and a picture of your target with eyes showing. If you have any of your target's personal concerns, add them too. Then, sew the slit shut. Take the fish outside and hang it upside down to a tree limb. Let it rot there. As it disintegrates, so will the gossip.

Stop Gossip Jar Spell

Place a name paper, a petition paper, and a picture of your target with eyes showing into a glass jar. If you have any of your target's personal concerns, add them too. Fill $^2/_3$ of the jar with the following gossip cessation plant parts and mineral:

- Alum (*Aluminum sulphate*)
- Chia Seed (*Salvia hispanica*)
- Slippery Elm (*Ulmus fulva*)

Fill the rest of the jar with water. Place a lid on the jar and shake daily while demanding that the gossipmonger cease talking about you.

Broom Magic

For centuries, broom magic and rituals have been widely used around the world in various metaphysical practices. Because the broom is used in a plethora of various magical purposes, this list will only contain the most popular uses by both old and new Hoodoo practitioners.

With the exception of the first two entries, which were personally relayed to me decades ago, the subsequent information is provided by Harry Middleton Hyatt's Hoodoo informants. These informants were descendants of the antebellum slaves and were interviewed by Hyatt almost one hundred years ago.

Defense Against a Human Curse

If someone sweeps the floor in front of you or under your chair, they are sweeping bad luck to you. If they sweep the floor as you are exiting, it is to symbolically ensure that you will never return to their home. To render these spells ineffective, simply spit on the broom.

Defense Against an Unwanted Spiritual Visitation

This spell is only successful if the entity is of a non-malicious nature. Take your broom and wave the bristles at the entity until you have chased it toward the door. Continuing to do so, open the door and scream: "Get out! Nobody invited you here!" Once you feel that the entity has left, slam the door shut. Draw a salt line and lean the broom brush side up at the door.

Bringing Good Luck into a New Home
If the first item that you bring into a new abode is a broom, it will protect you and bring you good fortune.

Bringing Good Luck to a New Marriage
One Hyatt informant said that a new bride can create a happy marriage and prevent anyone from cursing it with a broomstick. She is to simply jump over a broomstick immediately after her wedding. Another informant advises that both the bride and groom are to perform this act together.

Causing Yourself Bad Luck
Bad luck will bestow anyone who sweeps the floor after sundown or before the sun rises. Additionally, never sweep the dirt out the front door. Otherwise, you will sweep away all of your good luck.

Curing Warts
Rub a wart three times with three broom straws. Bury the broom straws in a wet muddy area and, as they decay, so will the warts.

Making Wishes
Let a broom fall. Immediately make a wish aloud, then, pick it up.

Preventing a Curse from a Witch
This spell was relayed by two different informants. If you see a magical practitioner coming your way with the intent of cursing you, lay a broom down parallel to the front door. Then, say, aloud: "Kiss my ass!" three times. That person will be unable to harm or bewitch you.

Preventing Death
Never rest a broomstick on a bed, or else the person who sleeps on it could die.

Sending Away Unwanted Company

This effective spell has been performed hundreds of times by both me and my mother . Rest a broom upside down, so that the bristles are on the top, by the door for which the company entered. They will soon become restless and will leave.

Business (Brick and Mortar) Improvement Magic

The application of these spells must be consistent with good customer service. All the business improvement spells in the world won't help if the customers are treated poorly.

Upon being treated poorly in stores, my selected products for purchase are left behind, followed by my signature statement of "If I wanted to be treated like dirt, I could hang out with my in-laws. At least their services are free."

So, remember: magic and behaviors must complement each other!

Citrine for Abundance

About ten years ago, this veterinarian's practice was declining. He begged me to help him to improve his business, without offering any sort of payment or compensation. Being a bleeding heart and not even questioning his character or competence, I agreed to help.

Since he offered no payment, my approach to this task was minimal. Because citrine crystals draw in abundance, they were placed in his patient files, appointment books, cash registers, near the front door, as well as the operating, x-ray, and examination rooms.

Within a month, his patient list doubled, and within three months, it tripled. Finally, his business was booming and became too heavy for one man to handle. So, he hired another veterinarian to assist him.

Sadly, no verbal or tangible gratuity was ever offered to me. In fact, he tripled his prices and his ego became over-inflated. The devastating news? His incompetence killed one of my dogs and sent another of my dogs and her three puppies to a different hospital. Later learning from others that he had killed a multitude of dogs from gross incompetence, his practice is now commonly referred to as "The Butcher House."

As a result of my failure to question why his practice was initially declining, as well as failing to investigate his true character, the loss of those animals' lives will always be on my heart. To this day, the guilt still haunts me.

But it also taught me a valuable lesson: investigate all aspects of a situation before delivering magical services.

Drawing Customers into your Store

Mix 2 tbsp of cinnamon (*Cinnamon spp.*) with 1 tsp of sugar. Do not use too much sugar, as it will also attract insects.

Lightly sprinkle this mixture, starting from both walkways toward your door. Finally, sprinkle the remaining mixture directly in front of the door.

Keeping a Steady Flow of Customers

Every day, before opening your business, rub magnet oil on the outside of your door frame. Do not rub oil on doorknobs or anything that the customer may touch, otherwise they will be appalled by the greasy coating. Also, rub the oil on the outside of your cash register.

Malachite for Money

Many spiritual store owners keep the crystal malachite in their cash registers to increase their cash input.

Nudging the Customers to Purchase Products

Boil 2 cups of water. Once the water bubbles, remove the pot from the stove. Steep about 1 tbsp of agrimony (*Agrimonia eupatoria*) in the water for three or five minutes. Strain the herb and let the solution cool. Once cooled, pour it into a spray bottle.

Spray the solution in the air and especially around the products for which you wish to sell. Respectfully return the herb to the ground, as close as possible to your store.

Candle Magic

As soon as we light a candle or oil lamp for ritual purposes, the flame pierces the veil between our mundane world and the spiritual realm. When this happens, it facilitates communication with entities through our verbalized words and through the tools and ingredients used in our spellwork. Additionally, that flame provides energy to the entities for whom we petition. Therefore, we are simultaneously opening a doorway to another realm as well as emitting power to energize both the spell and the spirits who are being petitioned.

For these reasons, candles ought to be treated with reverence and respect. The manner in which a candle is handled prior to lighting will also be transmitted into the spiritual realm. Thus, we must be mindful of both our moods and words when handling them.

Preparing a candle for spellwork consists of cleansing the candle and then inscribing, anointing, and sometimes, naming and baptizing it. To cleanse a candle, simply spray it with either Florida Water, holy water, whiskey, or a mixture of ½ tsp of salt to 1 cup of water. Inscribing the candle refers to taking a pencil and imposing your petition into the wax. Wide, free-standing candles ought to be anointed with either a condition oil or olive oil. If the candle is representing, or directed at, a target the person's name and birthdate is also inscribed into the wax.

Inscribing a Candle

The inscription on a thin taper candle will only contain the command. For positive spellwork, the candle is inscribed starting from the bottom and continuing toward the top. This direction represents attracting something to you such as love, success, money and all things favorable. Conversely, inscribing a candle starting from the top and continuing toward the bottom represents removal, banishing, or menacing requests.

The command that is inscribed on the candle, as well as on your petition paper, will correlate with the intention of your spell. If, for example, your desire is remove crossed conditions, your command of "banish negativity" would be inscribed on the candle nine to thirteen times from the top to the bottom in spiral fashion, without lifting your pencil in-between words. It would look something like this:

"banishnegativitybanishnegativitybanishnegativity
banishnegativitybanishneagtivity"

If you are working with a figural candle, inscribe the target's name, followed by their birthdate three times, once on each line. Then, turn it to the left and cross over the names with the command three times: one line beneath the next for a total of three lines. The result ought to look like a square that contains words. This is only written three times because, unless the candle is gigantic, there won't be enough surface area to inscribe the command for a total of nine or thirteen. However, you can also continue to write the command independently all over the surface of the candle to enhance your intentions.

If the spell does not involve another person, you can simply inscribe the command all over the candle. If desiring something for yourself, include your birth name and birthdate.

Candle Colors

Color imagery differs from one metaphysical practice to another. Around the year 1942, the color symbolisms below became the standard model for modern day Hoodoo practitioners.

- **White:** This is a neutral color which can replace any color in the spectrum. It is also used for blessings, purity, or when praying to God, the Father.
- **Black:** Employed for banishing ailments, people, situations. It is also the color of choice when performing negative spellwork.
- **Blue:** Light blue is my preferred color for healing. It is also utilized for peace, harmony, and forgiveness.
- **Brown:** Most commonly used for court cases.
- **Green:** All things pertaining to receiving money such as gambling, acquiring a job, asking for a raise at work, attracting customers to a business, etc.
- **Orange:** Used in both blockbuster and road opener spells. Lightning this candle color also helps to increase one's energy level.
- **Pink:** Although this color is engaged for romantic love, it is also employed to gain the love of a relative or friend. Also used in attraction and friendship spellwork.
- **Purple:** This color commands power, domination, mastery, ambition, and victory.
- **Red:** The color of choice for passionate love, lust, and sexual vigor.
- **Yellow:** The most commonly used color for any type of communication spellwork. Also employed for success magic.

- **Black over a red core (reversible):** If someone has jinxed, cursed, or hexed you, this candle is designed to return any crossed conditions to the sender. Below is a typical spell.

Return to Sender Spell

Cleanse your candle. Starting from the top and working your way down, inscribe the candle nine to thirteen times with the command: "Return to Sender."

Anoint the candle with either olive oil or a reversing condition oil. Immediately roll the candle in crab shell powder. Then, create a petition paper with the same command and place it underneath the candle.

Although many Hoodoo practitioners will set the candle over a mirror, if one is not available, a fireproof candle holder will suffice.

Double Action Candles

These are usually nine-inch taper candles that are half black, while the other half is of another color. Although the black side must first be burned, the wicks of these candles instead appear on the opposite side for which they are to be lit. Therefore, they must first be "butted." This means that the original wick is cut off and the wick on the black side is dug out from the candle to create a new one. It is a symbolic gesture to imply that all negativity will be banished first.

Although double action candles are now sold in an array of colors such as black/pink, black/orange, etc., the traditional candles are as follows:

- **Half black, half green:** The black portion of this candle is burned first to remove any crossed conditions in money matters. Then, the green portion burns last to attract money.
- **Half black, half red:** The black portion of this candle is burned first to remove any crossed conditions in matters of love. Then the red portion burns to attract love. Noteworthy is the fact that these colors are also available as glass encased candles. However, in the practice of Santeria, black and red are the colors of the entity Eleggua. The difference being that Eleggua's candle is red

over black, whereas the double action candle is black over red. Just ensure that the correct candle is being purchased.

- **Half Black, Half White:** The black portion of this candle is burned first to remove any crossed conditions. Then the white portion burns to attract blessings, good luck, improved health, etc. Below is an example of how some Hoodoo practitioners will utilize a double action candle to remove crossed conditions and summon blessings.

Remove Crossed Conditions Spell

Cleanse your candle. Starting with the black portion, begin inscribing the candle. From the top to down where the white portion begins, inscribe the words "Banish negativity" three times. Do not write on the white portion of the candle.

Turn the candle around and begin inscribing the white portion of the candle where the black portion ends. Starting from where the white portion begins, inscribe your candle upward five times with the word "blessings."

Anoint the entire candle with olive oil. Sprinkle the black side with the banishing herb asofoetida (*Ferula assa-foetida*), ensuring that all of it remains on the black portion of the candle.

Place a picture of yourself with eyes showing into a fireproof candle holder. Ensure that it is facing outward. Place the candle over your picture. Light the candle and pray.

For an in-depth exploration of candles, including preparation and candle communication, please see my book *Hoodoo Justice Magic.*

Types of Candles

Vigil Candles

A vigil candle is just another term for a glass encased candle. They are sold as three-day, five-day, seven-day and nine-day candles. Usually, the nine-day vigil candles correlate with the intention of performing a nine day prayer, also called a novena. One of my favorite uses for the nine-day vigil candle is to petition God Our Father for a favor. Remember to try and pray around the same time every day and do not extinguish the candle.

Novena To God the Father

"God, my Heavenly Father,
I adore You, and I count myself as nothing before Your Divine Majesty. You alone are Being, Life, Truth, and Goodness. Helpless and unworthy as I am, I honor You, I praise You, I thank You, and I love You in union with Jesus Christ, Your Son, our Savior and our Brother, in the merciful kindness of His Heart and through His infinite merits. I desire to serve You, to please You, to obey You, and to love You always in union with Mary Immaculate, Mother of God and our Mother. I also desire to love and serve others for the love of You. Heavenly Father, thank You for making me Your child in Baptism. With childlike confidence I ask You for the special favor:
(mention your request here)
I ask that Your will may be done. Give me what You know to be the best for my soul and for the souls of those for whom I pray. Give me Your Holy Spirit to enlighten me and to guide me in the way of Your commandments and Holiness while I strive for the happiness of Heaven, where I hope to glorify You forever. Amen."

Taper Candles

A taper candle is a long cylindrical candle available in a variety of sizes. For instance, chime candles are simply four-inch taper candles which are most commonly advertised. Six-inch and nine-inch candles are also readily available.

Please avoid the use of birthday candles in spellwork, as they can't be inscribed or dressed, and their combustible time is limited to just a few minutes. They neither give the practitioner enough time to pierce the veil between this world and the spiritual realm, nor do they provide enough power to energize both the spell and the spirits.

Self-Confidence Candle Spell

Obtain a purple taper candle, preferably either in a six-inch or nine-inch size, and cleanse it. Starting from the bottom of the candle and working your way to the top, inscribe the word "mastery" five times.

Anoint the candle with either olive oil or an appropriate condition oil. Then, immediately roll it in a powder made of High John the Conqueror Root (bindweed, jalap, king of the woods, king root, man root, man of the earth).

Place a picture of yourself with eyes showing into a fireproof candle holder. Ensure that it is facing outward. Place the candle over your picture. Light the candle and pray.

Figural Candles

Figural candles, often called "image candles," are those that are shaped or carved into the likeness of a symbol. They are preferred by many practitioners when working unusual or extremely strong spells because their visual symbolism is easy to see and, thus, helps the practitioners to focus on what they wish to manifest.

Figural candles are also available as effigies, which represent a specific person or people. Those that are shaped as a man or woman are frequently used in lieu of cloth, clay, or other forms of dolls. When implementing a candle as an effigy, as with dolls, it ought to be baptized in order to bring an essence of the target's spirit into the image. Once it is baptized, it need not be lit if your intent is to treat is as if it were a doll.

Money Candle Spell

Depending on your gender, obtain either a green male or female figural candle and cleanse it. Inscribe your birth name and birth-date on the candle, any place where it can be done, five times. Also inscribe the words "Money come to me" as many times as possible.

Name and baptize the candle. Next, anoint the candle with either an appropriate condition oil or olive oil. Then, immediately roll it in money herbs.

Obtain a picture of yourself with eyes showing and write your petition on the back. Then, place it into a fireproof candle holder, ensuring that it is facing outward. Place the candle over your picture. Light the candle and pray.

Communication Magic

Below are a few spells to either enhance one's own communication skills, change the type of communication occurring within the home, or to coax communication from another.

Change Crossed Words into Kind Words

If frequent arguments or crossed words are occurring in the home, change those harsh words into kind ones. Boil 2 cups of water. Once the water begins to bubble, remove the pot from the stove.

Immediately add 1 tsp each of the herb deer's tongue (*Liatris odoratissima*), dried red rose (*Rosa spp.*) petals, and/or buds. Allow the plant parts to steep for seven minutes, then strain them from the water and respectfully return them to the ground.

Once the tea has cooled off, pour it into a spray bottle. Spray all the rooms in your abode frequently. Pay special attention to the areas where most of the crossed words are occurring.

Eloquent Orator

Obtain either a yellow male or female figural candle, depending on your gender, and cleanse it. Inscribe your birth name and birthdate on the candle anywhere it can be done five times. Also inscribe the words "Eloquent speaker" as many times as possible.

Name and baptize the candle. Next, anoint the candle with either an appropriate condition oil or olive oil. Then, immediately roll it in the herb deer's tongue (*Liatris odoratissima*).

Obtain a picture of yourself with eyes showing and write your petition on the back. Then, place it into a fireproof candle holder, ensuring that your image is facing outward. Place the candle over your picture. Light the candle and pray.

Smooth Talker Spell

This spell is to speak words that are impressive to others.

Boil 1 cup of water. Once the water begins to bubble, remove the pot from the stove. Immediately add 1 tsp of the herb deer's tongue (*Liatris odoratissima*) and allow it to steep for seven minutes, then strain the water and respectfully return the herb to the ground.

Allow the tea to cool. It can also be refrigerated for future use. Prior to communicating with the one you wish to impress, lightly splash the potion around your mouth and on your forehead.

Talk To Me Spell

Ingredients

- A yellow or white skull candle
- ½ x ½ inch piece of torn brown paper bag for petition
- Metal pie plate
- Coasters
- Soldering iron (do not use inside the home)
- A melted chime candle of the same color as the skull candle
- A syringe or spoon to refill the skull candle
- Parrot feathers
- The herb deer's tongue (*Liatris odoratissima*)
- Olive oil or communication condition oil
- Powdered calamus root (*Acorus calamus*)

Instructions:

Cleanse the candle. With the soldering iron, bore a deep hole into the mouth of the candle. Parrots are "chatty;" thus, their feathers are commonly used in communication spellwork. So, stuff feathers into the mouth. Then, with your spoon, seal the feathers into the mouth with melted wax. Since the forehead represents the frontal lobe of the brain dominating speech, bore another hole into the forehead with the soldering iron. Fill that hole with deer's tongue and a small petition paper, stating something like: "Call (your name)" or "Contact (your name)." With your spoon, also seal that hole with melted wax.

With your pencil, inscribe the candle with the target's name. On the forehead, inscribe the same petition to call or contact you. Name and baptize that candle. Anoint the candle with oil and immediately roll in the powdered calamus root, which is a controlling component in spellwork.

Place the candle atop the metal pie plate, then place the plate over coasters. Light the candle and, every hour, talk to the candle as if it were a person while softly telling it to contact you.

What's Really on your Mind?

A truth-telling spell. It has been used to learn what a person is really thinking, especially if it's an ambiguous romantic interest.

Obtain a nine-inch taper candle and cleanse it. Then, starting from the bottom of the candle and working your way to the top, inscribe the words "(name of target) talk truthfully" seven times. Remember to inscribe the candle in a circular motion so that all sides of the candle contain words. Then anoint the candle with either an appropriate condition oil or olive oil.

Obtain a picture of your target with eyes showing. Write your petition over the target's forehead. Then, place it into a fireproof candle holder, ensuring that the image is facing outward. Place the candle over your picture.

Circle the candle holder with five communication crystals. You can use one of each of the crystals or a few to five of the same, depending on your desires.

Aquamarine for clear communication; emerald for smooth communications; blue lace agate to improve communication; amazonite to harmonize communication; and/or fluorite (any color) to also improve communication.

Light the candle and pray.

Court Case Magic

The most powerful prayers for those who have either been wrongly convicted of a crime or who wish for justice are Psalm 7 and Psalm 35. These psalms ought to be recited daily for nine consecutive days prior to the court appearance.

Time the novena to ensure that last day of prayer coincides with the night before the hearing.

However, it is my contention that prayers ought to begin many weeks prior to a court hearing, especially prayers appealing to both the Just Judge and St. Expedite. Adding a few Hoodoo spells into the mix doesn't hurt!

Let's first explore a couple of powerful prayers to the advocates of justice, followed by a few popular Hoodoo spells:

Just Judge

This ritual is popular amongst many Latin communities and Santeria practitioners. It is my personal "go-to" suggestion for not only people seeking justice, but also for attorneys wishing to win a trial. In most cases, if the client is being truthful, the ritual is successful.

The Just Judge is the manifestation of Jesus Christ as the ultimate judge who is fair in all matters of justice. Because Jesus Himself was unfairly judged, He understands injustice. He is most often called upon in Latin American Catholic folk magical practices. When situations are dire, it is believed that the Just Judge can be called upon to turn things around.

One month prior to the court appearance, obtain five or six glass-encased Just Judge candles. Widely available in Hispanic grocery stores, the candle is labeled *Justo Juez,* meaning "Just Judge" in Spanish.

With this ritual, you will be performing what is known as "a run of candles," or just "a run." It entails lighting one candle at a time while ensuring that a candle flame is always burning. Therefore, once all of the wax from the preceding candle is almost completely consumed, another candle is lit.

This continuity mimics the "continual flame" as stated in the Holy Bible, "And the fire upon the altar shall be burning in it; it shall not be put out: and the priest shall burn wood on it every morning, and lay the burnt offering in order upon it; and he shall burn thereon the fat of the peace offerings. The fire shall ever be burning upon the altar; it shall never go out" (Lev. 6.12–13).

At approximately the same time every day, kneel at the candle and recite the following prayer aloud.

Prayer to the Just Judge

"Dear Lord Jesus, You are the Just Judge, full of mercy and compassion. I come before you in this time of legal difficulty and uncertainty, seeking your divine justice
(Tell Jesus who you are and explain the case. Then, ask your petition)
I have explained the intricacies of my court case, and you see the truth that lies within. I entrust my legal matters into your hands, knowing that you are the ultimate source of righteousness. Please guide my

legal team, the judges, and all those involved in the legal process.
May their hearts be open to the truth and to your divine will.
I offer this prayer in Your Holy name, and believe in Your power
and authority over all things right and just. AMEN."

St. Expedite

When the opponent keeps taking another to court in order to cause delays and frustrations, it may be time to petition St. Expedite. For, as we know, he also helps to obtain expeditious solutions.

Light either a five-day or seven-day vigil candle to begin on a Thursday. Pray daily, and don't forget to offer him Sara Lee Pound Cake as a gratuitous gift.

Prayer To St. Expeditus for Court Cases

"St. Expeditus, I humbly beg thee to come to my aid so that thy
prompt and certain intercession will obtain for me, from our
Divine Lord, the grace of a happy and swift solution to the matter
which now concerns me.
(Explain your case and plead your petition here)
I do so without fear, being fully confident in the supreme wisdom of
Our Blessed Lord, and place my trust in Him without reservation,
being mindful that His will alone will be done. Holy Mary, Mother
of God, pray for me. St. Expeditus, your help in urgent matters,
pray for me. AMEN."

Apostles' Assistance

Take a brown paper bag and tear it in half. Avoid using any factory cuts on the paper. With a pencil, write the name of six of the Holy Apostles on one piece of paper and the other six apostles on the second paper. Fold the papers in half and wear one in each shoe when attending court. The Apostles will assist you in the court case matter.

Freezing the Mouths of Testifiers

Tear a piece of brown paper bag large enough to hold the names of anyone who may testify against you. Avoid using any factory cuts on the paper. With a pencil, write the names of those people on the paper and place it in between two bricks. On the day of the court appearance, place a bag of ice over the bricks to freeze their words.

Sour the Judge to your Opponent

Take a piece of brown paper bag and tear it in half. Avoid using any factory cuts on the paper. With a pencil, write the name of your opponent on one piece of paper and the judge's name on the other.

Place their names in a glass jar. If their pictures are available, also add those to the jar. Fill a third of the jar with spoiled milk, then add vinegar, but avoid overfilling the jar beyond two-thirds of its capacity.

Place a lid on the jar. Because both spoiled milk and vinegar produce gases, the jar could explode. Therefore, keep the jar outside or in a secluded area. Vigorously shake the jar at least twice a day while demanding that the judge hate your opponent.

Cursing and Crossing Magic

Although Psalm 37 of the Holy Bible is an uncrossing prayer, it meticulously describes what wicked people are capable of doing to another. How do they begin their quest to hurt virtuous people? They begin by coveting, as stated in Psalm 37: "The wicked watcheth the righteous, and seeketh to slay him."

In the beginning of this book, we learned how the Africans were coveted and then later kidnapped and brutally forced into slavery. Because there were no laws to protect these victims, their modes of justice relied on magical retaliation.

Nowadays, the righteous of all colors are coveted by bullies, thieves, liars, con artists, scammers, abusers, sociopaths, and psychopaths, while our legal system frequently fails to obtain justice for the victims. Thus, many again turn to magical retaliation for justice. Below are examples of vengeance spells. Please ensure that the magic is justified and the punishment is commensurate to the crime.

Car Accident Spell

Make a cloth doll of your target, ensuring that it is named and baptized. Place it under a tire of your car and run over it. Retrieve the doll and perform this spell as often as possible.

Goofer Dust Curse

This is a contact magical curse and can harm others who come into contact with this spell. Therefore, ensure that only the target will interact with it.

On the enemy's property, make a circle with the goofer dust. Then, make an "X" inside the circle while stating your curse. Walk away from it backward. When the target steps on it, the curse will take effect.

Gravely Handshake

Prior to encountering your target, rub your hands with graveyard dirt. Shake hands with the enemy, and that person will become ill. Immediately rinse your hands with either whiskey, Florida Water, holy water, or a salt and water mixture to rid yourself of the spiritual negativity.

Gravely Headache

If you're living with an abuser, put fresh graveyard dirt in their pillowcase every night. The target will suffer from headaches.

Nail Down the Enemy

This is a thirteen-day spell requiring a picture of the target, with eyes showing, and thirteen coffin nails. On the first day, place the picture facing the north side of a tree and hammer one coffin nail into it while verbalizing your restraining curse. Each subsequent day, drive another nail into the tree. After the thirteenth day, your target will become progressively weak and less able to harm you.

Eradicating Mischievous Entities Magic

Millions have viewed my appearance on the Warner Brothers/Discovery Network's award-winning documentary "Michigan Hell House." In a nutshell, it was about a family that had been attacked by malicious entities. It was my job to identify the types of entities that had performed the numerous ghastly acts of violence, as well as to identify the source of their emergence. My final task was to eradicate the lingering entities that continued to covet the property.

Although my mission was successful, many religious demonologists persisted to vehemently proclaim that a "Witch" did not have the authority to engage in spiritual eradication rituals. If this were true, why did the executive producer choose this Conjure woman/Hoodoo practitioner for the task? Because the executive producer knew what conjuring can do!

In his book, *Witchcraft Unchained*, author Craig Spencer eloquently answers this question. He states:

> "When it comes to Witchcraft and magic, we rarely think of the concept of "exorcism." It is true that the stigma exists wherein Witchcraft is considered evil and demonic and that Witches are going to end up like Linda Blair in The Exorcist; yet, Witchcraft has an intriguing history with exorcisms that is often missed in books on the Craft. That is the work of the conjurer. The word "conjurer" is often seen today as a word for calling on spirits alone, but this is not the full story. A conjurer has the power to both call upon and expel spirits. Both powers are important to the work of a conjurer and thus they are effectively the "exorcists" of the craft."

Learning to perform an effective demonic exorcism takes years of observation, study, and on-the-job training. However, if an entity is not of a demonic nature and is merely mischievous, there are methods to subside its activity or even eradicate it. Reciting Psalm 121 aloud ought to be performed numerous times a day and prior to sleeping.

Before performing any ritual, adjust your behaviors. Although easier said than done, avoid displaying anger or fear, because mischievous and malicious entities feed on these emotions. Instead, keep cool, calm, and collected while trying to make your environment not conducive to their comfort level. These entities despise:

- Fearlessness
- Fresh air
- Laughter
- Singing
- Sunlight

Bells

Hateful entities also despise the sound of bells ringing. This is because bells are usually rung prior to performing religious church activities, which malicious entities fear. Thus, they will usually flee to the sound. Therefore, on a frequent basis, ring as many bells as possible throughout your abode.

Entrap the Entity

Since entities are known to have a penchant for counting, you will lure the entity into the trap with grains of rice to count. Because they prefer hiding within objects resembling people, a small doll is laid upon the rice to provide the entity with security. The K-II EMF meter, which senses spiritual beings, will allow us to detect if the entity is within the trap. The duct tape will be used to ensure that the lid will not be dislodged.

For this trap, you will need:

- One K-II EMF (electromagnetic field) meter
- Rice
- 1 medium-sized container with a lid
- 1 small toy doll able to fit within the container.
- Duct tape

Pour a generous amount of rice into the container. Leave enough room to lay the doll over the rice, as well as being able to secure the lid once the entity is trapped.

Frequently check for possible activity within the container with the K-II meter by scanning it over the container. Once the entity is within the trap, the meter will display multiple lights. If the entity is aware of your presence, it will more often than not hide within the doll.

Immediately place the lid on the trap. Once again, use your K-II meter to ensure that the entity did not escape. If it is still within the container, secure the lid with a generous amount of duct tape.

The container must either be thrown into a river or buried in a cemetery.

Gregorian Chant Music

Several Catholic priests who perform exorcisms fervently profess that malicious entities cannot tolerate this music. Needless to say, my CD player, along with a selection of Gregorian chant CDs, are always with me when performing spiritual eradications. Although the chants are monotonous and sometimes annoying, they are indeed effective.

Salt Water

Poltergeist is a German word meaning "noisy ghost." Oftentimes, they make their noises by either tossing or throwing objects across rooms or at people. When this happens, try to identify the location from where the object was initially positioned. Most likely, that is where the entity is situated.

Boil two cups of water with ½ cup salt. When the solution cools, pour it into a spray bottle. Spray a generous amount of the solution at and around the last suspected location where the entity was stationed.

Tibetan Ghost Purging Incense Ritual

As previously discussed, Tibetan purging incense behaves as a spiritual "tear gas" that repulses and suffocates negative forces. What happens when human beings are exposed to tear gas? As an Air Force Combat Unit Veteran, I can tell you that being exposed to tear gas was a horrific experience.

The Air Force had many of us gathered in a large room with the doors and windows closed and locked. When that nasty tear gas was released, all of us attempted to flee, but we were locked in the room and couldn't escape. It felt as if impending doom was upon us because it felt as if we were inhaling fire. When the doors were finally opened, we all fled for our lives to escape those toxic fumes.

Thus, we do the same by enclosing the negative forces within a room, smoking them with the incense, then providing them with an escape route away from the home! Light a charcoal disc over your censer. When the charcoal turns grey in color, immediately close all your doors and windows. Then, place about ½ tsp of the incense into the concave portion of the charcoal disc. Keep additional incense on hand.

Perform this ritual one room at a time. Walk around the room with your censer, ensuring that the room is well-smoked by the incense. Then, immediately open one door or window and demand that the entities leave your home immediately. Allow about one minute before closing the window or door behind them. Repeat this ritual in every room and add more incense as needed.

Forgiveness Magic

It is oftentimes difficult for human beings to embrace the emotion of forgiveness. Thus, is important to perform these spells as often as possible to keep the energy at a steady output flow.

Calm Down!

My godfather in Santeria worked very hard to earn a living. Unfortunately, his wife would cash his paychecks and frivolously squander the money faster than he could make it. Her spending sprees infuriated my godfather and oftentimes caused his temper to explode.

But his anger was often alleviated with a little trick that his wife learned in Cuba. She would pour a one-ounce bottle of *Balsamo Tranquilo* (Tranquility Balm), a calming oil sold at almost all Hispanic botanicas, into a six-ounce glass of water. Next, she inserted a petition paper into the solution stating that my godfather's anger would subside. The glass was placed outside to evaporate and, within a day or two, he would completely forgive her bad behaviors.

In lieu of a petition paper, my preference is to instead obtain a picture of the target, with eyes showing. Then, write the petition on the backside of the picture and insert it into the solution. Once evaporation is completed, bury the picture, along with the remaining residual oil, in either the backyard or into the dirt of a houseplant.

Forgiveness of Sins

Hyssop (*Hyssopus officianalis*) is an herb of great antiquity and mentioned several times in both the Bible. It is a spiritual cleansing agent as well as the herb to use when seeking God's forgiveness.

Place two cups of water in a pot and place it on the stove. Turn the heat on high and once the water boils, immediately remove the pot from the stove. Add a heaping tbsp of hyssop into the water and allow it to steep for thirteen minutes. Then, strain the herb and set it aside.

Fill your bathtub with a comfortable temperature of water. Pour the hyssop solution into your bathtub. Remove your clothing and enter the bathtub with a printout of Psalm 51, which speaks of hyssop. While reciting this psalm aloud, try to completely immerse yourself in the water for a total of thirteen times, in between the recitation of the verses.

Don't forget to respectfully return the hyssop to the ground outside, as it is a gesture of returning it from whence it came.

Friends Again

The Holy Bible records that, in ancient times, there came from Gilead, beyond the Jordan, a substance used to heal and soothe. It was known as the Balm of Gilead (*Commiphora opobalsamum, Commiphora gileadens*). That name became symbolic as a great comforter with the power to soothe and heal. It is often used in many Hoodoo forgiveness and reconciliation spells.

Obtain an eight-ounce glass jar. Fill the jar to two-thirds of its capacity with confectioner's sugar. Add 1 tbsp each of balm of Gilead buds and the friendship herb, forget-me-not (*Myosotis spp.*), into the sugar and mix well.

Next, insert a small picture of yourself and your target into the jar. Ensure that the pictures are showing both parties' eyes. Add more sugar if necessary, so as to completely cover the pictures. Place a lid on the jar and gently shake it on a daily basis.

Heal the Emotional Pain

If you've hurt someone's feelings, obtain a six-inch or nine-inch light blue candle. Cleanse it, and, with a pencil, inscribe "forgive (your name)" seven times. Begin the inscription at the base of the candle and work your way toward the top.

Crush ¼ tsp each of the herbs forget-me-not (*Myosotis spp.*), passionflower (*Passifora incarnata*), and althea (*Althaea officianalis, Althaea spp.*). Mix the herbs together and set aside.

Anoint the candle with either olive oil or a healing condition oil. Then, immediately roll the candle in the crushed herbs.

Obtain a picture of your target with eyes showing. Write your petition over the image on their forehead, as it represents the frontal lobe of the brain that dominates speech and speaking. Then, place it into a fireproof candle holder, ensuring that the image is facing outward. Place the candle over your picture. Light the candle and pray.

Self-Forgiveness

Place your picture with eyes showing and your personal concerns into a jar filled with balm of Gilead buds. Cover the jar with a metal lid.

Obtain a four-inch pink taper candle and cleanse it. Starting from the bottom of the candle and working your way to the top, inscribe the words "forgive myself" into the candle three times. Then, anoint it with rose oil.

Place the candle atop the lid and light it. Recite the following prayer aloud:

Prayer For Self-Forgiveness

"Dear God, I know that You have forgiven me for my sins of (State your transgressions here). I thank You for Your unconditional love and grace. I am truly repentant and wish to overcome these tendencies. Now, Father, help me to forgive myself. Erase my guilt and create a new heart within me.
I love you. AMEN."

Although Sundays and Mondays are favorable days to perform this spell, it can be repeated any day and any time that it is necessary.

Good Luck Magic

Within our world, there are thousands of varying beliefs regarding good luck spells and charms. Keep in mind that the following customs are within the beliefs of Hoodoo practitioners.

There are numerous popular old time good luck charms and spells consisting of animal body parts. However, due to the practices of many mass manufacturers who ruthlessly torture and kill animals for the sake of profit, these charms and spells have been purposely omitted from the following list.

Coin Charm

Carrying a coin that is stamped with your birth year will bring good luck. Moreover, finding such a coin is exceptionally lucky.

Horseshoe

Nail a horseshoe over the outside of your doorway with the two prongs facing upward to draw in good luck. Conversely, if the prongs are facing the ground, it will prevent good luck from entering your abode.

Mercury Dime

Bore a small hole into a silver dime thread a string through it. Wear it around the waist to attract good luck. If worn as an anklet, it will prevent the bearer from being affected when stepping on anything that has been cursed.

Morning Magic

Step out of bed first with the right foot to bring good luck for the rest of the day.

New Year's Day

Eating cooked black-eyed peas on New Year's Day will bring good luck for the entire upcoming year.

New Year's Eve

Place a horseshoe in your pillowcase on New Year's Eve before going to sleep. It is said that the shoe will enchant the person with good luck for the entire upcoming year.

St. Joseph Beans

In the Catholic religion, 19 Mar. is the feast day of St. Joseph. On this day, elaborate altars are erected in honor of the saint. On most altars, especially amongst the churches with numerous Sicilian parishioners, one will see fava beans, or "lucky beans." After all, the items on the altar have been blessed by a Catholic priest. It is believed that the fava beans become empowered with the ability to provide good luck to those that carry them. Therefore, the beans are normally distributed once the celebratory services have been completed.

Salt and Red Pepper

Mix $^{1}/_{8}$ tsp each of salt and red pepper flakes. Place this mixture under your carpet to invite good luck into your abode.

Shoe Superstition

Always don your right shoe first to bring good luck in your daily endeavors.

Table Toss

As you sit down to eat, toss a small pinch of salt over your left shoulder before dining. It will bring good luck to not only yourself, but to those sitting at the same table.

Love Magic

Because "love makes the world go round," love magic accounts for a significant portion of almost all metaphysical practices throughout the world. Some of my personal favorites are those that involve ingestion spells because they are especially potent.

Follow Me

With a clean dry razor, shave either dry, flaking skin or callouses off the bottom of your foot. Do so in a delicate manner, as not to cut yourself. With a mortar and pestle, crush the dead skin into a powder. Add a little of this powder into warm or cold food that your target will ingest and that person will follow you.

Hairy Spell

Shave or cut a little hair from your left armpit. Then, cut some pubic hair that has grown from the right side of your genitalia. Place all of the hair into a small frying pan. Set the temperature of the stove on high in order to burn the hair into ashes. While the hair is burning, state your command aloud that your target will love you.

Once the hair has completely transformed into ashes, remove the pan from the stove and allow time for cooling. With your fingers, pulverize the ashes and add a little of this powder into the food that your target will ingest.

Love Necklace

As the name implies, love-vine *(Cassytha filiformis)* was widely used by both the African and African American slaves in love magic. One such spell involved allowing the vine to dry then pulverizing it. Add this powder, along with a personal concern of both yourself and the target, into a small flannel or cotton muslin bag. Wear the bag as a necklace, and the target will eventually love you.

Magnet Spell

This work will bind two people together. However, please do not perform this spell if one person does not know the other. When this occurs, the binding energies will not be shared by two people but will instead affect only one at full force.

- A small picture of yourself, with eyes showing.
- A small picture of your target, with eyes showing.
- 2 large, heavy-duty magnets.
- Honey
- Pink or red yarn

Smear a little honey, which will act as a glue, on the images of both pictures. Then, position the pictures together, face-to-face. Place a magnet on either side to further bind the targets together. Wrap this up in the yarn.

Because honey is sweet, it may attract insects. Therefore, place this spellwork in an isolated area free from insects.

Menstrual Blood Spell

This spell is notoriously popular amongst African Traditional Religions and their diasporas. It involves feeding a male target the menstrual blood of his admirer. However, there are several books, as well as websites, that have delivered misinformation regarding both the procedure, as well as the expected results. So, allow me to present the correct information:

The blood must be fresh for ingestion, do not save it for future use. Both my mother and my aunt had always instructed others to place a coffee cup under the vagina and allow three drops of blood to drip into the cup. Then, pour warm coffee into the cup, because hot coffee will burn the structural makeup of the blood, thus clotting it and forcing it to lose its spiritual life force. The other options given were to allow three drops of blood to drip onto a spoon and mix it with dark food, such as cake frosting or spaghetti sauce. No matter how the blood is served, it must be immediately ingested by the target.

Once the target has ingested the blood, he will initially become somewhat aloof toward the woman. Then, after a few hours, the spell will begin to work. Unfortunately, it is a short-lived spell, lasting for only about two to three days.

My mother warned me to never perform this spell more than once per menstrual cycle, as it could cause the target to lose his senses.

Money-drawing Magic

Because money is important in practically every single culture around the world, millions of people wear amulets to attract it. In addition to amulets, the wise ones also implement money spells. In fact, it is speculated that the three most common magical spells performed around the world are those for love, protection, and money!

Alfalfa

Keep about ½ tsp of dried alfalfa (*Medicago sativa*) in your wallet and you will never be without cash.

Baby Enchantment

Throughout history, the New Testament has been altered numerous times, mostly by monarchs and Church rulers. Many had done so for self-serving purposes, such as keeping people submissive and obedient not to God, but to these leaders themselves.

A prevalent and recurring theme amongst these altered biblical passages is that the practice of magic is forbidden by God. Yet, several magical practitioners were featured favorably. We have already explored the fact that one of the most predominant figures within the Holy Bible was Moses, a formidable magical practitioner, who was deeply loved by God.

When baby Jesus was born, three Magi followed a star to find him. Millions upon millions of people believe that this term simply means "wise men." It is instead a term derived from the word *magus,* meaning "sorcerer." These three men were magical practitioners, as well as astrologers, who followed an astrological event to find the baby. They brought to Jesus gifts of frankincense, myrrh, and gold. However, how they present these gifts to the baby is still a mystery. Maybe they did so in the same manner as this following old Hoodoo spell.

The first visitor of a newborn baby must gift it with a silver dime. Next, place the coin in the baby's left hand and guide its hand to grasp it. Do not allow the coin to drop. When the infant grows older, it will never become poor.

Bayberry Candle

One of my personal money spells is the use of a glass-encased bayberry candle. Whenever my psychic reading appointments begin to dwindle, this simple spell always significantly increases my workload.

Place a picture of yourself with eyes showing into a fireproof candle holder. Ensure that your image is facing outward. Place the candle over your picture. Light the candle and pray Psalm 23 aloud, then ask for money. Do not extinguish this candle while it is burning.

Bride's Financial Future

During her wedding, a bride must have folded money in her left shoe in order to have a financially prosperous marriage.

Check Book

This spell was extremely popular decades ago and very successful for me. However, it is only effective just one time.

Remove a blank check from your checkbook. Date it for one year from the day that you write the check. Example, if today's date is 14 Feb. 2025, the date would instead read 14 Feb. 2026.

The money is for you, so write your full birthname. Under the amount, write the amount needed. Do not get greedy and write for a vast sum of money. Just enough money to acquire something that you need, such as a car.

Under the signature portion, write "The Law of Abundance," and under the memo portion: "Leave the details to God." Slip the check back into the plastic portion of the checkbook and avoid looking at it.

Clothing
Many Cuban Santeros will sleep with red underwear on New Year's Eve for a financially prosperous upcoming year. Hoodoo practitioners say that wearing red clothing on any day of the year will attract money.

New Moon
Go outside and hold up money to the first night of new moon. Ask aloud that more money come to you. For the entire month or moon cycle, you will have more cash than usual.

New Year's Day Spell
Eating cooked cabbage on this day will ensure that you will not be without money for the upcoming year. Others say that a cooked head of cabbage must be served to four people in four equal portions.

Onion Peels
Burn onion peels in a cast iron pan and it will bring money to you.

Oyster Shell
Keep a piece of oyster shell in your left pocket to attract money.

Oil Lamp Magic

Although the earliest documented use of lamps occurred around 17500 BC by the ancient Egyptians, the widespread use of oil lamps began in Rome around 500 BC, and gained worldwide popularity. These lamps were created not only to produce light, but for usage in both religious and metaphysical practices. To this day, numerous sects of the African magico-religious practices and their diaspora continue the traditional use of oil lamps in ritual.

The old-style lamps throughout the world are either plain in appearance or ornately esthetic. In the practice of Santeria, we simply use a bowl made out of a dried gourd called a "*jicara*" (pronounced: he-cah-rah). It is filled with vegetable or olive oil and topped with a floating wick, called a "*mecha*" or "*mechita.*"

Since kerosene lamps are widely available in most stores, they are frequently used for spellwork. Ordinarily available are the flat wick kerosene lamps containing a bowl at the bottom, a burner in the middle, and a metal collar to secure the chimney to the bowl. The wick is flat and is adjusted with the knob adjacent to the metal collar.

There are both advantages and disadvantages to their usage:

Advantages

- Petition papers, pant parts, condition oils, and ritual items can be placed into the bowl.
- The flame is protected by the tall chimney and, therefore, less likely to be extinguished by the wind if placed outside.
- The cleanup does not involve scraping messy candle wax from the holder.
- They are easier to prepare than candles.

Disadvantages

- The bowl is small. Thus, less burning time.
- The chimney is made of fragile glass, so it must be handled in a gentle manner.
- The wick has to be adjusted frequently as it burns down.

While candles provide communicative comments through various behaviors and their wax distributions, oil lamps do not provide such feedback.

Never use mineral oil, rubbing alcohol, or pure gasoline as fuel for any oil lamp, as the vapors can pose serious health hazards. Additionally, these solutions are fire hazards which can cause explosions. Because olive oil is frequently mentioned in the Holy Bible, it is my preferred fuel for oil lamps.

No matter the type of oil lamp selected, here are the normal steps for the preparation, followed by a few spells:

1. Your your selected oil into the vessel, ensuring that it is only filled to two-thirds of its capacity. If desired, add a drop or two of candle wax dye and a few drops of an appropriate condition oil. Then, stir with a wooden implement.

2. Add the appropriate plant parts to the mix and stir again. Insert your folded petition papers, name papers, pictures, and, if possible, personal concerns. If desired, also add amulets, charms, medals, or other items representing your needs.

3. Light the wick, wait five minutes, then recite a Psalm or prayer aloud. Request your desires prior to closing the prayer with the word "Amen."

Blessing Oil Lamp

- **Plant Parts:** Blessing plant parts
- **Candle Wax Dye:** Blue
- **Prayer:** Psalm 145, a blessing Psalm

Love Oil Lamp

- **Plant Parts:** Love or attraction plant parts
- **Candle Wax Dye:** Pink for romantic love, red for passionate love
- **Prayer:** Psalm 23, prayed for love, luck, and money

Money Oil Lamp

- **Plant Parts:** Money drawing plant parts
- **Candle Wax Dye:** Green
- **Prayer:** Psalm 23, prayed for love, luck, and money.

Protection Oil Lamp

- **Plant Parts:** Protection plant parts (Note: avoid rue if pregnant)
- **Candle Wax Dye:** Black
- **Prayer:** Psalm 91, a strong protection prayer

Road Opener Oil Lamp

- **Plant Parts:** Road opener plant parts (add dirt from a crossroad, if desired)
- **Candle Wax Dye:** Orange
- **Prayer:** Psalm 65, a powerful road opening prayer

Protection Magic

Apotropaic magic (from the Greek αποτρέπειν, meaning "to ward off") is the original term for protection magic. Archeologists have discovered that protection rituals were practiced throughout the Ancient Near East, Ancient Greece, and Ancient Egypt. They did so to avert harm or misfortune instigated by the living or by evil entities.

To this day, people of all cultures around the world continue to practice protection rites. There are spells, rituals, and numerous objects to ward off evil entities, negative curses, and unwanted people. Even the most pious, God-fearing communities practice these rituals. For example, statues of gargoyles atop Catholic churches were placed there to ward off evil entities. Millions of others protect themselves through religious means, such as wearing sacred paraphernalia or through prayers, etc. No matter the approach, these examples remain as forms of protection magic.

Psalm 91 is one of the most powerful protection prayers within the Holy Bible, while Psalm 121 was specifically designed to ward off evil entities. Praying either or both Psalms while performing any of the spells below will greatly empower your intentions.

Averting Evil Entities from Entering your Home

Place dried rue (*Ruta graveolens*) in several cloth muslin bags and tie the drawstrings nine to thirteen times per bag. Hang these bags over every door and window in your abode. Do not work with rue if pregnant, as it is an aborticide.

Averting Evil People from your Property

As previously mentioned, the famous old saying states: "Evil cannot walk where basil has been." To protect your property, scatter dried basil (*Commiphora opobalsamum, Commiphora gileadens*) in and around your property. It will deter those with evil intentions from stepping on it.

Averting Evil People and Entities

Take a prayer card of St. Michael and place his image over an image of yourself with your eyes showing. Tape them together while reciting the prayer to St. Michael on the back of the card. Then, place this under a candle or statue of St. Michael.

Averting an Incubus or Succubus

Because Vick's Vapor rub contains camphor (*Camphora officinarum, Laurus camphora*), an odor that is repulsive to negative entities, it is widely used to deter them. Prior to going to sleep, rub the ointment on your inner thighs, avoiding the groin area. It will deter any sexual demonic entities from assaulting someone while sleeping.

Averting Magical Spells

Place dried red pepper flakes in a cloth muslin bag and tie the drawstring nine to thirteen times. Carry the bag in your left pocket and you will be protected from magical spells.

Send Away Magic

Send away spells are those employed to remove, dismiss, drive off, or keep a person or situation away. In my opinion, they are virtually innocuous, because the intent involves the least amount of harm to the target while attempting to thwart future confrontations. They are also ideal spells to cast for those fearing karmic or deity retribution.

Along with the following spells, praying either Psalm 94 or Psalm 105 aloud will greatly empower your desires.

Ant and Egg Spell

A Hyatt informant in Waycross, Georgia said to carry an egg to a red ant mound. Write on the egg who you want to leave and tell the egg and ants what you want them to do. Poke a hole into the egg and stick that end into the mound. This spell will take a while, because the egg will drip slowly. However, once the last of the egg has been eaten, that person will leave.

Bird Feather Spell

This is also a common spell in Santeria. If you find a feather belonging to a bird that takes flight, write the name of your target on it with a fine point marker. The feathers of pigeons are preferable, but any will suffice.

On a windy day, release the feather in a direction opposite of the target's residence or place of employment and say "As this bird takes flight away from here, so shall ____ (target's name)."

Coffin Spell

Place a picture of your target with eyes showing into a small makeshift or toy coffin. Then, close the lid. Bury this far from where the target lives or works and they will move away. Do not bury it in a cemetery, or the spell will cause harm to the target.

Dog Feces Spell

Open a clean small plastic container and fill it with fresh dog manure and a generous amount of cayenne pepper. With a disposable utensil, such as a stick or plastic object, stir well.

Tear a piece of brown paper bag, avoiding the factory folds. With a pencil, write the target's full birthname three times. Fold it way from you, turn it to the left, fold it away from you again, then repeat one more time for a total of three folds. Stick the paper deep into the dog manure and close the lid tight.

Bury this far from where the target lives or works and they will move away. Do not bury it in a cemetery, or the spell will cause harm to the target.

Foot Track Spell

Follow the target and obtain dirt from the left footprint. Place it in a small jar or bottle and cap it tightly. Throw this into a sewer, stream, or river.

Steady Work Magic

When performing steady work spells, try to include some of the techniques described in the portion entitled "Attraction Magic" to strengthen your chances of acquiring employment. Also remember to pray fervently prior to and during your pursuits. One of the most successful employment prayers to recite is as follows:

A Prayer for Employment

"God, our Father, I turn to you seeking Your divine help and guidance as I look for suitable employment. I need Your wisdom to guide my footsteps along the right path, and to lead me to find the proper things to say and do in this quest. I wish to use the gifts and talents you have given me, but I need the opportunity to do so with gainful employment. Do not abandon me, Dear Father, in this search, but rather grant me this favor I seek, so that I may return to you with praise and thanksgiving for Your gracious assistance.
Please grant this request through Christ, our Lord
(plead your petition here)
Amen."

Bringing Work into your Home

This spell is reminiscent of what a Conservative Jewish rabbi once told me. He said that, during ritual times, he blesses both wine and bread. Since wine is always blessed first, the bread is covered to ensure that its spirit does not know that the wine takes precedence. Thus, bread does, indeed, have awareness!

For this spell, take a piece of hard bread and tell it what you wish it to do. Place it in a large cloth muslin bag. Tie the drawstrings five times. Hang it over your kitchen door and it will bring work to your home.

Fear of Losing your Job
Carry a master root (*Imperatoria ostruthium*) at all times and pray Psalm 6 aloud at least three times a day.

Finding Job Prospects
While trying to identify potential employers, wear red pepper flakes in both of your shoes.

Preparing for the Interview
Once you've positioned an interview date, acquire a buckeye nut (*Aesculus spp.*) and sprinkle it daily with Hoyt's cologne. Bring the nut with you on the day of the interview.

Sitting with the Interviewer
Cut a tiny piece of white cotton cloth. Place only three grains of salt into it. When the interviewer turns away, quickly toss the salt toward the north side of the room.

Uncrossing Magic

The term "crossed conditions" usually implies that someone has cast a negative spell on another person, rendering that target "crossed." When this happens, the target will experience numerous signs, including, but not limited to: bad luck, obstacles, emotional and/or physiological distress, etc.

People can experience crossed conditions even if they were not victims of negative spellwork. They could have inadvertently picked up negative energies from other people or from environments that have been frequented. Other causes of crossed conditions could have been caused by shocking events, drug or alcohol abuse, or emotional/physiological illness.

In my book *Hoodoo Cleansing and Protection Magic,* the reader is provided with a complete understanding of how crossed conditions manifest, how to prevent them from occurring, and how to eradicate the problem. Of great importance is to pray Psalm 37 aloud while performing any uncrossing rituals as it is the most widely recited prayer for this purpose. Here are a few quick and easy solutions from my book, if the conditions are not severe:

Egg Cleansing

In many of the African magico-religions and diaspora, it is believed that an egg will absorb the negativity from within us through rolling it over our bodies. It is an ideal technique for removing minor attacks.

The technique requires gentle placement of the egg on top of your head then, slowly and carefully rolling it around and downward to your feet, while ensuring that it is rolled over all surfaces of the body.

Once the rolling has been completed, smash the egg into a toilet, a sewer, a flowing stream, or a river. Avoid ponds, lakes, or oceans, as they do not flow away from you.

Florida Water

Pouring Florida Water into a spray bottle and spraying the crown of your head daily will help to eradicate unwanted negative energies.

Holy Water

Pour holy water into a spray bottle. Immediately after bathing and before donning your clothes, spray your entire body with it. When not in use, keep the holy water refrigerated to avoid bacterial growth.

Internal Cleansing

The herb nettle (*Urtica dioica*), also known as "stinging nettle," contains both spiritual as well as health values. The spiritual value offered by nettle is that it contains uncrossing or jinx-breaking properties. As an added bonus, it also contains certain nutrients that help to build our immune system.

Boil a cup of water. Once it bubbles, remove the pot from the stove. Add 1 teaspoon of nettle to the water and steep for nine minutes. Strain the herb from the water and drink the tea. Sugar may be added. It is recommended to drink one cup for thirteen consecutive days.

Rue Soap

Rue eradicates negative energies and has protection properties. Bathe as you normally do with any soap but state your petition aloud while bathing. A simple command could be: "Cleanse and protect my energy fields." Then, rinse off the soap and towel dry.

This concludes the basic introduction to the craft of Hoodoo/Conjure. Although it will take years of study and practice to master, you're on your way! Remember, it also took many years for the slaves of the antebellum period to integrate their original African magico-religious practices into the environmental and cultural atmosphere of North America. Therefore, in order to attain mastery of the craft, we all must continue to study and seek out elders to guide us.

Because Hoodoo practitioners have integrated scriptures from the Holy Bible, the final chapter will provide you with many prayers that will fortify your spellwork.

CHAPTER EIGHT

COMPLIMENTARY PSALMS FOR YOUR SPELLS AND RITUALS

A psalm is defined as a sacred song or poem used in worship. From a metaphysical perspective, psalms are incantations that directly summon God to plead for His assistance with specific needs.

My elders used to say that, whether sung or verbalized, psalms are ultimately translated into the spiritual world as melodies that must be delivered in their entirety. It is akin to turning on the radio and hearing one line of a song, as opposed to the entire piece. Attempting to convince God by taking the time to persuade Him with an entire song rather than with merely a verse or two will yield better results. Therefore, psalms ought to be delivered in their entirety in order to gain God's favor.

Since ancient times, it is believed that burning frankincense is a symbol of prayer ascending directly to God. Because the psalms are prayers to Him, burning frankincense during the prayers optimizes your chances of achieving His assistance. Pulverized incense is not recommended, due to the possible introduction of other chemicals into the powder. Instead, burn the resin.

The Book of Psalms contains 150 poems, speculatively written mostly by Moses, as well as King David and his prophets. However, only twenty-one of these incantations are provided to complement the aforementioned spells and rituals throughout this book. But, before reciting any prayer to God, there are three important points to remember:

- Unlike praying to other entities, such as saints, we never make any promises of gratuitous gifts to God. He has everything because He created everything.
- As stated numerous times throughout this book, pray out loud to output energy.
- Prior to closing the prayer with the word "amen," tell God who you are, the problem, and your respectful request.

Abundance, Love, Luck, and Blessings

Psalm 23

The Lord is my shepherd; I shall not want.
He maketh me to lie down in green pastures:
he leadeth me beside the still waters.
He restoreth my soul:
he leadeth me in the paths of righteousness for his name's sake.
Yea, though I walk through the valley of the shadow of death, I will fear no evil: for thou art with me; thy rod and thy staff they comfort me. Thou preparest a table before me in the presence of mine enemies: thou anointest my head with oil; my cup runneth over.
Surely goodness and mercy shall follow me all the days of my life:
and I will dwell in the house of the Lord forever. Amen.

Binding Enemies

Psalm 94

O Lord God, to whom vengeance belongeth; O God,
to whom vengeance belongeth, shew thyself.
Lift up thyself, thou judge of the earth: render a reward to the proud.
Lord, how long shall the wicked, how long shall the wicked triumph?
How long shall they utter and speak hard things?
and all the workers of iniquity boast themselves?
They break in pieces thy people, O Lord, and afflict thine heritage.
They slay the widow and the stranger, and murder the fatherless.

Yet they say, The Lord shall not see, neither shall the God of Jacob regard it. Understand, ye brutish among the people: and ye fools, when will ye be wise? He that planted the ear, shall he not hear? he that formed the eye, shall he not see?
He that chastiseth the heathen, shall not he correct?
he that teacheth man knowledge, shall not he know?
The Lord knoweth the thoughts of man, that they are vanity.
Blessed is the man whom thou chastenest, O Lord, and
teachest him out of thy law;
That thou mayest give him rest from the days of adversity,
until the pit be digged for the wicked.
For the Lord will not cast off his people, neither will
he forsake his inheritance.
But judgment shall return unto righteousness:
and all the upright in heart shall follow it.
Who will rise up for me against the evildoers?
or who will stand up for me against the workers of iniquity?
Unless the Lord had been my help, my soul had almost dwelt in silence.
When I said, my foot slippeth; thy mercy, O Lord, held me up.
In the multitude of my thoughts within
me thy comforts delight my soul.
Shall the throne of iniquity have fellowship with thee,
which frameth mischief by a law?
They gather themselves together against the soul of the
righteous, and condemn the innocent blood.
But the Lord is my defence; and my God is the rock of my refuge.
And he shall bring upon them their own iniquity, and shall cut
them off in their own wickedness; yea, the Lord our God shall cut
them off. Amen.

Psalm 140

Deliver me, O Lord, from the evil man:
preserve me from the violent man;
Which imagine mischiefs in their heart;
continually are they gathered together for war.
They have sharpened their tongues like a serpent;
adders' poison is under their lips. Selah.
Keep me, O Lord, from the hands of the wicked; preserve me

from the violent man; who have purposed to overthrow my goings.
The proud have hid a snare for me, and cords; they have spread
a net by the wayside; they have set gins for me. Selah.
I said unto the Lord, Thou art my God: hear the
voice of my supplications, O Lord.
O God the Lord, the strength of my salvation, thou
hast covered my head in the day of battle.
Grant not, O Lord, the desires of the wicked: further
not his wicked device; lest they exalt themselves. Selah.
As for the head of those that compass me about, let the
mischief of their own lips cover them.
Let burning coals fall upon them: let them be cast into
the fire; into deep pits, that they rise not up again.
Let not an evil speaker be established in the earth:
evil shall hunt the violent man to overthrow him.
I know that the Lord will maintain the cause of
the afflicted, and the right of the poor.
Surely the righteous shall give thanks unto thy name:
the upright shall dwell in thy presence. Amen.

Blessings

Psalm 145

I will extol thee, my God, O king; and I will
bless thy name for ever and ever.
Every day will I bless thee; and I will praise
thy name for ever and ever.
Great is the Lord, and greatly to be praised; and
his greatness is unsearchable.
One generation shall praise thy works to another,
and shall declare thy mighty acts.
I will speak of the glorious honour of thy majesty,
and of thy wondrous works.
And men shall speak of the might of thy terrible acts:
and I will declare thy greatness.
They shall abundantly utter the memory of thy
great goodness, and shall sing of thy righteousness.
The Lord is gracious, and full of compassion;

slow to anger, and of great mercy.
The Lord is good to all: and his tender mercies are over all his works.
All thy works shall praise thee, O Lord; and thy saints shall bless thee.
They shall speak of the glory of thy kingdom, and talk of thy power;
To make known to the sons of men his mighty acts,
and the glorious majesty of his kingdom.
Thy kingdom is an everlasting kingdom, and
thy dominion endureth throughout all generations.
The Lord upholdeth all that fall, and raiseth
up all those that be bowed down.
The eyes of all wait upon thee; and thou givest
them their meat in due season.
Thou openest thine hand, and satisfiest the desire of every living thing.
The Lord is righteous in all his ways, and holy in all his works.
The Lord is nigh unto all them that call upon
him, to all that call upon him in truth.
He will fulfil the desire of them that fear him: he also
will hear their cry, and will save them.
The Lord preserveth all them that love him:
but all the wicked will he destroy.
My mouth shall speak the praise of the Lord: and
let all flesh bless his holy name for ever and ever. Amen.

Court Cases

Psalm 7

O Lord my God, in thee do I put my trust: save me
from all them that persecute me, and deliver me:
Lest he tear my soul like a lion, rending it in
pieces, while there is none to deliver.
O Lord my God, If I have done this; if there be iniquity in my hands;
If I have rewarded evil unto him that was at peace with me;
(yea, I have delivered him that without cause is mine enemy:)
Let the enemy persecute my soul, and take it; yea, let him tread down
my life upon the earth, and lay mine honour in the dust. Selah.
Arise, O Lord, in thine anger, lift up thyself because of the rage of mine
enemies: and awake for me to the judgment that thou hast commanded.
So shall the congregation of the people compass thee

about: for their sakes therefore return thou on high.
The Lord shall judge the people: judge me, O Lord, according
to my righteousness, and according to mine integrity that is in me.
Oh let the wickedness of the wicked come to an end; but establish the
just: for the righteous God trieth the hearts and reins.
My defence is of God, which saveth the upright in heart.
God judgeth the righteous, and God is
angry with the wicked every day.
If he turn not, he will whet his sword;
he hath bent his bow, and made it ready.
He hath also prepared for him the instruments of death;
he ordaineth his arrows against the persecutors.
Behold, he travaileth with iniquity, and hath conceived
mischief, and brought forth falsehood.
He made a pit, and digged it, and is fallen
into the ditch which he made.
His mischief shall return upon his own head, and
his violent dealing shall come down upon his own pate.
I will praise the Lord according to his righteousness: and
will sing praise to the name of the Lord most high. Amen.

Psalm 35

Plead my cause, O Lord, with them that strive with me:
fight against them that fight against me.
Take hold of shield and buckler, and stand up for mine help.
Draw out also the spear, and stop the way against them that
persecute me: say unto my soul, I am thy salvation.
Let them be confounded and put to shame that seek after my soul:
let them be turned back and brought to confusion that devise my hurt.
Let them be as chaff before the wind: and let
the angel of the Lord chase them.
Let their way be dark and slippery: and let
the angel of the Lord persecute them.
For without cause have they hid for me their net
in a pit, which without cause they have digged for my soul.
Let destruction come upon him at unawares; and let his net that

he hath hid catch himself: into that very destruction let him fall.
And my soul shall be joyful in the Lord: it shall rejoice in his salvation.
All my bones shall say, Lord, who is like unto thee, which deliverest the
poor from him that is too strong for him, yea, the poor
and the needy from him that spoileth him?
False witnesses did rise up; they laid to my charge things that I knew not.
They rewarded me evil for good to the spoiling of my soul.
But as for me, when they were sick, my clothing was sackcloth: I humbled
my soul with fasting; and my prayer returned into mine own bosom.
I behaved myself as though he had been my friend or brother: I bowed
down heavily, as one that mourneth for his mother.
But in mine adversity they rejoiced, and gathered themselves together:
yea, the abjects gathered themselves together against me,
and I knew it not; they did tear me, and ceased not:
With hypocritical mockers in feasts, they
gnashed upon me with their teeth.
Lord, how long wilt thou look on? rescue my
soul from their destructions, my darling from the lions.
I will give thee thanks in the great congregation:
I will praise thee among much people.
Let not them that are mine enemies wrongfully rejoice over
me: neither let them wink with the eye that hate me without a cause.
For they speak not peace: but they devise deceitful
matters against them that are quiet in the land.
Yea, they opened their mouth wide against
me, and said, Aha, aha, our eye hath seen it.
This thou hast seen, O Lord: keep not silence: O Lord, be not far
from me. Stir up thyself, and awake to my judgment,
even unto my cause, my God and my Lord.
Judge me, O Lord my God, according to thy
righteousness; and let them not rejoice over me.
Let them not say in their hearts, Ah, so would we have it:
let them not say, We have swallowed him up.
Let them be ashamed and brought to confusion together
that rejoice at mine hurt: let them be clothed with shame
and dishonour that magnify themselves against me.

Let them shout for joy, and be glad, that favour my righteous cause: yea, let them say continually, Let the Lord be magnified, which hath pleasure in the prosperity of his servant.
And my tongue shall speak of thy righteousness and of thy praise all the day long. Amen.

Cursing and Crossing

Psalm 109

Hold not thy peace, O God of my praise;
For the mouth of the wicked and the mouth of the deceitful are opened against me: they have spoken against me with a lying tongue.
They compassed me about also with words of hatred; and fought against me without a cause.
For my love they are my adversaries: but I give myself unto prayer.
And they have rewarded me evil for good, and hatred for my love.
Set thou a wicked man over him: and let Satan stand at his right hand.
When he shall be judged, let him be condemned: and let his prayer become sin.
Let his days be few; and let another take his office.
Let his children be fatherless, and his wife a widow.
Let his children be continually vagabonds, and beg: let them seek their bread also out of their desolate places.
Let the extortioner catch all that he hath; and let the strangers spoil his labour.
Let there be none to extend mercy unto him: neither let there be any to favour his fatherless children.
Let his posterity be cut off; and in the generation following let their name be blotted out.
Let the iniquity of his fathers be remembered with the Lord; and let not the sin of his mother be blotted out.
Let them be before the Lord continually, that he may cut off the memory of them from the earth.
Because that he remembered not to shew mercy, but persecuted the poor and needy man, that he might even slay the broken in heart.
As he loved cursing, so let it come unto him: as he delighted not in blessing, so let it be far from him.
As he clothed himself with cursing like as with his garment,

so let it come into his bowels like water, and like oil into his bones.
Let it be unto him as the garment which covereth him, and
for a girdle wherewith he is girded continually.
Let this be the reward of mine adversaries from the
Lord, and of them that speak evil against my soul.
But do thou for me, O God the Lord, for thy name's
sake: because thy mercy is good, deliver thou me.
For I am poor and needy, and my heart is wounded within me.
I am gone like the shadow when it declineth:
I am tossed up and down as the locust.
My knees are weak through fasting; and my flesh faileth of fatness.
I became also a reproach unto them: when they
looked upon me they shaked their heads.
Help me, O Lord my God: O save me according to thy mercy:
That they may know that this is thy
hand; that thou, Lord, hast done it.
Let them curse, but bless thou: when they arise,
let them be ashamed; but let thy servant rejoice.
Let mine adversaries be clothed with shame, and let them cover
themselves with their own confusion, as with a mantle.
I will greatly praise the Lord with my mouth;
yea, I will praise him among the multitude.
For he shall stand at the right hand of the poor, to
save him from those that condemn his soul. Amen.

Exorcism

Psalm 121

I will lift up mine eyes unto the hills, from whence cometh my help.
My help cometh from the Lord, which made heaven and earth.
He will not suffer thy foot to be moved:
he that keepeth thee will not slumber.
Behold, he that keepeth Israel shall neither slumber nor sleep.
The Lord is thy keeper: the Lord is thy shade upon thy right hand.
The sun shall not smite thee by day, nor the moon by night.
The Lord shall preserve thee from all evil: he shall preserve thy soul.
The Lord shall preserve thy going out and thy coming
in from this time forth, and even for evermore. Amen.

Drive Away Enemies

Psalm 94

O Lord God, to whom vengeance belongeth; O God,
to whom vengeance belongeth, shew thyself.
Lift up thyself, thou judge of the Earth: render a reward to the proud.
Lord, how long shall the wicked, how long shall the wicked triumph?
How long shall they utter and speak hard things?
and all the workers of iniquity boast themselves?
They break in pieces thy people, O Lord, and afflict thine heritage.
They slay the widow and the stranger, and murder the fatherless.
Yet they say, The Lord shall not see, neither
shall the God of Jacob regard it.
Understand, ye brutish among the people:
and ye fools, when will ye be wise?
He that planted the ear, shall he not hear?
he that formed the eye, shall he not see?
He that chastiseth the heathen, shall not he correct?
he that teacheth man knowledge, shall not he know?
The Lord knoweth the thoughts of man, that they are vanity.
Blessed is the man whom thou chastenest,
O Lord, and teachest him out of thy law;
That thou mayest give him rest from the days
of adversity, until the pit be digged for the wicked.
For the Lord will not cast off his people,
neither will he forsake his inheritance.
But judgment shall return unto righteousness:
and all the upright in heart shall follow it.
Who will rise up for me against the evildoers?
or who will stand up for me against the workers of iniquity?
Unless the Lord had been my help, my soul had almost dwelt in silence.
When I said, My foot slippeth; thy mercy, O Lord, held me up.
In the multitude of my thoughts within
me thy comforts delight my soul.
Shall the throne of iniquity have fellowship
with thee, which frameth mischief by a law?
They gather themselves together against the

soul of the righteous, and condemn the innocent blood.
But the Lord is my defence; and my God is the rock of my refuge.
And he shall bring upon them their own iniquity, and shall cut
them off in their own wickedness; yea, the Lord
our God shall cut them off. Amen.

Psalm 105

O give thanks unto the Lord; call upon his name:
make known his deeds among the people.
Sing unto him, sing psalms unto him: talk ye of all his wondrous works.
Glory ye in his holy name: let the heart
of them rejoice that seek the Lord.
Seek the Lord, and his strength: seek his face evermore.
Remember his marvellous works that he hath done;
his wonders, and the judgments of his mouth;
O ye seed of Abraham his servant, ye children of Jacob his chosen.
He is the Lord our God: his judgments are in all the Earth.
He hath remembered his covenant forever, the word
which he commanded to a thousand generations.
Which covenant he made with Abraham, and his oath unto Isaac;
And confirmed the same unto Jacob for a law,
and to Israel for an everlasting covenant:
Saying, Unto thee will I give the land of
Canaan, the lot of your inheritance:
When they were but a few men in number;
yea, very few, and strangers in it.
When they went from one nation to another,
from one kingdom to another people;
He suffered no man to do them wrong:
yea, he reproved kings for their sakes;
Saying, Touch not mine anointed, and do my prophets no harm.
Moreover he called for a famine upon the
land: he brake the whole staff of bread.
He sent a man before them, even Joseph, who was sold for a servant:
Whose feet they hurt with fetters: he was laid in iron:
Until the time that his word came: the word of the Lord tried him.
The king sent and loosed him; even the ruler

of the people, and let him go free.
He made him Lord of his house, and ruler of all his substance:
To bind his princes at his pleasure; and teach his senators wisdom.
Israel also came into Egypt; and Jacob sojourned in the land of Ham.
And he increased his people greatly; and
made them stronger than their enemies.
He turned their heart to hate his people,
to deal subtilly with his servants.
He sent Moses his servant; and Aaron whom he had chosen.
They shewed his signs among them, and wonders in the land of Ham.
He sent darkness, and made it dark; and
they rebelled not against his word.
He turned their waters into blood, and slew their fish.
Their land brought forth frogs in abundance,
in the chambers of their kings.
He spake[sic], and there came divers sorts
of flies, and lice in all their coasts.
He gave them hail for rain, and flaming fire in their land.
He smote their vines also and their fig trees;
and brake the trees of their coasts.
He spake[sic], and the locusts came, and
caterpillers,[sic] and that without number,
And did eat up all the herbs in their land,
and devoured the fruit of their ground.
He smote also all the firstborn in their land,
the chief of all their strength.
He brought them forth also with silver and gold:
and there was not one feeble person among their tribes.
Egypt was glad when they departed:
for the fear of them fell upon them.
He spread a cloud for a covering; and fire to give light in the night.
The people asked, and he brought quails,
and satisfied them with the bread of heaven.
He opened the rock, and the waters gushed out;
they ran in the dry places like a river.
For he remembered his holy promise, and Abraham his servant.

And he brought forth his people with joy, and his chosen with gladness:
And gave them the lands of the heathen:
and they inherited the labour of the people;
That they might observe his statutes, and keep his laws.
Praise ye the Lord. Amen.

Forgiveness of Sins

Psalm 51

Have mercy upon me, O God, according to thy lovingkindness: according unto the multitude of thy tender mercies blot out my transgressions.
Wash me throughly from mine iniquity, and cleanse me from my sin.
For I acknowledge my transgressions: and my sin is ever before me.
Against thee, thee only, have I sinned, and done this evil in thy sight:
that thou mightest be justified when thou
speakest, and be clear when thou judgest.
Behold, I was shapen in iniquity; and in sin did my mother conceive me.
Behold, thou desirest truth in the inward parts: and
in the hidden part thou shalt make me to know wisdom.
Purge me with hyssop, and I shall be clean:
wash me, and I shall be whiter than snow.
Make me to hear joy and gladness; that the
bones which thou hast broken may rejoice.
Hide thy face from my sins, and blot out all mine iniquities.
Create in me a clean heart, O God; and renew a right spirit within me.
Cast me not away from thy presence; and
take not thy Holy Spirit from me.
Restore unto me the joy of thy salvation;
and uphold me with thy free spirit.
Then will I teach transgressors thy ways;
and sinners shall be converted unto thee.
Deliver me from bloodguiltiness,[sic] O God, thou God of
my salvation: and my tongue shall sing aloud of thy righteousness.
O Lord, open thou my lips; and my mouth shall shew forth thy praise.
For thou desirest not sacrifice; else would I
give it: thou delightest not in burnt offering.

The sacrifices of God are a broken spirit: a broken
and a contrite heart, O God, thou wilt not despise.
Do good in thy good pleasure unto Zion:
build thou the walls of Jerusalem.
Then shalt thou be pleased with the sacrifices of righteousness,
with burnt offering and whole burnt offering: then shall
they offer bullocks upon thine altar. Amen.

Gossip Cessation

Psalm 12

Help, Lord; for the godly man ceaseth; for
the faithful fail from among the children of men.
They speak vanity everyone with his neighbour: with
flattering lips and with a double heart do they speak.
The Lord shall cut off all flattering lips, and
the tongue that speaketh proud things:
Who have said, With our tongue will we prevail;
our lips are our own: who is lord over us?
For the oppression of the poor, for the sighing of the needy,
now will I arise, saith the Lord; I will set him in
safety from him that puffeth at him.
The words of the Lord are pure words: as silver
tried in a furnace of earth, purified seven times.
Thou shalt keep them, O Lord, thou shalt preserve
them from this generation forever.
The wicked walk on every side, when the vilest men are exalted. Amen.

Psalm 120

In my distress I cried unto the Lord, and he heard me.
Deliver my soul, O Lord, from lying lips, and from a deceitful tongue.
What shall be given unto thee? or what
shall be done unto thee, thou false tongue?
Sharp arrows of the mighty, with coals of juniper.
Woe is me, that I sojourn in Mesech, that I dwell in the tents of Kedar!
My soul hath long dwelt with him that hateth peace.
I am for peace: but when I speak, they are for war. Amen.

Group Troublemakers

Psalm 1

Blessed is the man that walketh not in the counsel
of the ungodly, nor standeth in the way of sinners,
nor sitteth in the seat of the scornful.
But his delight is in the law of the Lord; and
in his law doth he meditate day and night.
And he shall be like a tree planted by the rivers of water,
that bringeth forth his fruit in his season; his leaf also shall not
wither; and whatsoever he doeth shall prosper.
The ungodly are not so: but are like the
chaff which the wind driveth away.
Therefore the ungodly shall not stand in the judgment,
nor sinners in the congregation of the righteous.
For the Lord knoweth the way of the righteous: but
the way of the ungodly shall perish. Amen.

Healing (Emotional and Physical)

Psalm 41

Blessed is he that considereth the poor: the
Lord will deliver him in time of trouble.
The Lord will preserve him, and keep him alive;
and he shall be blessed upon the Earth: and thou
wilt not deliver him unto the will of his enemies.
The Lord will strengthen him upon the bed of
languishing: thou wilt make all his bed in his sickness.
I said, Lord, be merciful unto me: heal my
soul; for I have sinned against thee.
Mine enemies speak evil of me, When shall he die, and his name perish?
And if he come to see me, he speaketh vanity: his heart
gathereth iniquity to itself; when he goeth abroad, he telleth it.
All that hate me whisper together against
me: against me do they devise my hurt.
An evil disease, say they, cleaveth fast unto him:
and now that he lieth he shall rise up no more.

Yea, mine own familiar friend, in whom I trusted,
which did eat of my bread, hath lifted up his heel against me.
But thou, O Lord, be merciful unto me, and
raise me up, that I may requite them.
By this I know that thou favourest me, because
mine enemy doth not triumph over me.
And as for me, thou upholdest me in mine integrity,
and settest me before thy face forever.
Blessed be the Lord God of Israel from everlasting,
and to everlasting. Amen, and Amen.

Impending Job Loss

Psalm 6

O Lord, rebuke me not in thine anger,
neither chasten me in thy hot displeasure.
Have mercy upon me, O Lord; for I am weak:
O Lord, heal me; for my bones are vexed.
My soul is also sore vexed: but thou, O Lord, how long?
Return, O Lord, deliver my soul: oh save me for thy mercies' sake.
For in death there is no remembrance of thee:
in the grave who shall give thee thanks?
I am weary with my groaning; all the night make
I my bed to swim; I water my couch with my tears.
Mine eye is consumed because of grief;
it waxeth old because of all mine enemies.
Depart from me, all ye workers of iniquity;
for the Lord hath heard the voice of my weeping.
The Lord hath heard my supplication;
the Lord will receive my prayer.
Let all mine enemies be ashamed and sore vexed:
let them return and be ashamed suddenly. Amen.

Protection

Psalm 91

He that dwelleth in the secret place of the most
High shall abide under the shadow of the Almighty.

I will say of the Lord, He is my refuge and
my fortress: my God; in him will I trust.
Surely he shall deliver thee from the snare of the
fowler, and from the noisome pestilence.
He shall cover thee with his feathers, and under his
wings shalt thou trust: his truth shall be thy shield and buckler.
Thou shalt not be afraid for the terror by
night; nor for the arrow that flieth by day;
Nor for the pestilence that walketh in darkness;
nor for the destruction that wasteth at noonday.
A thousand shall fall at thy side, and ten thousand
at thy right hand; but it shall not come nigh thee.
Only with thine eyes shalt thou behold
and see the reward of the wicked.
Because thou hast made the Lord, which is my
refuge, even the most High, thy habitation;
There shall no evil befall thee, neither shall
any plague come nigh thy dwelling.
For he shall give his angels charge over
thee, to keep thee in all thy ways.
They shall bear thee up in their hands,
lest thou dash thy foot against a stone.
Thou shalt tread upon the lion and adder: the
young lion and the dragon shalt thou trample under feet.
Because he hath set his love upon me, therefore will I deliver
him: I will set him on high, because he hath known my name.
He shall call upon me, and I will answer him: I will be with
him in trouble; I will deliver him, and honour him.
With long life will I satisfy him, and shew him my salvation. Amen.

Road Opener

Psalm 65

Praise waiteth for thee, O God, in Sion:
and unto thee shall the vow be performed.
O thou that hearest prayer, unto thee shall all flesh come.
Iniquities prevail against me: as for our transgressions,
thou shalt purge them away.

Blessed is the man whom thou choosest, and causest to approach unto
thee, that he may dwell in thy courts: we shall be satisfied with the
goodness of thy house, even of thy holy temple.
By terrible things in righteousness wilt thou answer us, O God of our
salvation; who art the confidence of all the ends of the
Earth, and of them that are afar off upon the sea:
Which by his strength setteth fast the
mountains; being girded with power:
Which stilleth the noise of the seas, the
noise of their waves, and the tumult of the people.
They also that dwell in the uttermost parts are afraid
at thy tokens: thou makest the outgoings of the
morning and evening to rejoice.
Thou visitest the Earth, and waterest it:
thou greatly enrichest it with the river of God,
which is full of water: thou preparest them corn,
when thou hast so provided for it.
Thou waterest the ridges thereof abundantly:
thou settlest the furrows thereof: thou makest it soft
with showers: thou blessest the springing thereof.
Thou crownest the year with thy goodness; and thy paths drop fatness.
They drop upon the pastures of the wilderness:
and the little hills rejoice on every side.
The pastures are clothed with flocks; the valleys
also are covered over with corn; they
shout for joy, they also sing. Amen.

Uncrossing

Psalm 37

Fret not thyself because of evildoers, neither be
thou envious against the workers of iniquity.
For they shall soon be cut down like the
grass, and wither as the green herb.
Trust in the Lord, and do good; so shalt thou
dwell in the land, and verily thou shalt be fed.

Delight thyself also in the Lord: and he shall
give thee the desires of thine heart.
Commit thy way unto the Lord; trust also
in him; and he shall bring it to pass.
And he shall bring forth thy righteousness
as the light, and thy judgment as the noonday.
Rest in the Lord, and wait patiently for him:
fret not thyself because of him who prospereth in his way,
because of the man who bringeth wicked devices to pass.
Cease from anger, and forsake wrath:
fret not thyself in any wise to do evil.
For evildoers shall be cut off: but those that wait
upon the Lord, they shall inherit the Earth.
For yet a little while, and the wicked shall not be: yea,
thou shalt diligently consider his place, and it shall not be.
But the meek shall inherit the Earth; and shall
delight themselves in the abundance of peace.
The wicked plotteth against the just, and
gnasheth upon him with his teeth.
The Lord shall laugh at him: for he seeth that his day is coming.
The wicked have drawn out the sword, and have
bent their bow, to cast down the poor and needy,
and to slay such as be of upright conversation.
Their sword shall enter into their own heart,
and their bows shall be broken.
A little that a righteous man hath is better
than the riches of many wicked.
For the arms of the wicked shall be broken:
but the Lord upholdeth the righteous.
The Lord knoweth the days of the upright:
and their inheritance shall be forever.
They shall not be ashamed in the evil time:
and in the days of famine they shall be satisfied.
But the wicked shall perish, and the enemies of the
Lord shall be as the fat of lambs: they shall consume;
into smoke shall they consume away.

The wicked borroweth, and payeth not again:
but the righteous sheweth mercy, and giveth.
For such as be blessed of him shall inherit the Earth;
and they that be cursed of him shall be cut off.
The steps of a good man are ordered by the
Lord: and he delighteth in his way.
Though he fall, he shall not be utterly cast down:
for the Lord upholdeth him with his hand.
I have been young, and now am old; yet have I
not seen the righteous forsaken, nor his seed begging bread.
He is ever merciful, and lendeth; and his seed is blessed.
Depart from evil, and do good; and dwell for evermore.
For the Lord loveth judgment, and forsaketh not his saints;
they are preserved for ever: but the seed
of the wicked shall be cut off.
The righteous shall inherit the land, and dwell therein forever.
The mouth of the righteous speaketh wisdom,
and his tongue talketh of judgment.
The law of his God is in his heart; none of his steps shall slide.
The wicked watcheth the righteous, and seeketh to slay him.
The Lord will not leave him in his hand,
nor condemn him when he is judged.
Wait on the Lord, and keep his way, and he
shall exalt thee to inherit the land:
when the wicked are cut off, thou shalt see it.
I have seen the wicked in great power, and
spreading himself like a green bay tree.
Yet he passed away, and, lo, he was not: yea,
I sought him, but he could not be found.
Mark the perfect man, and behold the upright:
for the end of that man is peace.
But the transgressors shall be destroyed together:
the end of the wicked shall be cut off.
But the salvation of the righteous is of the Lord:
he is their strength in the time of trouble.
And the Lord shall help them, and deliver them:
he shall deliver them from the wicked,
and save them, because they trust in him. Amen.

Victory

Psalm 59

Deliver me from mine enemies, O my God:
defend me from them that rise up against me.
Deliver me from the workers of iniquity,
and save me from bloody men.
For, lo, they lie in wait for my soul: the mighty are gathered
against me; not for my transgression, nor for my sin, O Lord.
They run and prepare themselves without my
fault: awake to help me, and behold.
Thou therefore, O Lord God of hosts, the God of Israel,
awake to visit all the heathen: be not merciful
to any wicked transgressors. Selah.
They return at evening: they make a noise
like a dog, and go round about the city.
Behold, they belch out with their mouth: swords
are in their lips: for who, say they, doth hear?
But thou, O Lord, shalt laugh at them; thou
shalt have all the heathen in derision.
Because of his strength will I wait
upon thee: for God is my defence.
The God of my mercy shall prevent me:
God shall let me see my desire upon mine enemies.
Slay them not, lest my people forget: scatter them by
thy power; and bring them down, O Lord our shield.
For the sin of their mouth and the words of their
lips let them even be taken in their pride:
and for cursing and lying which they speak.
Consume them in wrath, consume them,
that they may not be: and let them know
that God ruleth in Jacob unto the ends of the Earth. Selah.
And at evening let them return; and let them
make a noise like a dog, and go round about the city.
Let them wander up and down for meat,
and grudge if they be not satisfied.
But I will sing of thy power; yea, I will
sing aloud of thy mercy in the morning:

for thou hast been my defence and refuge in the day of my trouble.
Unto thee, O my strength, will I sing: for God is my defence, and the God of my mercy. Amen.

Psalm 86

Bow down thine ear, O Lord, hear me: for I am poor and needy.
Preserve my soul; for I am holy: O thou my God, save thy servant that trusteth in thee.
Be merciful unto me, O Lord: for I cry unto thee daily.
Rejoice the soul of thy servant: for unto thee, O Lord, do I lift up my soul.
For thou, Lord, art good, and ready to forgive; and plenteous in mercy unto all them that call upon thee.
Give ear, O Lord, unto my prayer; and attend to the voice of my supplications.
In the day of my trouble I will call upon thee: for thou wilt answer me.
Among the gods there is none like unto thee, O Lord; neither are there any works like unto thy works.
All nations whom thou hast made shall come and worship before thee, O Lord; and shall glorify thy name.
For thou art great, and doest wondrous things: thou art God alone.
Teach me thy way, O Lord; I will walk in thy truth: unite my heart to fear thy name.
I will praise thee, O Lord my God, with all my heart: and I will glorify thy name for evermore.
For great is thy mercy toward me: and thou hast delivered my soul from the lowest hell.
O God, the proud are risen against me, and the assemblies of violent men have sought after my soul; and have not set thee before them.
But thou, O Lord, art a God full of compassion, and gracious, long suffering, and plenteous in mercy and truth.
O turn unto me, and have mercy upon me; give thy strength unto thy servant, and save the son of thine handmaid.
Shew me a token for good; that they which hate me may see it, and be ashamed: because thou, Lord, hast holpen me, and comforted me. Amen.

CONCLUSION

My personal sentiments regarding book-writing is comparable to giving birth to a child and raising it into adulthood. Initially, there's excitement, followed by a plethora of emotions, including worry, grief, hardships, and lastly, pride. Writing the conclusion is similar to watching the little baby grow into maturity and finally leaving the nest. It's a bittersweet journey in which all of you have shared with me, and for that, I thank you.

However, before ending this journey, it is of the utmost importance to remind everyone that the African slaves and their descendants had suffered tremendous cruelty and oppression. To this day, millions are still treated harshly. Most of my African and African American friends and clients tell me their personal and despicable stories regarding racism.

Remember that this craft was brought to us by the slaves of the antebellum period, thus making them the founders and forefathers of Hoodoo. If we choose to immerse ourselves in Hoodoo, we must neither disrespect their descendants, nor exploit the craft.

Many people enjoy higher social standings due to their hereditary connections to esteemed ancestors who had either endured treacherous journeys, became founders or forefathers, or had rich and diverse historical familial backgrounds. We now know that the African Americans also have rich and diverse historical familial backgrounds. Their ancestors were also founders and forefathers in particular arenas. But, rather than enjoying a higher social standing for the same reasons, many are instead met with racism.

So, if you plan to practice the craft, you must RESPECT THE PEOPLE and their generational (and current) struggle!

BIBLIOGRAPHY

Adams, A.J. "Seeing Is Believing: The Power of Visualization," *Psychology Today,* 3 Dec. 2009. www.psychologytoday.com/us/blog/flourish/200912/seeing-is-believing-the-power-visualization.

Aderet, Ofer. "The Uncomfortable Truths of Jewish Life in the U.S. South,"*Haaretz,* 22 Jun. 2021, www.haaretz.com/us-news/2021-06-22/ty-article-magazine/.premium/slave-owners-confederates-and-wrestlers-jews-of-the-u-s-south-in-the-showcase/0000017f-da74-dea8-a77f-de766f7c0000.

Anderson, Jeffrey E. *Conjure in African American Society.* Louisiana State UP, 2005.

Barnwell, R. G. "Coolies as a Substitute for Negroes." in *Debow's Review: Agricultural, Commercial, Industrial Progress, and Resources* (Aug. 1866) vol. 2, no. 2, August 1866, name.umdl.umich.edu/acg1336.2-02.002.

Battle, Mary. "American Indian Slavery in Carolina." *Lowcountry Digital History Initiative,* ldhi.library.cofc.edu/exhibits/show/africanpassageslowcountryadapt/sectionii_introduction/american_indian_slavery_caroli.

Boyd, Herb. *African History for Beginners.* Danbury: For Beginners, LLC., 1994.

Brown, Karen McCarthy. *Mama Lola: A Vodou Priestess in Brooklyn.* University of California Press, 1991.

Butler, Alban. *Lives Of the Saints: For Every Day of The Year.* Tan Books, 1955.

"Capture and Captives." *Slavery and Remembrance: A Guide to Sites, Museums, and Memory.* The Colonial Williamsburg Foundation: 2025, slaveryandremembrance.org/articles/article/?id=A0003.

Chireau, Yvonne P. *Black Magic: Religion and The African Conjuring Tradition.* University of California Press, 2006.

Collins, Robert Keith. "How Africans Met Native Americans During Slavery." *Contexts* 19.3 (Sep. 2020): 16-21 Available: https://doi.org/10.1177/1536504220950396.

Cooley, Charles Horton and Hans-Joachim Schubert. *On Self and Social Organization.* University of Chicago Press: 1998.

Dessens, Nathalie. "Saint-Dominque Refugees." Oxford Bibliographies, 19 Dec. 2012. Available: doi.org/10.1093/OBO/9780199730414-0107.

Douglass, Frederick. Narrative of the Life of Frederick Douglass: An American Slave, Written by Himself. Boston: The Anti-Slavery Office. 1845.

Fatunmbi, Awo Falokun, et. al. *Family Spirit: The Ifa Concept of Egun.* Brooklyn: Athelia Henrietta Press, Inc. 2006.

Ferris State University. "Africa Before Slavery." *FSU Jim Crow Museum,* jimcrowmuseum.ferris.edu/timeline/africa_before.htm.

Gifford, Paul. *African Christianity: Its Public Role.* Bloomington and Indianapolis: Indiana University Press, 1998.

Griffith, James S. Folk Saints of the Borderlands: Victims, Bandits, and Healers. Rio Nuevo Publishers, 2003.

Guiley, Rosemary Ellen. *The Encyclopedia of Saints.* New York: Facts on File, Inc, 2001.

Gudrun. "Prayer to St. Expeditus for Court Cases/Urgent Matters." *Prayers4reparation,* prayers4reparation.wordpress.com/author/prayers4reparation/.

Haskins, Jim. *Voodoo & Hoodoo.* Old Bethpage: Original Publications, 1978.

Higgins, Abigail. "40 Years a Slave: The Extraordinary Tale of an African Prince Stolen From His Kingdom." *History,* 8 Feb. 2019, www.history.com/articles/african-prince-slavery-abdulrahman-ibrahim-ibn-sori.

The Holy Bible. King James Version, Rev. Edition. Translated by Thomas Nelson. 1976.

Hopler, Whitney "Angel Prayers: Praying to Archangel Gabriel." *Learn Religions,* 6 Jan. 2019, www.learnreligions.com/praying-to-archangel-gabriel-124252.

Hyatt, Harry Middleton. "Hoodoo-Conjuration-Witchcraft-Rootwork." Comp. Catherine Yronwode, *Lucky Mojo Curio Co.: Hoodoo in Theory and Practice,* www.luckymojo.com/hyatt.html.

"Joan of Arc." *Daily Prayers,* www.daily-prayers.org/angels-and-saints/prayers-to-saint-joan-of-arc/#:~:text=Holy%20Saint%20Joan%2C%20compassionate%20to,me%20through%20this%20difficult%20time.

Lovasik, Lawrence G. *New Picture Book of Saints: Illustrated Lives of the Saints For Young and Old.* Totowa: Catholic Book Publishing Corporation, 1979.

Mayer, John. "Praying for the Intercession of Moses? Can Catholics ask for the Prayers of Those who Lived Before Christ?" *Catholic 365,* 2 Jul. 2018, www.catholic365.com/article/9037/praying-for-the-intercession-of-moses-can-catholics-ask-for-the-prayers-of-those-who-lived-before-christ.html.

Mills, David Charles. *Unholy: the Slaves Bible.* Ghetto Kids Enterprises, 2009.

Michigan Hell House. Directed by Steven T. Shippy. Workaholic Productions for Warner Brothers/Discovery Network, 2021.

Mills, David Charles. *Unholy: The Slaves Bible.* Ghetto Kids Enterprises, 2009.

Noegel, Scott B. "Moses and Magic: Notes on the Book of Exodus." In *Journal of the Ancient Near Eastern Society 24,* 45–49, 1996.

O'Neil, Aaron. "Black and Slave Population in the United States 1790–1880." *Statista,* 12 Aug. 2024, www.statista.com/statistics/1010169/black-and-slave-population-us-1790-1880/.

Ogren, Brian. *Kabbalah and the Founding of America.* New York: New York UP, 2021.

Omaritian, Stormie. "Praying to Forgive Yourself, God, and Others." *Faith Gateway,* faithgateway.com/blogs/christian-books/praying-to-forgive-yourself-god-and-others.

"Patron Saints A-Z." *Catholic Online,* 2025, www.catholic.org/saints/patron.php.

Perrault, Alix. "Vodou and the Loas." *The Vodou Element.* VP Books, 2004.

Pope, Hugh. "Guardian Angel." *The Catholic Encyclopedia.* New York: Robert Appleton Company, 1910.

"Prayer for Education Success-Academic Success in Exams." *Pray Ray Prayer Journal*, prayray.com/prayer-for-education-success/. Available at: www.newadvent.org/cathen/07049c.htm.

"A Prayer for Employment." *Eternal World Television Network*. Global Catholic Network: 2025, www.ewtn.com/catholicism/devotions/prayer-for-employment-326.

"Prayer to the Holy Spirit." *Catholic Online*, www.catholic.org/prayers/prayer.php?p=336.

"Prisoner's Prayer to Saint Maximilian Kolbe." Maximilian Kolbe Mission: Addiction Prayer Ministry, maxkolbemission.wordpress.com/prisoners-prayer-to-saint-maximilian-kolbe/.

Raboteau, Albert J. Slave Religion: The "Invisible Institution" in the Antebellum South. New York: Oxford UP, 1978, 2004.

Roberts, Alaina E. "How Native Americans Adopted Slavery from White Settlers." *Al Jazeera*, 27 Dec. 2018, www.aljazeera.com/opinions/2018/12/27/how-native-americans-adopted-slavery-from-white-settlers.

Sarna, Jonathan D. "The Mystical World of Colonial Jews." *Mediating Modernity*, Ed. Lauren B. Strauss, et al. Detroit: Wayne State UP, 2008. 185–94.

Schnurr, Dennis. *Novena for Justice and Peace*. Catholic Campaign for Human Development: Break the Cycle of Poverty, Build Community. US Catholic Conference Publishers, 1998.

Spencer, Craig. *Witcraft Unchained: Exploring the History & Traditions of British Craft*. Crossed Crow Books, LLC, 2023.

"St. Rita." *Catholic Online*, Your Catholic Voice Foundation: 2025, www.catholic.org/saints/saint.php?saint_id=205.

Stagnaro, Angelo. "What You Need to Know About St. Benedict and His Medal." *National Catholic Register*, 11 Jul. 2020, www.ncregister.com/blog/what-you-need-to-know-about-st-benedict-and-his-medal.

The Torah: The Five Books of Moses. Third Edition, Philadelphia: The Jewish Publication Society, 1992.

"The Transatlantic Slave Trade." *Equal Justice Initiative*. https://eji.org/report/transatlantic-slave-trade/.

"Trans-Atlantic Slave Trade—Database." *Slave Voyages*, xwww.slavevoyages.org/voyage/database.

Webster, Richard. "Amulets, Talismans, & Charms." Llewellyn, 19 Apr. 2004, www.llewellyn.com/journal/article/583?srsltid=AfmBOopkxNqa7tND9n-UjwRLV5N7sf6ZULfmeYdoTbWN-TLLe68RPT72.
"Where the False Claim That Jews Controlled the Slave Trade Comes From." *My Jewish Learning*, www.myjewishlearning.com/article/jews-and-the-african-slave-trade/.
Williams, Alex. "How Many Crystals Are There in the World?" *Speeli*, 31 Jan. 2024, www.speeli.com/how-many-crystals-are-there-in-the-world/.
Yronwode, Catherine. *Hoodoo Herb and Root Magic: A Materia Magica of African-American Conjure*. Lucky Mojo Curio Company, 2002.
Zohary, Michael. *Plants of the Bible*. Press Syndicate of the University of Cambridge, 1982.